The St. Lucie Press
Total Quality Series™

BOOKS IN THE SERIES:

Total Quality in HIGHER EDUCATION

Total Quality in PURCHASING and SUPPLIER MANAGEMENT

Total Quality in INFORMATION SYSTEMS and TECHNOLOGY

Total Quality in RESEARCH and DEVELOPMENT

Total Quality in MANAGING HUMAN RESOURCES

Total Quality and ORGANIZATION DEVELOPMENT

Total Quality in MARKETING

MACROLOGISTICS MANAGEMENT

For more information about these books call St. Lucie Press at (407) 274-9906

Series Editor • Frank Voehl
Series Development Editor • Sandy Pearlman

Total Quality in

INFORMATION SYSTEMS AND TECHNOLOGY

By
Jack Woodall, MBA
Vice President and COO
Management Systems International
Boca Raton, Florida

Deborah K. Rebuck, MBA
CEO and Founder
Maximum Business Automation
Tampa, Florida

Frank Voehl
President and CEO
Strategy Associates, Inc.
Coral Springs, Florida

S_L^t

St. Lucie Press
Delray Beach, Florida

Phone: (407) 274-9906
Fax: (407) 274-9927

S^{t}L

Published by
St. Lucie Press
100 E. Linton Blvd., Suite 403B
Delray Beach, FL 33483

TABLE OF CONTENTS

SERIES PREFACE

The St. Lucie Press Series on Total Quality originated in 1993 when some of us realized that the rapidly expanding field of quality management was neither well defined nor well focused. This realization, coupled with America's hunger for specific, how-to examples, led to the formulation of a plan to publish a series of subject-specific books on total quality, a new direction for books in the field to follow.

The essence of this series consists of a core nucleus of eight new direction books, around which the remaining books in the series will revolve over a three-year period:

- Education Transformation: *Total Quality in Higher Education*
- Respect for People: *Total Quality in Managing Human Resources*
- Speak with Facts: *Total Quality in Information Systems and Technology*
- Customer Satisfaction: *Total Quality in Marketing*
- Continuous Improvement: *Total Quality in Research and Development*
- System Transformation: *Total Quality and Organization Development*
- Supplier Partnerships: *Total Quality in Purchasing and Supplier Management*
- Cost-Effective, Value-Added Services: *Total Quality and Measurement*

We at St. Lucie Press have been privileged to contribute to the convergence of philosophy and underlying principles of total quality, leading to a common set of assumptions. One of the most important deals with the challenges facing the transformation of the information systems and technology area for the 21st century. This is a particularly exciting and turbulent time in this field, both domestically and globally, and change may be viewed as either an opportunity or a threat. As such, the principles and practices of total quality can aid in this transformation or, by flawed implementation approaches, can bring an organization to its knees. A total of $60 billion a year is spent in this area.

As the authors of this text explain, the total quality orientation redefines managerial roles and identifies new responsibilities for the traditional function to come to grips with. The information systems/information technology professional's role now includes strategic input and continual development of the strategic planning system to increase customer satisfaction both now and in the future. The full meaning of these changes is fully explored in light of the driving forces reshaping the systems environment.

As Series Editor, I am pleased with the manner in which the series is coming together. Its premise is that excellence can be achieved through a singular focus on customers and their interests as a number one priority, a focus that requires a high degree of commitment, flexibility, and resolve. The new definition of the degree of satisfaction will be the total experience of the interaction—which will be the determinant of whether the customer stays a customer. However, no book or series can tell an organization how to achieve total quality; only the customers and stakeholders can tell you when you have it and when you do not. High-quality goods and services can give an organization a competitive edge while reducing costs due to rework, returns, and scrap. Most importantly, outstanding quality generates satisfied customers, who reward the organization with continued patronage and free word-of-mouth advertising.

In the area of abstracts, we are indebted to Richard Frantzreb, President of Advanced Personnel Systems, who has granted permission to incorporate selected abstracts from their collection, which they independently publish in a quarterly magazine called *Quality Abstracts*. This feature is a sister publication to *Training and Development Alert*. These journals are designed to keep readers abreast of literature in the field of quality and to help readers benefit from the insights and experience of experts and practitioners who are implementing total quality in their organizations. Each journal runs between 28 and 36 pages and contains about 100 carefully selected abstracts of articles and books in the field. For further information, contact Richard Frantzreb (916-781-2900).

We trust that you will find this book both usable and beneficial and wish you maximum success on the quality journey. If it in some way makes a contribution, then we can say, as Dr. Deming often did at the end of his seminars, "I have done my best."

Frank Voehl
Series Editor

AUTHORS' PREFACE

This book breaks tradition in its treatment of information technology, also known as information systems. Its purpose is to educate business and technical personnel at all levels on how to bridge the communication and quality gaps between their respective areas. The intent is to provide a guideline for actions to be taken before getting into the "nuts and bolts." Acting before preliminary planning costs money, especially when expensive technology is involved.

Many business managers believe the technology area should be excluded in company planning. Traditionally, technology has been viewed as a costly overhead area that rarely delivers on time or within budget. Properly used, technology is an investment rather than an expense. On the flip side, many technicians invariably want the newest technology regardless of cost. Our intent is to show how a company can gain a competitive edge when the technical and business areas work in harmony. This book covers proven, successful methods.

We would like to acknowledge and express our gratitude to organizations and individuals who provided additional information and experiences. A special thanks to the Data Processing Management Association, Dr. Roger McGrath, Jr., University of South Florida, Penn State, University of Miami, Warfields Business Record, American City Business Journals, and the Data Interchange Standards Association. There were other individuals who provided support (they know who they are), but an extra special thank-you to Pat Woodall and Joe Burke for their patience.

We encourage you to contact us to share your success and concerns.

Jack Woodall
Deborah K. Rebuck
Frank Voehl

THE SERIES EDITOR

Frank Voehl has had a twenty-year career in quality management, productivity improvement, and related fields. He has written more than 200 articles, papers, and books on the subject of quality and has consulted on quality and productivity issues, as well as measurement system implementation, for hundreds of companies (many Fortune 500 corporations). As general manager of FPL Qualtec, he was influential in the FPL Deming Prize process, which led to the formation of the Malcolm Baldrige Award, as well as the National Quality Award in the Bahamas. He is a member of Strategic Planning committees with the ASQC and AQP and has assisted the IRS in quality planning as a member of the Commissioner's Advisory Group.

An industrial engineering graduate from St. John's University in New York City, Mr. Voehl has been a visiting professor and lecturer at NYU and the University of Miami, where he helped establish the framework for the Quality Institute. He is currently president and CEO of Strategy Associates, Inc. and a visiting professor at Florida International University.

On the local level, Mr. Voehl served for ten years as vice chairman of the Margate/Broward County Advisory Committee for the Handicapped. In 1983, he was awarded the Partners in Productivity award for his efforts to streamline and improve the Utilities Forced Relocation Process, which saved the state of Florida some $200 million over a seven-year period.

THE AUTHORS

Jack Woodall, MBA, is vice president and chief operating officer of Management Systems International in Boca Raton, Florida. As a consultant in total quality management, he participates in the assessments of clients' total quality management needs, identification of initial and successive interface areas, and total deployment programs.

Mr. Woodall received his Masters in Business Administration from the University of Miami and attended the Program for Management Development at the Harvard Business School.

His strong management skills are enhanced by his involvement as a major contributor in the development and implementation of FPL's total quality management system and the Deming examination. He is an expert in total quality management deployment technology and methodologies.

Mr. Woodall assisted in the implementation of the University of Miami's Institute for the Study of Quality in Manufacturing and Services and served as a director for the institute. He participated in study missions and steering committee meetings in Japan and has studied under Drs. Asaka, Kano, Kondo, Kuragane, and Makabe. He has also served on numerous committees and held positions of leadership within professional and user computer organizations.

Deborah K. Rebuck, MBA, is the CEO and founder of Maximum Business Automation in Tampa, Florida. Her firm specializes in planning, management, training, and bridging the gap between the business and technical worlds. The company provides personnel who can address both technical and business issues. Ms. Rebuck is a results-oriented business and computer professional with solid experience and achievements working within various corporate environments. She has over fifteen years of solid management experience with major Fortune 100 companies. Her background includes both domestic and international experience in major projects.

Ms. Rebuck received her Masters in Business Administration, magna cum laude, and Bachelor of Science, summa cum laude, in management and marketing from Tampa College in Tampa, Florida. She also holds a certificate in computer programming from Lear Siegler in Washington, D.C.

Her experience in key troubleshooting roles has earned her a reputation as a results-oriented individual. She focuses on business solutions, using information technology as an enabler, rather than letting technology drive the solution.

CHAPTER 1

HARNESSING THE POWER OF INFORMATION TECHNOLOGY THROUGH TOTAL QUALITY: AN OVERVIEW OF TECHNOLOGY, QUALITY, AND INFORMATION

TECHNOLOGY: THE GREAT ENGINE OF CHANGE

Technology is arguably the most powerful and definitive force in the development of modern civilization. Fueled by scientific development and discovery, the evolution of technology is synonymous with the history of man's struggle to improve his condition on the planet, his sheer will and desire to reach beyond the limitations of the day and create altogether new, unprecedented ways of traveling, treating the ill, communicating, working, creating, and entertaining. Technology has transformed, and continues to transform, the way we live and move and think. Quite succinctly, technology has and continues to transform *what we are.*

Technology is so deeply embedded in the human psyche that it is an extension of man himself, of his desire to exercise control over the environment and wield the materials of the world to his advantage. Beginning with the first flint and stone, the first rudimentary wheel, technology has shaped the way we think of ourselves, the way we interact with one another, and the way we control the natural environment. It is as much a cause as an effect of human and planetary evolution. It is used by the good to build and create and by the evil to destroy and violate.

Technology is not static. It moves in spurts and sometimes waves of discovery and innovation. Like a tornado, its course is often unpredictable and dangerous. Like shattering glass, it can break off in a thousand directions, spawning a huge network of subinnovations and spinoffs, each with its own unique shape, form, and application. How, for example, can we begin to assess the impact of Gutenberg's printing press, Watt's steam engine, or Franklin's lightning conductor on the development of civilization?

Technology rarely acts alone. Discoveries, advances, and innovations often merge and combine to engender new applications, new products that would not be possible without the important contribution of each separate technological development. Guns, for instance, would never have come into existence if gunpowder, formerly used by the Chinese for fireworks, was not combined with the matchlock, the flintlock, and subsequent advances in gunpowder-ignition mechanisms. Electricity, without developments in generation, transmission, and distribution, would never have found its way into almost every household in the developed world. And oil, the precious fuel of the industrial age, would never have become so vitally important apart from the combustion engine, would never have even been extracted in mass quantities apart from drilling technologies, would never have been refined without processing technologies, and would never have been consumed on a mass scale apart from the literally thousands of parallel technological developments undergirding the commercialization of energy and oil-powered transmission and travel.

Technology has the power to ravage old inventions on a global scale, rendering them useless and obsolete, while simultaneously laying the groundwork for entirely new ways of constructing, moving, communicating, and living. Who, for example, in today's gas-powered society remembers the horse and buggy? Who can fathom survival without the toilet, the calculator, or the telephone? While all these innovations were spawned in the spirit of their archaic precursors—the outhouse, the slide rule, the telegraph—they represent quantum, nonlinear leaps in how sewage is disposed, numbers are crunched, and messages are sent. How many of us still use the Morse code?

Clearly, technological innovation has the power to change the lives of millions in one overarching swoop. In fact, the economic destinies and living conditions of entire nations have been and continue to be radically altered by significant technological breakthroughs. As technology evolves, mutates, and permeates the world, it holds great potential and possibility for the future and, for better or for worse, leaves the lives of millions, even billions, hanging in the balance.

THE BEHAVIOR OF TECHNOLOGY

Sometimes technology develops in increments and sometimes by leaps and bounds, a phenomenon we can trace by looking briefly at the history of building materials and techniques from pre-industrial to industrial times. From earth to timber to clay to stone to iron to steel, a quick study of this evolution affords us a glimpse into the behavior of technology—how it sometimes progresses in small, linear steps and how sometimes, in one large, quantum leap, it jumps beyond itself, breaking through all the old assumptions and their concomitant constraints.

In early times, Paleolithic men, when caves were not available, made cave-like dwellings built into the ground from timber, earth, and, some believe, animal bones. Later, Neolithic men made above-the-ground structures from timber and animal hide and bones. In the Near East (which had less timber), dried clay, reeds, and palm leaves were used to construct entire villages east of the Tigris and in Jericho during the Stone Age, a time when various uses of clay were developed and proliferated as a staple element of construction.

Further developments in building technology awaited the introduction of stone by the Egyptians, who cut out and transported large blocks as heavy as 1,000 tons for use in the construction of pyramids and temples. According to T.K. Derry and Trevor Williams,[1] authors of A *Short History of Technology*, stone was also used later, in the first millennium B.C. by Assyrian king Sennacherib, to build a stone canal through which water was transported to Nineveh from a point 50 miles away.

These developments in stone-based construction did not replace earlier clay- and wood-based techniques overnight, much as modern-day technological developments do not instantly replace their predecessors. As with any new technological development, there is an incubation period during which the new technology is applied experimentally and sporadically. After this initial period of development, when the new materials and techniques are tested and refined, there comes a time when the new surpasses the old, at first overshadowing it and, eventually, rendering it secondary or obsolete. At just the right time, when the market is ready, the emerging technology is catapulted to the forefront.

In the case of stone, for hundreds of years it was combined with clay and brick and wood in construction. The Cretans, for example, used stone rubble for the bottom of their palace walls, sun-dried brick for the upper part, stone piers for the first-floor supports, and timber for the frame. Eventually, however, due to superior strength and durability, incremental accelerations in stone- and cement-based construction technologies during the Renaissance and post-Renaissance periods largely replaced the early clay-based building materials.

The introduction of iron, on the other hand, represented a leap in building and construction. Used for framework, roofwork, cement reinforcement, and, as early as 1779, for bridge building, iron ushered in a new era of building materials. At a time when multi-story mill buildings were made with solid plank floors and wooden beams and posts, the use of iron greatly reduced the threat of fire (and the cost of fire insurance!) and introduced an element of strength and flexibility theretofore unachievable. The cast-iron frame, sometimes reaching 70 feet, foreshadowed the modern type of structure that in no way relied on the walls to bear the weight of the structure.

Finally, cheap steel, even stronger and less rigid than its iron predecessor, was introduced as a structural material in the 1870s. While at first most steel was consumed by the railways for track, later it was approved by the British Board of Trade for use in bridge building. In America, the world's leader in cheap steel output, the innovative new material was used at first in the upper stories of enormously tall buildings as high as 14 stories and later in the construction of all-steel-framed skyscrapers, some as high as 386 feet. So revolutionary was this new-age material that the 21-story Masonic Temple built in 1892 in Chicago was described as one of the 7 wonders of the world.

In much the same way as earlier advances, the advent of steel combined with related technological advances to yield entirely new ways of constructing buildings and civil infrastructures. The invention of reinforced concrete for foundations and hydraulic lifts for elevators, for example, combined to make possible that stretching, formerly unimaginable structure we now call a skyscraper. It is this "technological clustering" phenomenon that has transformed society with such menacing power and sheer force and that promises to continue its upward trend for as long as humans inhabit the earth.

The legacy of building materials is, of course, long and detailed enough to fill many more pages. It is only mentioned here, with the aid of a simple, pre-industrial age example, to illustrate the developing nature of technology: how it moves, jumps, and clusters to change the way we live and make our living.

Technology is an essential and foundational element of virtually every facet of life, including building and construction, travel and communications, energy, entertainment, and industry. As such, the way it is managed and applied becomes a matter of critical importance that has far-reaching implications for consumers, businesses, and society at large. But before we discuss these implications and explore how total quality and technology, specifically information technology, work together to create competitive advantage, let us for a moment explore the power of technology.

THE POWER OF TECHNOLOGY

With the advent of industrialization and urbanization, the sheer number of technological developments multiplied and proliferated as rapidly as the very populations inhabiting our burgeoning city-states, the great symbols of modern civilization.

In architecture and construction, travel and transportation, tools and devices, agriculture, medicine, and communications, industrial-age advances were made at a pace and on a scale never before witnessed by human life. What we see with the advent of industry, in short, is an acceleration of change that is explosive beyond comprehension. In his seminal work, *Future Shock*, futurist Alvin Toffler[2] quotes eminent economist and imaginative social thinker Kenneth Boulding, who asserts: "The world of today [1970]...is as different from the world in which I was born as that world was from Julius Caesar's" (p. 13).

What Toffler is trying to get across is that during the industrial era, the pace of life quickened so dramatically that the world was literally transformed in the span of just one single person's lifetime. In an era when the mode of transportation went from the automobile to the rocket in just 40 years, technology had asserted itself as an undisputed engine of change and had set in motion a never-ending cycle of development that would change the world, and change it again, and change it again.

Although much of the key technological innovations of the past century are hidden from the view of the common person, they have the power to influence and shape our very consciousness, the way we act and interact, the way we view ourselves, raise our children, organize socially, transact business, retire, and, in short, live on the planet.

Who, for example, contemplates the vast and complex communications networks spanning our globe? Yet who is not affected by the ability to pick up a telephone anywhere in the world and call wherever they want to? Who thinks about the system of roads, railways, shipping lanes, and airways—the distribution channels—encircling the industrialized world? Yet who is not able to sit down and, all in one meal, enjoy meat from Argentina, wine from Italy, cheese from France, strawberries from California, and coffee from Jamaica? Who can fathom the intricate systems of water treatment, sewage, and drainage that lie just below the surface of our great metropolitan cities? Yet how many go one day in America without washing or bathing or without flushing unwanted waste down the toilet? And what person considers the vast and powerful electrical systems that energize our planet; the subways, tramways, and mass transit systems that lace our cities; the cables that run under our oceans or the pipelines that carry oil across vast distances? These are the core elements, the infrastructure of the industrial age, that have shaped and defined our planet and the lives of its inhabitants.

At a very basic level, then, technology forms and shapes the way we view ourselves, our role in the world, our relationships with others, and our view of nature and the world. Sometimes driven by very deliberate, planned developments and sometimes by unexpected, serendipitous ones, the grand scheme of technological progress unfolds before our very eyes and rages forward at ever-increasing speeds, changing and transforming and leaving in its wake new realities.

Yet in all their wondrous glory, the techno-developments that have been discussed heretofore are what futurist Alvin Toffler calls "second wave" innovations—foundational and key elements of industrial society. They do not approximate or come close to the technological explosion of the information era, the third great wave of human history that has been forming slowly since the 1950s and at blinding speed since around the mid-1980s.

It is on these information-age developments that this book will focus— how they shape and define the economic environment, how they literally structure and restructure whole industries and businesses, how they change the structure of competition, and how they affect the way we manage, the decisions we make, and the operating environment in which we make those decisions. From the way we plan to the way we communicate to the way we hire, train, design, purchase, produce, deliver, and distribute—technology and total quality work hand in hand to achieve organizational objectives and priorities.

Technology, however, does not develop in a vacuum. It is both a cause and result of a rapidly changing and evolving world, and it is inextricably connected to social and organizational developments and developments in the theory and practice of management. (For additional information, see Abstract 1.1 at the end of this chapter.)

THE RISE OF ORGANIZATIONAL SOCIETY, MANAGEMENT THEORY, AND TOTAL QUALITY

Industrial-era technological advances were paralleled by other important advances in the size of markets, the scale of production, the organization of productive enterprise, and the science of management. Together, these coalesced to spark the birth of quality control and to establish an economic system that, in order to function and sustain itself, required higher levels of standardization and control all along the value-added chain.

What we witness in this period is a series of explosions—in population, markets, technology and know-how, scientific discovery, organizational and institutional sophistication, and management methodologies. We see the train of development set in motion during the Renaissance gathering momentum and progressing with ever-increasing, even exponential, speed. If

Galileo Galile, Rene Descartes, Francis Bacon, and Leonardo DaVinci defined and paved the way for the new society, those who came later—Isaac Newton, Adam Smith, Frederick Taylor, Walter Shewhart, and Edwards Deming—made it happen. What we see, in short, is a new society unfolding before us.

Essentially, a flurry of productive activity occurred in the mid-18th century, fueled by the collision of multiple factors: the further organization and institutionalization of European society, the continuing emphasis on humanism and the role of man in exercising power and control over the environment, the proliferation of scientific thinking and methods, the increasing influence and exponential effect of technological innovation, such as steam power, and increased demand for industrial output (England's population doubled between 1750 and 1820).

Output of rubber from Brazil (the world's main supplier of the raw material) grew, for example, from 31 tons in 1827 to 27,650 in 1900, a dramatic rate of growth brought on in part by the advent of vulcanization, advances in transportation and distribution, and rapidly increasing demand. Similar order-of-magnitude advances were made in mining, agriculture, textiles, iron and steel, chemicals, industrial machinery, pottery and glass, printing and photography, canning, refrigeration, and food processing and preservation—to name a few. In literally hundreds of areas, the face and inner workings of industry were transforming.

Around the late 19th and early 20th century, the locus of work shifted from the family to the factory, and the beginnings of large-scale production took root. To meet demand—the sheer volume of output—industrialists sought economies of scale and restructured the production process to include greater division of labor, more centralized discipline and regulation, and hierarchical planning and control. New products, new processes, new machinery, new production techniques, new markets, and new management and organizational forms combined to fashion a new world order and undeniably instituted new requirements for controlling the uniformity and quality of inputs and outputs throughout an ever-lengthening value chain. In short, an increasingly complex production process required greater organization and coordination, more varied human skills (labor and management), and new methods and techniques of quality control.

And so began the legacy of total quality: in close connection with concurrent developments in technology, production, organization, and management. As we enter the future, then, the challenge for total quality is to maintain and improve this important relationship between technology; the tools, techniques, and raw materials of production; and the management methods employed to organize, bridle, control, and plan the value-added process of information-intensive businesses and business functions.

Before delving into the specifics of total quality—what it is, how it developed, and how it is applied in an information systems environment—

let's explore the characteristics of the emerging information society, the new applications of information technology, and the challenges facing organizations as they do business in an increasingly information-driven economy.

THE AGE OF INFORMATION

If the world was transformed by industry, it was transformed yet again by information. In today's environment of techno-wizardry, the innovations of yesterday—the printing press, the cotton gin, the telegraph, the railroad, the combustible engine—evoke a languid response and wane greatly in comparison to the present onslaught of information-age innovations bombarding our minds and lives at every juncture.

With all their power to transform the world, most industrial-age technological innovations relied primarily on mechanics, not information. With the rapid rise of the service economy and information-driven technology, however, the information quotient has grown exponentially and continues to increase at breakneck speed.

Already, the world is well into what futurist Alvin Toffler calls the third great phase of human history—the information age—about which he eloquently penned the following words in *The Third Wave:*[3]

> For Third Wave civilization, the most basic raw material of all—and one that can never be exhausted—is information, including imagination. Through imagination and information, substitutes will be found for many of today's exhaustible resources although this substitution, once more, will all too frequently be accompanied by drastic economic swings and lurches.
>
> With information becoming more important than ever before, the new civilization will restructure education, redefine scientific research and, above all, reorganize the media of communication. Today's mass media, both print and electronic, are wholly inadequate to cope with the communications load and to provide the requisite cultural variety for survival. Instead of being culturally dominated by a few mass media, Third Wave civilization will rest on inter-active, de-massified media, feeding extremely diverse and often highly personalized imagery into and out of the mindstream of the society.
>
> Looking far ahead, television will give way to "indi-videon"— narrow-casting carried to the ultimate: images addressed to a single individual at a time. We may also eventually use drugs, direct brain-to-brain communication, and other forms of electro-

chemical communication only vaguely hinted at until now. All of which will raise startling, though not insoluble, political and moral problems.

The giant centralized computer with its whirring tapes and complex cooling systems—where it still exists—will be supplanted by myriad chips of intelligence, embedded in one form or another in every home, hospital, and hotel, every vehicle and appliance, virtually every building-brick. The electronic environment will literally converse with us.

With eerie accuracy, Toffler's words, articulated in 1980, pinpoint the reality of 1995 and beyond. From outer space to cyberspace in just one generation, the world of the past 30 years has seen, and absorbed, more change than all previous generations combined! In essence, the transition from industrial society to information society, now complete, is a revolution unprecedented in human history. With ever-quickening modes of transportation, ever-pervasive networks of data communications, and ever-increasing options, the world as we once knew it is changing before our eyes: it is becoming smaller, more personalized, and more interconnected and the boundaries of space and time are blurring. (For additional information, see Abstract 1.2 at the end of this chapter.)

Information and its by-product, knowledge, have firmly established themselves as the undisputed engines of the new economy. The spectacular productivity improvements of the past 50 years, in conjunction with the rapid rise of service- and information-intensive businesses and business functions, have caused tectonic shifts in the structure of the world economy that have hurled information into center stage and relegated labor- and capital-intensive businesses and business functions to a secondary, even tertiary, position in the economic pecking order.

Eminent management guru Peter Drucker,[4] in *Post-Capitalist Society*, offers the following comments about the decline of manufacturing and labor-driven business activity:

When Frederick Taylor started to study work, nine out of ten working people did manual work, *making or moving things;* in manufacturing, in farming, in mining, in transportation. Forty years ago, in the 1950's, people who engaged in work to make or move things were still a majority in all developed countries. By 1990, they had shrunk to one fifth of the workforce. By 2010, they will form no more than one tenth. The Productivity Revolution has become a victim of its own success. From now on, what matters is the productivity of non-manual workers.

Essentially Drucker has articulated the end of capitalism, or at least capitalism in its original form. He and others, like Alvin Toffler, Robert Reich, and Tom Peters, have made it their business to understand the stream of change that promises to turn into a flowing river and, at some point not far in the future, a gushing rapid of info-possibility—cybernetic galaxies yet unexplored.

In this brave digital world, information will replace capital and labor as the primary factor of production. Already, the presence and availability of information technology is transforming formerly labor- and capital-intensive industries such as farming and manufacturing. Italian businessman Vittorio Merloni, whose company makes 10 percent of all washing machines, refrigerators, and other household appliances sold in Europe, says, "We need less capital now to do the same thing. The reason is that knowledge-based technologies are reducing the capital needed to produce, say, dishwashers, stoves or vacuum cleaners"[5] (p. 89). Among other applications, Mr. Merloni is using information technology to reduce high-cost inventory and speed factory responsiveness to the market.

In hundreds of thousands of companies, information is assuming a greatly expanded role. Even in Germany, where manufacturing is still king, information technology has made its way into the center of business life. At premier toolmaker Trumpf, although apprentices still devote most of a year to hand-filing metal, one-third of the company's research staff is comprised of software engineers, according to Tom Peters.

In *Liberation Management*, Peters[6] (pp. 113–114) outlines a few examples of how information technology is changing or more accurately—radically altering—the way business is conducted. Among these are the following:

- *Business Week*, July 1991—"In the future, U.S. apparel factories will need automated sewing equipment to remain competitive with overseas competitors. But one question that raises is quality control. Now, researchers at the Georgia Institute of Technology in Atlanta have designed electronic 'ears' that enable sewing machines to supervise their own work and check for mistakes....Broken or worn needles have a distinctive sound, or acoustic signature. Computer analysis of those signatures reveals that the amplitudes increase in proportion to how badly the needle is worn. When the sewing machine hears this, they trigger a flashing light that notifies a human operator that maintenance or adjustments are necessary."

- Consultant Stan Davis and professor Bill Davidson in *2020 Vision*—"Cattle were sold in stockyards in the industrial economy, but video auctions on an electronic network could mean that stockyards would go the way of the old-fashioned cattle drive. Superior Livestock Auction of Fort Worth uses satellite transmission, television cameras and computerized buying networks to auction steers that never leave the ranch until they are sold."

- A Coors promotional stunt reported in the *Toronto Globe and Mail,* May 26, 1992—"A microchip inside a container nestled within a can of Coors Light enables it to 'talk.' When exposed to light, it is supposed to say, 'You win!,' and then describes the prize, items like stereos and compact disks, valued in excess of $1 million."

The business of sewing machines, cows, and beer will never be the same. All will be transformed, in one way or another, by the power of information technology.

Even in the grocery business, information technology has become a core and essential element, a prerequisite for survival. Through optical scanning technology, long checkout lines and errors in accounting have been minimized. The Universal Product Code or bar code (the small black box of lines and numbers that appears on everything from applesauce to laundry detergent) has forever changed the way products are packaged, distributed, stocked, sold, and ordered. According to Toffler, bar coding has become nearly universal in the United States, with fully 95 percent of all food items marked by the distinctive little symbol. In France, by 1988, 3,470 supermarkets and specialty department stores were using it. In West Germany, 1,500 food stores and 200 department stores employed scanners. From Brazil to Czechoslovakia and Papua New Guinea, there were 78,000 scanners at work as far back as 1988.[5]

As with virtually any application of information technology, however, the examples above represent only the infant stages of the information age, the first babbling expressions of just-born technology. In supermarkets and retail stores, for example, consumers may soon find themselves navigating their way through aisles lined with "electronic shelves." Instead of paper tags indicating the price of items, they will find blinking liquid crystal displays with digital price readouts. The implications are staggering. In addition to automatically changing thousands of prices from a remote location, the new displays would provide nutritional and other information at the touch of a button and even elicit market research information from the consumer.

In retail, Wal-Mart is setting the electronic pace by requiring all its vendors to be tied into its system of electronic data exchange. Simply through the use of integrated computer-to-computer systems, Wal-Mart's suppliers know when the retailer is running low on specific products and send new inventory automatically—without any order being placed, without any unnecessary handoffs or steps in between.

What we are moving toward is a seamless connection between consumers and manufacturers. According to George Fields, chairman and CEO of ASI Market Research (Japan), "distribution no longer means putting something on the shelf. It is now essentially an information system." Distribution, he notes, "will no longer be a chain of inventory points, passing goods along the line, but an information link between the manufacturer and the consumer"[5] (p. 105).

In this environment, "prosumers"—a term coined by Alvin Toffler[3] in *The Third Wave*—become actively engaged in product design. Using CAD/CAM software, for instance, the day when prosumers will be able to participate in the design of their vehicles at the dealer's workstation may not be too far off in the future. A prosumer can preselect the body structure, drive train components, and suspension components and can tailor the car's lighting system or instrument panel layout to fit personal preferences. And, perhaps most impressive, the car can be delivered within three days after the order is placed.

In countless instances, across the board, information technology is redefining how companies conduct business and succeed in the marketplace. From the development of new information-related products and services such as personal computers and software development; to the design of new noninformation-related products such as automobiles, stereo systems, and razor blades; to the construction of prototypes; to the invention of new products; to the "smartening" of everything from sewing machines to elevators to shopping carts to machine tools to buildings, the role and economic significance of information technology are rapidly expanding.

Information is, in short, taking over the world. According to Davis and Davidson,[7] authors of *2020 Vision*, by the year 2020, 80 percent of business profits and market value will come from that part of the enterprise that is built around info-businesses. In this world of heightened info-possibility, those who know how to develop, acquire, and utilize information for their companies and their customers will outpace and outsmart their competitors and win in the game of global competition. Today's business leaders unequivocally understand that when it comes to information, there are no options: either you get it, develop it, and use it to your best advantage or fall into the abyss of a forgotten age.

Consider the following words of Alex Mandl, an executive in the transportation company CSX, as quoted in *Powershift*, by Alvin Toffler:[5]

> The information component of our service package is growing bigger and bigger. It's not just enough to deliver products. Customers want information. Where their products will be consolidated and deconsolidated, what time each item will be where, prices, customs information, and much more. We are an information-driven business (p. 76).

Everywhere, the importance of information is growing, even exploding. In every sector of the economy and in every business function and activity, information is creeping, and sometimes leaping, into center stage. The rules of the game are changing. Restructuring, reengineering, revitalization, and even total quality management methods are of little help in today's high-tech society without the speed and power of information technology and information systems. In boosting productivity and profitability, in improving quality and reliability, in lowering costs, and in increasing customer responsiveness, information is critical.

In a world where antiballistic missiles can, at a speed of more than several thousand miles per hour, hone in and make final real-time trajectory adjustments while in flight before obliterating their moving targets; where, in the United States alone, more than 400 million customers book flights on daily domestic flights annually; where entire libraries full of data are transmitted over great distances in a matter of minutes; where, all in the space of 12 seconds, the word *moshimoshi* is spoken in Japanese and translated into Japanese text by one computer, which then passes it on to another computer that translates it into English and sends it via modem to yet another computer, which reads the text and synthesizes the English word "hello"; in this world, the role of information technology—and its possibilities—is skyrocketing.[5,6]

So deeply and significantly has information changed the corporate landscape that the very character of the organization and the way it produces and delivers value is changing too. Old paradigms are tumbling, falling by the wayside. Outmoded concepts of work, rigid organizational hierarchies and structures, excessive division of labor, and large-batch production—once the hallmarks of industry—are now going the way of the dinosaur.

A new era is upon us, one in which organizations are flat and flexible; bureaucracies, hierarchies, and rigid structures are dissolving; labor and business activity is increasingly cross-functional; and production is fast and made-to-order in small batches—all trends made possible and undergirded by the presence and proliferation of information-based technologies. What we are witnessing, in a nutshell, is the integration of previously separated, disjointed market and organizational functions. The boundaries are blurring—between consumers and producers, between suppliers and customers, between departments and functions within the organization.

In this environment, the average life span of new products is drastically declining, cycle times of everything from invoice processing to field repairs are falling sharply, and the time required to complete value-added activities continues to plummet. In this environment, Japanese automakers are actively pursuing the "72-hour car"; Citicorp Mortgage is processing loans in 15 minutes; Sony Corporation is churning out a different model of its Walkman about once every three weeks; market and competitive intelligence data are gathered, processed, and acted on in week-long cycles; and salesmen in the field are digitally connected with the production floor so that as soon as orders are placed, production begins. Developing before us is a new organizational culture, fueled and driven by information, where there is a premium on speed and flexibility and where, all at once, the needs and wishes of greatly varied customers—from housewives to Hare Krishnas—can be met with accuracy, precision, and impeccable timing. (For additional information, see Abstract 1.3 at the end of this chapter.)

THE CULTURE OF CHANGE

The world, and the corporation, is becoming less static and more dynamic. "We do not seek permanence," says Matsushita Corporation's Chief of Design Masatoshi Naito. "...Consumption is a continuous cycle of new products replacing old products, everything is in a process of change, nothing endures"[6] (p. 3). Indeed, today, the only constant is change. Even change itself has changed: it happens faster, its implications reach further, and its power to render today's products and services obsolete is growing stronger by the day. "The nineties will be a decade in a hurry, a nanosecond culture," says vice-chairman of Northern Telecom David Vice. "There'll be only two kinds of managers [and organizations]: the quick and the dead"[6] (p. 59).

Throughout the developed world, the culture of change is taking root and shaping the way we think, plan, make, sell, service, and structure our organizations and value-added networks. The creation, coordination, transmission, management, and use of information and information-based technologies will keep pushing the world toward one huge, interconnected economic system already foreshadowed by the rising regional economies of the Pacific Rim, the European Union, the Americas, and several other regional economic alliances.

The challenge, then, for information systems executives is to apply their craft and develop their systems in a way that will best perpetuate and facilitate the fluid and open business environment we find unfolding before us. It is in this permanently ephemeral world that the instruments and intelligence of the information age find life and purpose and are employed to ensure the continued success of the ever-transforming corporation. And it is in this culture of perpetual change and permanent flexibility that the instruments and methods of total quality are applied in conjunction with the proliferating information technologies and their myriad applications.

Before we discuss how total quality and information technology work together to maximize organizational effectiveness, let's go one step further in our overview of information technology in the information age. Let's look briefly at a few of the key emerging technologies—how they are impacting individual consumers; how they are being used by companies to create competitive advantage; how, in short, they are altering the present and forming the future.

NETWORKS, SATELLITES, AND SUPERHIGHWAYS

Like the railroads, highways, canals, and electrical and telephone systems of the industrial age, the emerging information networks promise to rewrite the rules for doing business in the information age. Networks have always been at the center of technological and civilizational progress, have always spurred drastic changes in the way goods and services are brought to market, and, at a fundamental level, have changed the way business is transacted.

Can we attempt to describe what kind of coordination and control is necessary to run today's enterprises—modern railways, airports, telecommunications networks? Since 1850, the world population has more than quadrupled, the speed at which man can travel has increased from 100 miles per hour to more than 18,000, and systems—from power to transportation to telecommunications—have proliferated, grown in complexity, and forever reconfigured the course of civilization.

Today, the new information networks are rewiring the planet. Although these emerging networks build on the cables and wires laid and strung during the industrial era, they are changing, improving, and replacing these systems with altogether new ones that promise to hurl the world—and all that is in it—into a new reality. Known to many as cyberspace, the emerging reality is one in which previously only imagined possibilities are materializing in our midst.

Consider TRON Pilot Intelligent House, for example, located in Tokyo. You approach the TRON house, located in the heart of Tokyo, and the lights turn on. You drop your briefcase in a bin in the closet, and it is whisked away by a conveyor belt and stored in the basement. Later, you turn on a video monitor and scroll through pictures of as many as ten similar cases, each containing a unique set of contents, and pick the one you want. You select it and, presto, it is whisked back into your closet bin. The house is so sophisticated that you can draw your bath by phone before leaving the office. Cooking a meal is as simple as punching a couple of buttons on the combination oven/VCR, with a video showing you how to prepare the meal. Sprinklers automatically turn on and water the plants. There is even a "smart" toilet that adjusts the strength, direction, and temperature of the water spewing from the bidet, and the attached computer conducts a detailed urinalysis and blood-pressure test. Controlled by wires, cameras, and sensors running through the walls and ceilings, the pilot smart home is a product of collaboration between 18 Japanese companies, including Nippon Telegraph & Telephone Corporation, Mitsubishi Electric Corporation, and Seibu Department Store Ltd.[6]

But the smart home is only the beginning, a narrow slice of the burgeoning info-sphere. Also just over the horizon lies the much-publicized "interactive, multimedia revolution," the great confluence of television, computers, telephones, faxes, and video cameras. Inside this smart home, so the vision holds, there will be an electronic epicenter, a section of the living room parceled off for nothing more than the electronic machinations of those family members who are young enough or technologically astute enough to navigate themselves through the cybernetic world invading their homes.

Want to call up a movie from a library of thousands using a menu displayed on the television screen? Want to buy a wedding gift by selecting the wedding department, searching for gifts in a certain price range, paying for your selection, and arranging for pickup or delivery all with the touch of a few buttons on your telephone or remote control device? Want your phone calls digitized and your callers pictured in a little box on your TV screen? Want to study the third baseman during a ball game, while others view the batter? Play Street Fighter or NBA Jam with another video game junkie located hundreds of miles away? Surf 500 channels? Replay that action scene? Design and customize your own clothing?

Well, say the experts, in the not-too-distant future, you will be able to do all this and more. It will be made possible by glass fibers that can carry as much as 250,000 times more data than the old copper wires, space satellites that beam information in large batches to regional earth stations, and home-based "smart boxes" that manage and coordinate incoming and outgoing data. The electronic superhighway is on its way.

Yet as much as the so-called Infobahn or I-way is giving birth to a cornucopia of novel applications and possibilities for the private user, the real potential lies in the corporate sector, where businesses and organizations are capitalizing on the commercial opportunities presented by the unfolding information age.

In retail, trade, manufacturing, electronics, construction—in virtually every business sector—the growing data-sphere is revolutionizing how market and customer data are gathered and used and how products and services are made, distributed, sold, and serviced. Some companies, such as those in telecommunications, computers, and fiber optics, are transforming the marketplace while at the same time transforming themselves. MCI, for example, while building the new communications infrastructure also expects to employ that infrastructure in conducting its business. Similarly, Corning Glass Works, maker of fiber-optic cables, will benefit from the very cables it makes and sells. And Intel, maker of the much ballyhooed Pentium chip, will use it to run its own personal computers.

More than any other, however, the software companies stand to cash in on the coming revolution, for it is they that will shape and define the underlying structure of the emerging business environment. It is their contributions that promise to be even more important and impressive than the fibers, cables, and satellites through which their bits and mips race at raging speeds. It is for the brain of the information economy that the coming commercial battles will be fought, for it, more than anything, will determine the character and course of the coming cyber-culture.

All these companies—MCI, Corning, Intel—and thousands more are the pioneers of the information frontier, the engineers of the information age. They are on the vanguard of change, and it is their special contributions that will raise the entire economic machinery—from market research to product and service design to raw material extraction and processing to production, sales, and after-sales service—to a new level. It is their contributions that will enable companies in all sectors to design more quickly, produce more efficiently, and simply do what they do better. (For additional information, see Abstract 1.4 at the end of this chapter.)

The real revolution, then, is not taking place in our living rooms. It is being shaped and formed in the boardrooms, from England to Japan. It is changing the way companies do business, the way they act and interact with their suppliers, customers, shareholders, regulators—every last constituent, institution, or organization with which they come in contact. In a nutshell, information is transforming the very heart of the modern corporation.

While there is not space enough here to cover the entire spectrum of new systems, applications, products, machines, robots, tools, gadgets, and devices used in business and brought on by the information revolution, a few examples of current corporate information infrastructure developments are in order. These are the networks and mega-networks that undergird and make possible the budding info-revolution.

Local Area Networks

Local area networks are popping up everywhere, connecting PC users in one building or complex. From the tiny business with two or three computers to larger ones that employ hundreds, local area networks are revolutionizing the way people communicate and work together. Through electronic mail, for example, Richard Pogue, a managing partner of a global law firm, keeps communications "personal, collegiality high and far-flung offices part of the team." E-mail, according to Pogue, lets people converse with him who otherwise might be too intimidated to drop by his office. And while a memo may sit in his briefcase for weeks, the psychology of wanting to wipe that screen clean impels Pogue to respond almost instantly to his 35 to 40 daily electronic messages.[6] From quarterly financial data to information about the wellness program, E-mail is changing the way people communicate within the corporation.

Bulletin Boards and Databases

Bulletin boards and databases covering such diverse interests as new legislation, stock market performance, education for the handicapped, and the weather are available for online perusal and interaction. With only a PC and modem, these networks allow the individual user to tap into specific sources of information and, in many cases, download that information onto a floppy or hard drive. Through a small window the size of a monitor, bulletin boards and databases enable the user to view and experience vast infoscapes and to interact with any of the hundreds of thousands of other users planet-wide.

Just one such available information utility is Minitel, a system developed by France Telecom, a government-owned telephone company. With 18 percent of all French households hooked up to Mintel through terminals provided free of charge, citizens can access a variety of paid services: travel information, news, banking interest rates, online shopping, and the wildly popular "messagerie rose," an adults-only fantasy line.[8]

Of course the network of networks, the ultimate bulletin board, is Internet, an interconnected group of networks connecting academic, research, government, and commercial institutions from within the United States and in more than 40 countries worldwide. Research house Dataquest reports: "Somewhere between 20 and 30 million people around the globe use the Net more or less regularly. The graphical portion called the World Wide Web is stocked with more than 22 million pages of content, with over 1 million more pages added each month."[9]

Collaborative Networks (Computer-Augmented Collaboration)

These are special electronic tools designed to support the process of collaboration so vital in the present business climate, where there is a premium on team power—the process by which people unite their minds and skills to tackle problems and issues, design new products, configure new systems, or write business plans. For example, computer-generated shared space is a good way to get people to participate playfully in meetings. A large screen becomes a community computer screen where everyone can write, draw, scribble, type, or otherwise offer information for community viewing. It is shared space. People can produce on it or pollute it. Traditional conversational etiquette does not apply here. One person may write a controversial message on the community screen while another talks about something else. Ostensibly, this may not seem revolutionary, but exploring ideas and arguments in the context of shared space can completely transform conversation. The software injects a discipline and encourages people to create, visually and orally, a shared understanding with their colleagues. The technology motivates people to collaborate.[6]

Electronic Data Interchange Systems

The object here is intimacy, or connectivity. The means is electronic data interchange (EDI) systems—electronic connections that greatly ease the burden of interacting with suppliers, customers, and other entities within and external to the organization. By electronically integrating key functions, such as invoicing, scheduling, and material requisitions, the value-added chain is made tighter and stronger at key linkage points. Inventories are reduced, engineering data are exchanged, work scheduling is improved, distribution networks are streamlined, market feedback and research are collected, and many of the former costs associated with coordination, communication, and linkage are greatly reduced. More and more companies are bringing EDI systems on line. The big auto companies, for instance, now refuse to do business with suppliers that are not equipped for electronic interaction.

Expert Systems

These systems are able to do much more than store and organize data in rigid categories, recall facts and figures, and package outputs for the user. Through extensive programming, expert systems can approximate *intelligence*. In addition to storing facts, they determine and change the relationships between those facts. As new information becomes available, the knowledge base (the database of the expert system) can reorganize and repackage its outputs to reflect the new input obtained. Although still far from perfect, expert systems have saved millions of man-hours and dollars in fields as diverse as medicine, manufacturing, and insurance.

For example, Digital Equipment Corporation's XCON, perhaps the most successful expert system in commercial use today, has been configuring complex computer systems since 1980. The system's knowledge base consists of more than 10,000 rules describing the relationship among various computer parts. It reportedly does the work of more than 300 human experts, with fewer mistakes. Other expert systems include MYCIN, a medical system that outperforms many human experts in diagnosing diseases.[8]

Parallel Systems and Neural Networks

In the quest for speed and power, parallel processing machines use multiple processors to work on several tasks at the same time. The technology is especially promising for such applications as speech recognition, computer vision, and other pattern-recognition tasks. Some supercomputers, called Connection Machines, use as many as 64,000 inexpensive processors in parallel to execute thousands of instructions simultaneously in the achievement of complicated tasks, such as those required by expert systems.

One complex parallel system is the neural network, which utilizes thousands of simple processors called neurons and which approximates the parallel structure of the human brain. Instead of processing information in linear, sequential steps according to a set of rules, neural networks are able to process information concurrently and distributively and, in doing so, learn by trial and error—somewhat like the way humans learn. In effect, they train themselves and form habits based on their past experience. Some neural networks, for example, are intelligent enough to narrow or widen themselves as a function of how much electronic traffic they find pulsing through their systems. That would be like an interstate widening and narrowing itself automatically based on how many cars it found rolling across its surface!

Already, neural networks are being used at banks to recognize signatures on checks and at financial institutions to analyze complicated correlations between hundreds of variables and the performance of the Standard and Poor's 500 index. In the future, researchers are hopeful that the nets may provide hearing for the deaf and sight for the blind.

Corporate Virtual Workspaces

The information revolution is so important that it may end up redefining every aspect of corporate life, including the very space in which companies operate. The corporate competitive advantage will lie in the acquisition and use of information. Companies have the ability to be dispersed geographically and replace existing physical facilities. Employees can now work from home or other mobile locations. Permanent office space will no longer be a necessity. Sales and marketing can take place using the information highway, otherwise known as cyberspace.

Corporate virtual workspaces, neural networks, expert systems, EDIs, the Internet—these are the elements of the information infrastructure that promises to change the way we conduct business in the post-capitalist age. These are the systems that will define the structure, character, and behavior of the info-corporation. Add to these the throngs of information-based technological innovations—computer-integrated manufacturing, computer-aided design, digital image processing, optical character and automatic speech recognition, three-dimensional modeling, virtual reality, hypermedia, digital video, computer vision, xerography, and liquid crystal and plasma displays—and you have an info-society complete with info-products from the most commonplace to the most advanced and bizarre. How many are aware, for example, that scientists have constructed tiny robots the size of large insects to handle maneuvers in spaces too small for human involvement, or that in the field of microtechnology, scientists have already produced motors no more than the width of two human hairs? Some day, they say, these microscopic machines might be crawling around inside the human body, searching out and destroying aberrant cells like those that cause cancer.

From the living room to the local ATM to the factories and offices of corporate America—and everywhere in between—the power and presence of information are linking up the planet, connecting and integrating people, companies, and nations and changing and redefining the very foundation upon which modern civilization was built and upon which the economy of industrial society was formed. Today, we rely not so much on railroads, highways, airways, and shipping lanes (the infrastructure of the industrial age) as we rely on satellites, optical cables, computers, and modems (the infrastructure of the post-industrial age). Like an expansive convolution of interlocking spider webs girdling the globe—networks within networks within networks—the new information infrastructure is becoming something like the neurological system of the planet.

Just how vast and pervasive the cyber-frontier will become is not a question for the novice or recreational thinker; it is a question asked by tough-minded businesspeople whose destinies are certain to be swept into the swirling vortex of information-driven change and whose futures will depend on their ability to navigate and manage their way through the ever-thickening info-sphere. (For additional information, see Abstract 1.5 at the end of this chapter.)

THE NEXUS OF INFORMATION TECHNOLOGY AND TOTAL QUALITY

Background and History

Without detailing the history and legacy of total quality (a topic addressed in Chapter 4), it is enough for our purposes here to simply establish that, from the beginning, the quest for quality has influenced our behavior and the outputs of our labor. From the terra-cotta sculptures of Babylon to the pyramids of Egypt to the self-contained cities of Greece and Rome—and beyond—the quest to create and maintain quality has permeated the tasks to which man has applied his hands. As the architects of civilization, and as the perpetuators of art and industry, humans have always been galvanized by the drive to produce works of distinctive form and function. The quest for quality is, in short, embedded in the human soul.

It is the evolving soul of man, then, that has driven and defined the course of quality throughout the ages. In ancient times, the quality of man's products was guided by a sense of enchantment, wonder, myth, and mysticism; the gods were in complete control, and the work of humans merely reflected their omnipresence and omnipotence. In Classical times, the quality of art and industry reflected an increasing emphasis on technological know-how, in addition to a continuing emphasis on the spiritual verities of existence, as evidenced in the great temples and ornate and intricate shrines of Greece and Rome.

During the Renaissance, we begin to see a dramatic shift in the nature of man and, commensurately, in the nature and application of quality. With growing attention to material life and science, man's sense of quality began to shift from the spiritual to the practical. Instead of applying his aesthetic sensibilities to works of art, he increasingly applied his analytical sensibilities to the accelerating sciences. In the important pursuits of medicine and invention, for example, quality was becoming increasingly synonymous with utility and function, not beauty and form.

Yet it was not until the advent of industry that quality began to grow into a science unto itself. Spurred by the advent of mass production and hierarchical organizations, the quest for quality turned completely material and reflected the nature and character of the unfolding industrial culture. Quality, like everything, began to conform with the scientific paradigm. In accordance with developing markets, production methods, organizational structures, and management theory, quality, like the whole of society, grew out of the tinkering stage and passed into the stage of economic necessity. The age of mass production and consumption—the consumer society—had arrived, and with it came the imperative to manage and control the processes by which products were churned off the production line.

From this point on, we are quite familiar with the trajectory of quality control. It was first applied in the form of statistical process control to ensure product uniformity and to prevent defects. Next, it was expanded to include the people-oriented processes of quality circles and quality teams. After this, the blossoming methods and techniques of quality control were applied in the nonproduction areas, such as procurement, delivery, and other services, including information systems. And finally, as pioneered by the Japanese in the 1950s, quality methods and principles had become so pervasively applied that they evolved into what is today called total quality management, or total quality.

Integration through Total Quality

Why is total quality so important in today's world, where at the touch of a few buttons we can launch rockets into outer space, where our factories are populated with robots and smart machinery, and where soon we will be able to use our television sets to get an education, pay our bills, and participate in town meetings?

The answer is that as smart as our machines are and as powerful as our information might be, we still live in a world dominated by the behavior and movement of people and the organizations to which they belong. Computers, although they can help us perform complex, detailed analyses and tasks, cannot think strategically, consider the moral implications of their actions, or even begin to comprehend the work to which they are applied. In short, they cannot manage.

Total quality, on the other hand, encompasses the whole. It is an overall management framework through which to integrate the various elements of a successful organization: strategy, policy, planning, information systems, project management—all the activities required to run today's large, complex organizations. In this capacity, total quality plays the role of integrator, focusing the entire organization in one direction, coordinating the plans and actions of hundreds of otherwise fragmented organizational sections and functions, controlling the processes and outputs all along the value-added chain, and improving the business by increments and, when necessary, by leaps and bounds.

There is, then, a unique synergy between total quality and information technology: when they are properly applied together, they can catapult an organization into new levels of market strength. Total quality and information systems work together to reduce defects, decrease cycle time, improve safety, improve delivery, increase reliability, and increase customer service and satisfaction.

The power and miracle of information technology is simply only as good as the structures and processes of the organization in which it is applied. Many companies are implementing high technology merely to become technical innovators or leaders. They are doing so without rethinking their corporate goals and objectives. They are using technology as the instant business solution without matching technology to their corporate strategy and plans. Without aligning new technology with the corporate strategy, the solution often becomes more complex and expensive.

The danger we encounter with technology is that if we do not change the way we do business at a fundamental level, it only allows us to do the *wrong things* faster. According to Michael Hammer,[10] the nation's forerunning expert on business reengineering, technology without business process redesign is, at best, a poor allocation of resources and, at worst, a good way to automate yourself out of business. The irony is that although we have made great and amazing advances in technology, many of us still follow business processes that were invented long before the advent of the computer, modern communications, and other technological innovations.

Many business processes and methods were designed to compensate for a time when we lived in relative technological poverty. Although we are now technologically affluent, we often find it difficult to break out of the old way of thinking: that certain processes, certain methods by which business is conducted—methods that were invented decades ago—are set in stone. The practical result, according to Hammer, in the information technology industry is that many of these archaic assumptions are now deeply embedded in automated systems.

The key point about technology and total quality, then, is that both need to reflect the possibilities of an advanced technological age, not the constraints of an age gone by. When this occurs, the results can be staggering. Consider the following organizations that used total quality in conjunction with information technology to gain an edge in the marketplace:

- IBM Credit reduced the amount of time it takes to approve a customer's credit application from seven days to four hours while achieving a hundredfold improvement in productivity.[10]
- Federal Mogul, a billion-dollar auto parts manufacturer, reduced the time to develop a new part prototype from 20 weeks to 20 days.[11]
- Mutual Benefit Life, a large insurance company, halved the costs associated with underwriting and issuing policies.[11]
- The IRS achieved a 33 percent rise in the amount of tax dollars collected from delinquent taxpayers with half its former staff and a third fewer branch offices.[11]
- Ford reduced the number of people involved in paying vendors from 500 to 125. In some parts of the company, like the Engine Division, the head count for accounts payable is just 5 percent of its former size.[10]
- Eastman Kodak slashed its product development process for its 35-mm single-use camera nearly in half while reducing its tooling and manufacturing costs by 25 percent.[10]

For additional information, see Abstract 1.6 at the end of this chapter.

What we learn from these companies, and what we will demonstrate in the chapters that follow, is that the role of information technology in a total quality effort is secondary, not primary. It is a means to an end, not an end in itself. We will learn that, like a thoroughbred horse, information technology must be bridled and harnessed by the effective application of total quality principles and methodologies. We will learn how executives and corporate leaders apply total quality to the information technology function and how information technology, in turn, supports the company's strategic intent and improvement objectives.

ENDNOTES

1. Derry, T.K. and Williams, Trevor I. (1961). *A Short History of Technology.* New York: Oxford University Press.
2. Toffler, Alvin (1970). *Future Shock.* New York: Bantam.
3. Toffler, Alvin (1981). *The Third Wave.* New York: Bantam.
4. Drucker, Peter F. (1993). *Post-Capitalist Society.* New York: HarperCollins.
5. Toffler, Alvin (1990). *Powershift.* New York: Bantam.
6. Peters, Tom (1992). *Liberation Management.* New York: Alfred A. Knopf.
7. Davis, Stan and Davidson, Bill (1991). *2020 Vision.* New York: Simon and Schuster.
8. Beekman, George (1994). *Computer Currents.* Redwood City, CA: Benjamin Cummings.
9. "Taming the Internet." *U.S. News and World Report.* Spring Tech Guide, April 29, 1996.
10. Hammer, Michael and Champy, James (1993). *Reengineering the Corporation.* New York: HarperCollins.
11. Davenport, Thomas (1993). *Process Innovation: Reengineering Work Through Information Technology.* Boston: Harvard Business School Press.

ABSTRACTS

ABSTRACT 1.1
ACHIEVING TOTAL QUALITY THROUGH INTELLIGENCE

Fuld, Leonard M.
Long Range Planning, February 1992, pp. 109–115

Information—in whatever form—can empower employees to make continuous improvements in product and process, contends the author, by monitoring customers, competitors, and suppliers. He describes the complexities of information sharing at Corning, where 25,000 employees at 90 locations throughout the world must communicate about 60,000 products and services. A "Corrective Action Team" was formed to conduct an information audit. This resulted in a computer-based "Information Exchange Intelligence System" that allows information entry and access throughout the company. Cost per user is lowered by making the system accessible to all employees, and instead of funneling all information through the company's information systems department, data can be entered by any system user in a standard format. By creating a personal electronic file folder, any time new information that matches a user's request is fed into the system, it is entered into the user's folder for viewing the next business day. A sidebar to the article, based on a survey of over 200 large companies, highlights six principles for building an information system for total quality. The bulk of the article discusses the way information flow is important to the five key factors assessed by Baldrige Award examiners:

1. Customer focus

2. Meeting commitments

3. Process management and elimination of waste

4. Employee involvement and empowerment

5. Continuous improvement

The author gives examples from a number of companies, such as Xerox, M&M Mars, Johnson & Johnson, IBM, GTE, and Milliken.

ABSTRACT 1.2
KEIRETSU IN AMERICA

Kinni, Theodore B.
Quality Digest, December 1992, pp. 24–31

The author is a well-known business writer who presents a concise and intriguing look at one of the key features of Japan's success—an integrated marketing and sales/purchasing/supplier quality management system: *keiretsu.* The opening frame sets the stage with a simple well-directed statement: "Corporate Communism? Industrial war machines? As U.S. business comes to terms with dealing with Japan Inc. on home turf, it's time we understood how our new neighbors do business." The reason, according to Kinni, is that Japanese business interests hold a sizable stake in over 1,500 U.S. factories, a fact which is confirmed by the Japan External Trade Organization.

Keiretsu is the Japanese system of conglomerates which cross-market and trade heavily with one another, dating back to the Meiji Restoration of 1868. The author quotes Robert Kearns in describing how an American *keiretsu* structured along the lines of the Mitsubishi or Sumitomo group might operate: "Such a group would be worth close to a trillion dollars. Each of the 30 or so lead companies would own a piece of each other, would do business among themselves and meet once a month for lunch and discuss matters." *Keiretsu* members share in the economies of large-scale operation, says the author, such as low-cost capital at rates of 0.5 percent to 1.5 percent interest. Membership in a *keiretsu* virtually guarantees a market for one's goods, since other member companies own large stakes in each other's companies, and the value of their investments depends on the long-term success and growth of the member firms. According to Kinni, "the *keiretsu* system is an ideal structure for rapid and secure economic growth and a major reason for Japan's economic success since World War II." After describing how the system operates, the author turns to examples of the *keiretsu* way, which means allowing a foreign group to eventually own about 30 percent of one's company stock and, to some extent, dictate the organization's future. Some U.S. companies, like Timken Co., are building structures reminiscent of the *keiretsu* on their own, such as the "supplier city" in Perry Township, Ohio, which will bring its suppliers within arm's reach. What does the future hold?

Invasion or evolution? The author uses observers and "experts" to sum up the final arguments. "As the Japanese investments in this country mature, their plants and equipment will age, their employees will grow more expensive, and the playing field will level. Perhaps the *keiretsu* will learn a new respect for the individual and will begin to temper its authoritarian structures." On the other hand, he believes that U.S. corporations can learn much from the business practices of the *keiretsu*, with its efficient cross-marketing and supplier relationships. The best way to come to terms with *keiretsu*, he concludes, is to think of it as an immigrant, not an invader, with gifts to offer and lessons to learn—for those wise and gracious enough to know how to use them.

Overall, this is a most worthwhile article on an often misunderstood topic. As America moves further along in its understanding of the "extended enterprise," businesses will see themselves as members of a global network, whose aim will be to optimize the value chain through mutual relationships built on trust. Illustrations and models are provided, although the citations are from 1978 and 1986 material.

ABSTRACT 1.3
THE LAW OF PRODUCING QUALITY

Wollner, George E.
Quality Progress, January 1992, pp. 35–40

Most large-scale efforts to bring total quality (TQ) into organizations fail, says the author. Top leadership commitment is the key to success, he contends, and commitment is determined by appropriate incentives. The author expounds two important laws of producing quality:

- Achieving TQ is a matter of incentive.

- More quality is produced when it brings organizational leaders more of the success they desire.

He cites Soviet production policies as examples of disincentives. "While TQ can be an effective tool for redesigning or eliminating nonproductive processes," he says, "the first step has to be in the elimination of the wrong incentives." Almost every failed TQ effort results from an organization's perception that the TQ process is not worth it, he concludes. The key is for the leader to "consistently and continuously measure the three TQ success objectives (increasing customer satisfaction, increasing employee satisfaction, and decreasing unit costs) and link employees' important rewards to their achievements." He mentions the power of noneconomic incentives such as employee empowerment, recognition, self-esteem, and pride in work, as well as monetary incentives. The author introduces the term "incentive controller" as the person or group who has the power to provide or withhold the prized incentives that an organization or individual seeks. "When the incentive controller and the end consumer are the same, and competitive conditions prevail, the market produces quality well," he says. But when incentive controllers are stockholders or politicians, for example, short-term gain can rob long-term advantage. The author discusses the role of TQ leaders in realigning the organizational incentive system. In every case of successful TQ, he says, three critical events occur:

1. The leaders of the organization experience an irresistible incentive to improve product quality.

2. They transform this challenge into a compelling vision that is attractive to the work force.

3. They make it in everyone's best interest to use TQ as the way to achieve the vision.

The article concludes with a simple "TQ Success Forecaster." (©*Quality Abstracts*)

ABSTRACT 1.4
THE NEW SOCIETY OF ORGANIZATIONS

Drucker, Peter F.
Harvard Business Review, Vol. 70 Issue 5, September/October 1992, pp. 95–104

Peter Drucker opens this article with gusto in the opening sentence of the first paragraphs: "Every few hundred years throughout Western history, a sharp transformation has occurred. In a matter of decades, society altogether rearranges itself—its world view, its basic values, its social and political structures, its arts, its key institutions." Our age is such a period of transformation, which began with the G.I. Bill of Rights, giving to each American soldier returning from World War II money to attend a university, something that Drucker feels would have made no sense at the end of World War I. This signaled the shift to a knowledge society, in which land, labor, and capital become secondary and knowledge became *the* product. For Drucker's managers, the dynamics of knowledge imposes one clear imperative—every organization has to build the management of change into its very structure. Every organization must learn to exploit its knowledge to develop the next generation of applications from its own successes, and it must learn to innovate.

If the organization is to perform, it must be organized as a team. For more than 600 years, no society has had as many competing centers of power as the one in which we now live. Change is the only constant in an organization's life. Drucker is always the master storyteller, with his tales of Japanese business development (the soccer team), the Prussian army vs. Henry Ford's assembly line (models of teams), PTAs at suburban schools (perfunctory management), university freedom (the autonomous centers of power), who will take care of the common good (unresolved problems of the pluralistic society), and the failure of socialism/communism (leading to cohesive power of knowledge-based organizations). This is Drucker's thirtieth article for *Harvard Business Review* and undoubtedly one of his best.

ABSTRACT 1.5
THE NEW BOUNDARIES OF THE "BOUNDARYLESS" COMPANY

Hirschhorn, Larry and Gilmore, Thomas
Harvard Business Review, Vol. 70 Issue 3, May/June 1992, pp. 104–115

The opening lines of the first two paragraphs clearly set the stage for this interesting and thought-provoking article on organizational boundaries which are meant to be defined in the eyes of the beholders: the institutional leaders and IS/IT support staff. "In an economy founded on innovation and change, one of the premier challenges of management is to design more flexible organizations. For many executives, a single metaphor has come to embody this managerial challenge and to capture the kind of organization they want to create: the corporation without boundaries." From this vision of Jack Welch to the "data feelings" of the alert IS/IT manager, a wide variety of challenging topics are covered: (1) challenges of flexible work; (2) remapping organizational boundaries of authority, tasks, politics, and identity; (3) the authority vacuum; and (4) downsizing with dignity.

The authors point out, however, that managers should not assume that boundaries may be eliminated altogether. Once the traditional boundaries of hierarchy, function, and geography disappear, a new set of boundaries become important and must be dealt with. These new boundaries are more psychological than organizational, and instead of being reflected in a company's structure, they must be enacted over and over again in a manager's *relationships* with bosses, subordinates, and peers. The four new important boundaries are the authority boundary, task boundary, political boundary, and identity boundary. The article ends with a plea for getting started and is enhanced by an interesting mini-study on "The Team that Failed." The implications for IS/IT are for renewed networking within as well as outside of the enterprise. A shortcoming is that references are not provided.

ABSTRACT 1.6
HEROES ON THE HELP DESK: REDEFINING THE STRATEGIC
ROLE OF SUPPORT

Murtagh, Steve and Sheehan, R. William
Fortune, April 15, 1996, pp. 69–85

Although positioned as an advertisement/editorial, the authors and principals of Renaissance Partners, Inc. have put together a provocative piece of reading on how effective IT support services are saving their client organizations millions and improving customer satisfaction at the same time. Although help desks have been around for almost 20 years, assisting customers and internal staff with PC and other technical problems, not everybody is happy with the concept. As computers have made their way from the glass palace to the desktop, the cost of supporting the infrastructure has risen faster and higher than anyone expected, contend the authors. Global expenditures for technical services and support have exceeded $175 billion in 1995, and the percentage of the IT budget that goes to support services, rather than to operations and development, averages 57 percent and is climbing.

Clearly, a new approach is required, one that strategically redefines and repositions the help desk to sit astride not one but three critical processes: contacts, incidents, and problems. Thus, the function must be reengineered to best satisfy these three processes. A number of companies are profiled and their attempts documented:

- *Clorox*—Reengineered IT support services to create measurable strategic value and short-term tactical results, with a goal of reducing the hidden cost of IS/IT support services by 50 percent.

- *Florida Power & Light*—Developed a training program to familiarize employees with basic PC/LAN concepts, resulting in a reduction of calls by some two-and-one-half times.

- *IBM*—Created a special support service for external customers to provide effective help desk functions such as assessment, automation services, integration support, and operations assistance.

- *Vantive Corporation*—The fastest growing publicly traded software company in the customer interaction market and the leading provider of integrated customer interaction software covering automated sales, marketing, customer service, defect tracking, field service, and internal help desk functions.

- *Software Artistry, Inc.*—Develops and markets a product called SA-Expertise which provides support management tools required to link operations such as help desk, network management, asset-change management, and end-user empowerment.

- *Clarify, Inc.*—Provides systems to assist clients with product support call management, help desk management, product change requests, and inventory control.

- *Entergy Corp.*—Used the Quality Action Teams approach, coupled with natural work teams, to completely reengineer its 13 help desk operations in three states into a single "Command Theater" operation and double the number of calls processed with a 15 percent reduction in staff.

- *Taco Bell*—Used the SCORE system to separate help desk support from the IT group in order to become more focused on the business of supporting restaurants.

- *Magic Solutions, Inc.*—Has worked with over 27,000 organizations worldwide, including the White House, to improve help desk operations, and recently rated number one by *Software Digest.* Features embedded artificial intelligence to assist help desk professionals in solving complex problems and shorten the support cycle.

- *Remedy Corporation*—Developed the Action Request System to help track and resolve support requests in the over 2,000 PC and UNIX computing environments in 35 countries, involving some 1,000 customers.

- *NASCO*—Used the Bendata HEAT software system to centralize and revamp its help desk operations, including the education of customers on tools, services, correct usage, and options available.

CHAPTER 2

UNDERSTANDING THE INFORMATION TECHNOLOGY ORGANIZATION

Technology is often known for its jargon, acronyms, and newly created word definitions. The term "information technology" usually creates confusion because it has various names and functions. There are no set naming rules or conventions. A company's senior management will usually name a departmental area based upon preference. The "buzz name" is not important; the function performed and the results realized are.

Before proceeding, let's clarify some confusing interchangeable terms and their usages. The first are information technology (IT) and information systems (IS). Some say that IT is the technical equipment used, and IS is the method of delivering the information. One accepted definition of IT is the application of technology to business processes, gathering data and creating information that is valuable to managers who make business decisions.[1] It does not matter whether a company calls the function IT, IS, data processing, or some other name, as long as everyone in the company uses the same terminology. IT will be used in this text, but some endnotes refer to IS. The two terms are interchangeable.

Other perplexing terms are data and information. Again, these are basically the same. The primary difference is their usefulness. One definition of data is "a representation of facts, concepts, or instructions in a formalized manner suitable for processing."[2] Information is defined as data assembled in a usable form and beneficial to person(s) using it. Purists are specific about the usage of these terms, but most individuals use them interchangeably. Technology is not necessary to generate information, and some information is best derived manually. Information was being created long before computers were invented.

Technology has developed over time and will continue to change. The functions and roles of IT are continually changing as a result of this revolution and evolution.

REVOLUTION AND EVOLUTION OF INFORMATION TECHNOLOGY

The First Computers

Data-processing devices have progressed over the centuries, from counting on fingers and toes to the abacus to slide rules to calculators to electronic computers. The first computers were primarily used for scientific purposes and have advanced over the years from business to personal use.

Calculating and computing devices exist in digital and analog forms. The difference between the two forms is that the analog device measures and the digital device counts. Analog computers were subject to systematic errors but were very fast. The first mechanical analog computers were introduced in the 1920s, but it was not until the mid-1940s that digital computers were introduced. IBM and Harvard University teamed in 1938 to build a general-purpose digital computer, the Automatic Sequence Controlled Calculator, also known as the Mark I. The Mark I computer was installed in 1944 as the first fully automatic computer. It was huge (it filled a room) and consisted of thousands of relays connected by mazes of wire. This computer was considered a success, but it was also a failure because it was slow—the Mark I was only a hundred times faster than a human using a mechanical calculator. The Mark I was put to work calculating gunnery tables during World War II.

Computers have continually improved since the Mark I was introduced. The computer evolution has caused a continual change in technology and the business environment. The computer age can be thought of as two eras.

Era One

The first technology era was from the 1950s to 1980s. Until the 1980s, technology was primarily used to automate *existing* business functions and reduce clerical costs. The basic IT structure was hierarchical, with walls built within functions and between companies. IT systems were designed to support individual companies and their business functions with minimal or no cross-company integration of information. It was a rare occasion for companies to share software with customers or team with a competitor to enhance industry technology. This era can be subdivided into five generations, each of which provided major technical advancements.

First Generation: Late 1940s to Late 1950s—The computers were large, required a controlled room temperature, and operated using vacuum tubes. The input methods were paper tape or punch cards. These computers were primarily used for scientific calculations.

Second Generation: Late 1950s to Mid 1960s—Transistors replaced vacuum tubes, which allowed for a smaller, modular-designed computer. The ability to teleprocess and transmit data to another computer via telephone lines was introduced. The development of large databases with long-distance linkups connected by terminals also began. Major corporations, which were the only ones that could afford a computer, started using it for business purposes.

Third Generation: Mid 1960s to Late 1960s—Major changes occurred during this generation. Miniature integrated circuits replaced transistors. The computer became smaller, and processing speeds were reduced to billionths of a second. Other advancements were optical scanners, magnetic ink character readers, and larger storage devices.

Computers were enhanced by the addition of additional languages and a "multi-programming" capability which made the computer capable of handling simultaneous processing of independent functions. The remote processing concept was introduced, which allowed a terminal to directly access the computer from various off-site locations.

Fourth Generation: Early 1970s to Early 1980s—This was the personal computer (PC) age. Microprocessors replaced integrated circuits and allowed the computer to become smaller, faster, and more powerful. The mini- and micro-computer era began. Smaller businesses were now able to consider purchasing computers and automating their business processes.

Fifth Generation: Early 1980s to Late 1980s—Manufacturers developed "chips" customized for each computer's specific needs. The PC was given the power of mainframe computers. Costs came down, and the computer became affordable for most businesses and some individuals. This generation saw the development of robotics and the growth of electronic data interchange (EDI).

Era Two

The second era started in the late 1980s, and it is difficult to see when it will end. Technology has now come to play an important role in supporting business development. Technology advances have enabled companies to interact. In a special supplement about the second era in IT, *Business Week*[3] mentions that the traditional IT system should be changed to reflect the new enterprise. Like the new enterprise, it is open and networked. It is modular and dynamic and based on interchangeable parts. It technically empowers users by distributing intelligence and decision making. Yet, through standards, it is integrated, moving enterprises beyond system islands (and their organization equivalents) of the first era. It works the way people do, ignoring boundaries among data, text, voice, and image, and provides a backbone for team-oriented business structures. The IT paradigm shift is bringing about fundamental change in technology in just about everything regarding the technology itself and its application to business. *Organizations that do not make this transition to the new paradigm will fail.* They will become irrelevant or cease to exist. The new IT enables enterprises to have a high-performance team structure, to function as integrated businesses despite high business unit autonomy, and to reach out and develop new relationships with external organizations—to become "extended enterprises."

This text provides the foundation to support the IT Era Two. Firms must start using technology to develop new business opportunities and include the IT functions when reviewing business processes. Basically, they must rethink how to better utilize technology *effectively* to enhance company growth and profits. (For additional information, see Abstract 2.1 at the end of this chapter.)

Technology Trends

Computers and the methods used to gather and process data will continue to improve and change. Technology touches every individual, whether at work, play, or home. With the technical advancements being made, hardware is waiting for the software and peripheral devices to catch up. Peripherals include data storage devices and various input/output devices. It is impossible to predict the technological future except to say that "electronic communications" appear to be the next trend. The technical area is wide open for innovation and creativity, as people are becoming more imaginative as to the application of technology.

Business functions such as accounting and inventory control have been around for centuries, and people have had time to adjust to them. However, the slow development of such functions cannot be compared with the technical advances that have occurred over the past 50 years. Small wonder that people do not fully understand the rapidly developing technology of our own era. Rather than inculcate training and development of personnel to accommodate an ever-changing technology, most companies simply try a new method, and if it is unsuccessful, they try something else.

Change should be an improvement. Often it is merely an extension of an earlier method or technique. Only the name is changed to reflect a new and improved version of an old method, even though the old method was inefficient. An example is object-oriented design, an approach where a reusable, modular design is to be created. Although the term "object-oriented" is new, it is actually the modular, reusable program routines in use since the early 1970s.

Well-known management consultant Peter Drucker had the following to say about business executives and computer technology:[4]

> There are still a good many businessmen around who have little use for, and less interest in, the computer. There are also still quite a few who believe that the computer will somehow replace man or become his master. Others, however, realize by now that the computer, while powerful, is only a tool and is neither going to replace man nor control him. The trick lies in knowing both what it can do and what it cannot do. Without such knowledge, the modern executive can find himself in real trouble in the computer age.

This statement was made in 1966. It still holds true today, even with all the advances made over the past 25 years.

INFORMATION TECHNOLOGY ORGANIZATIONAL FUNCTIONS

Organization Overview

A popular conception of IT is, "All those expensive machines and people are overhead! They speak a language all their own." This is partially true. It does cost time and money to invest in machines and people. But that is not overhead; it is an investment in the future. The IT profession is a specialty and requires skilled expertise. Compare IT professionals with accountants or lawyers; they also speak a unique language. The IT profession is even more complex as there are multiple professions and functions within it. There is an additional communication barrier between the functional units within IT. Application programmers speak a different jargon than telecommunications specialists, and they become frustrated with one another, just as a businessperson does when dealing with a "techie."

From the outside, the IT organization looks like a single entity, but it is actually comprised of separate functional units. Each functional unit plays a distinct role, and all need to work together as a cross-functional team.

FUNCTIONAL UNIT DESCRIPTIONS

The IT area basically consists of four functions (Figure 2.1), regardless of the size of the company. The number of people supporting IT usually depends on the size, budget, and work volume of the company.

The four basic IT functions are:

- Telecommunications
- Data center
- Applications support
- Information administration

The name of the functional unit and work responsibilities performed vary from company to company. For example, the applications support function has been called information systems, management information systems, business systems development, data processing, etc. The point is that no one name is correct; it is the job function being performed that is critical.

Telecommunications

This functional unit adds to and maintains any technically driven communications. The telecommunications function usually installs the company telephone system and keeps it working. When a company is involved with electronic interchange, whether it be installing workstations or transmitting data from one location to another, this functional area is involved. Whenever telephones, cabling, wiring, or computer networks are included, this functional unit should be an active participant. This unit includes two subfunctional units:

Communications (Voice and Data)—Monitors and installs telephones and any data communications devices. Evaluates and installs cables to connect workstations or terminals, for example.

Computer Networks—Builds and maintains the network that is used to transmit data or information from one location to another. Makes certain the different computers can "talk" to one another and determines the best route for the data to travel for security and expediency.

Data Center

This function maintains the computer facilities. The data center includes the computer hardware, peripherals, and the software that tell the computer what to do (not to be confused with application business software). Data center subfunctions include:

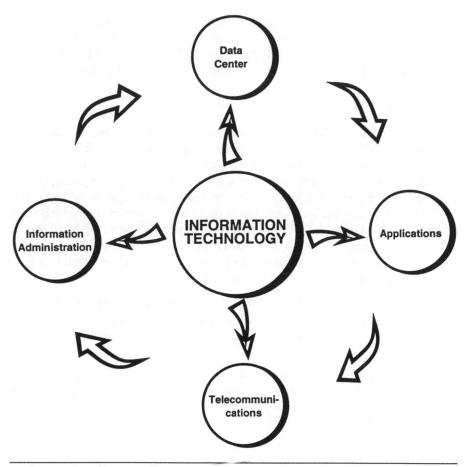

Figure 2.1 Information Technology Basic Functions.

Operations Support—Monitors the computer and ensures that there are no computer processing interruptions to the business.

Systems Support—Improves computer efficiency, maintains the computer operating software, and stays abreast of new advances. Includes monitoring space, where data are stored, and data security.

Production Support—Plans and schedules the work to be completed by the computer. Ensures all data inputs are prepared and the outputs are distributed on time to the customers. This unit is often responsible for ensuring that computer-related documentation is completed and for enforcement of standards.

To further complicate matters, it is important that cross-functional team-work occurs *within* the data center functional unit. For example, production support informs the operations support area what work must be processed, when it must be completed, and how it is to be delivered to the customer.

Applications Support

This functional unit is usually the one most visible to the business customer (also known as the end user). Applications support is responsible for building and maintaining business support computer software, such as payroll, inventory, accounts payable, sales forecasting, and so on. Depending on the size of the company and the number of business computer systems, the traditional applications support area is divided into subgroups which support computer systems in various business departments (e.g., all the financial computer systems are under one subgroup which supports the financial department. This provides better customer support but hinders an integrated process team approach. The subfunctions include:

Business Support—Interacts with the business and represents the business applications processing. Consists of the analysts, programmers, and project team managers who design, code, test, and implement projects and changes for the company.

Data Base—Administers, maintains, and analyzes data and information used by the business applications processing in an integrated, centralized manner.

Information Administration

Information administration is usually a separate functional unit in larger companies, but it should be considered a necessary function for small firms. The smaller company usually handles this function within applications support. This functional unit is the central location for business and technology coordination. It provides computer assistance (also known as the help desk) to the centralized business user. It integrates information, plans technical strategy, provides security, and does business recovery planning. This unit is the central technical watchdog and helper.

Help Desk—Provides assistance when business or technical units require any help relating to a technical concern. A centralized contact point.

Security/Audit—Monitors the information and regulates who can access what information in the computer systems.

Business Recovery—Maintains a contingency plan supporting how business will be conducted if the automated systems should become unavailable. This function includes planning for a temporary interruption to business and major disasters for all IT support functions and business processes.

Strategic Planning—Works with the company to define the vision and goals in order to generate a technology strategic plan.

Miscellaneous Support Systems

Over the years, various miscellaneous information support systems have evolved. They are generated by business users to avoid the IT organization, especially for ad hoc reporting. These areas are referred to as "private sand boxes," and they cause great difficulty for the IT area. They generally develop in response to business users' impatience with IT's long response times. There is nothing wrong with having different support systems, but when it comes to business recovery planning, security, data integrity, and information integration, they create a nightmare for IT and business decision makers. These functions include but are not limited to decision support systems, executive support systems, and expert systems.

The term decision support system was coined in 1971. It allowed organizations to distinguish between the bulk of structured data-processing activities (such as sales orders or managing payroll) and the use of information and IT to support the less structured tasks of managers.[5] Additional versions of decision support systems were spawned as vendors sold new products and decided to call them something else. Other names include, but are not limited to, executive information systems and group decision support systems. Results range from a spreadsheet to graphical displays.

Information should be under a central control. Total quality is sacrificed with multiple information centers. Multiple centers of information lead to redundant information, unpredictable results, reporting inconsistencies, and poor to no security (or business recovery planning). A firm cannot be forced to keep all support system functions under IT, but the importance of coordination with IT cannot be overstated. This is where teamwork comes into play. If a department has the funds to purchase software and hardware, then it should work as a team with IT to coordinate effort and receive support. IT should adopt a positive attitude and begin offering solutions to the end user. Without teamwork, communication breaks down and inefficient use of technology will be a recurring difficulty until organizational barriers come down.

DESCRIBING THE INFORMATION TECHNOLOGY PROFESSIONAL

An IT professional is defined is anyone who works in or is employed in a technical field profession. This can be within any of the functional units. Each person within IT is considered a professional, regardless of position or function.

Image Projected by Information Technology

Unfortunately, a stereotypical image of the IT professional is someone who is:

- Egotistical
- Nontraditional
- Loyal only to the computer
- Highly paid compared to other business functions
- Unconventional in appearance
- Speaks a strange language
- Acts strangely

The following is a true story about a management misunderstanding as to what IT work entails. A senior manager walked through the computer department and asked why a particular person just sat there, staring into space. The senior manager voiced the opinion that this person ought to be reprimanded and told to get to work immediately. The individual in question was a programmer, one of the best, who was thinking through a programming problem. The individual had been called in to work on a problem that had to be corrected before the start of the business day. He had been on-site from 1:00 a.m. to 3:00 a.m. The senior manager did not understand that most IT work is not observably busy, but requires thinking, planning, and off-hours support. This adds to the complexity of managing or working with IT professionals; sometimes it is difficult to know if they are working. This should be judged by the work produced and its quality.

Role and Characteristics

The IT professional must be a visionary in order to anticipate future technological trends. No one really knows what new and great product will be introduced next. Professionals must continually stay abreast of marketing trends and future product announcements. IT should design and implement systems using modular methods and offer flexibility to meet changing business needs.

Each IT professional should possess the following general characteristics:

- Team player
- Friendly
- Open-minded
- Accept change and challenge
- Trainable
- Business and technical solution oriented
- Ethical and moral
- Patient
- Good communicator (oral and written)

This seems like a tall order, but the IT professional of the future must interact with the business and technical functional areas to provide what is best for the entire company instead of just what is best technically or personally. The ethical and moral necessities are included because the individual has access to secure data and other confidential information. The concept of total quality stresses teamwork, being innovative, and customer service ("users"). If IT professionals do not possess these characteristics, a company cannot succeed in implementing total quality.

IT managers generally advance from the technical ranks and thus do not have the same leadership and management expertise as business managers. This is changing as IT managers realize the need for business management education and training. To properly function with business managers, IT managers must articulate technical issues in a meaningful way to those who control the business, understand how to solve the problems of others, and motivate subordinates to work as a team.

Types of Positions

The IT profession has created new specialized job types. Each is its own specialty and requires continual training due to constant technical advancements and changes. They are listed by functional unit but could report elsewhere in a company. The exhibits at the end of this chapter detail the possible skill descriptions for IT professionals. This is far from an inclusive list but touches on the most common job types. Table 2.1 shows a comparison between manufacturing and IT positions when generating a product. (For additional information, see Abstract 2.2 at the end of this chapter.)

Information Technology Manager—This position in larger companies is sometimes called the chief information officer (CIO) or IT director. This person is responsible for coordinating and leading *all* IT functions in the organization.

Table 2.1 Position and Function Comparison: Manufacturing to Information Technology

IT position	Manufacturing position	Function performed
Systems analyst	Design engineer	**Designs** the product
Programmer	Production engineer	**Builds** the product
End user	Customer	**Uses** the product

Telecommunications

Telecommunication Analyst—This relatively new position is the position of the future. This person should be responsible for the company's computer networks in terms of security and business recovery, system and network tools, and wireless technologies.

Telecommunication analysts are involved with electronic data interchange, distributed processing, and are data "traffic cops." Data networks become congested, similar to highway systems, but the result is "data jams" instead of "traffic jams."

Data Center Support

Computer Operator—Monitors the computer and ensures that all is functioning properly.

Production Control Analyst—Responsible for the day-to-day data center scheduling and ensures that work is completed on time.

Applications Support

Project Team Manager—Responsible for a team of IT personnel who support a project. Interfaces with the business customers. Prepares status reports and project plans. Interfaces with the other IT functions.

Systems Analyst—A person with analytical skills, a problem solver. Interfaces with the end user, obtains business requirements, designs the computer system, and assists with testing and system conversion planning. This individual must know the company products and services, policies and procedures, and regulatory considerations. Systems analysts interact with the other IT functional units and work with the programming team(s).

Programmer—Designs, codes, and tests software programs. The programmer of the 1990s is a computer analyst who is also becoming a business analyst who interfaces with the business users.

Data Analyst—Plans and designs the technical data base. Maintains and secures any data dictionary or software support that involves the data.

Information Administration

Systems Integrator—This individual ensures that technical and business needs are met. This position is a liaison between technical functional units, the company, its suppliers, and the business users. Systems integrators make certain that information is integrated and that all financial and legal ramifications are considered. This position could be part of the role of the systems analyst (explained above) in smaller firms.

Strategic Planner—Responsible for developing a company-wide operating plan and a long-term strategic plan by optimizing the return on investment of technical resources. Provides guidance and direction to implement the overall technical goals and objectives of the company.

Performance Measurements

Firms usually look at company profitability as the primary measurement criterion for performance evaluations and offering incentives. This trend appears to be changing. Celia Berk, who heads employee programs and training for Reuters company operations in North and South America, has stated:[6]

> ...we decided that if you measure yourself just by financial re-
> sults, you can't tell if you're creating an opportunity for rivals.
> Now the company measures itself on client satisfaction, employee
> effectiveness and satisfaction, operating efficiency, and contribu-
> tion to shareholder value, in that order.

Performance measurement criteria are changing and in many instances are being forced to change. With more employees working at home, thanks to technology, the former scenario of showing up for work on time, working hard, and receiving a good review will no longer hold true.

IT employees should be evaluated on their willingness to learn new techniques, the quality of work produced, their business knowledge, customer (end-user) satisfaction, and their teamwork abilities. If someone is working an excessive number of hours, the reason why should be investigated. For example, is the extra time due to problems not uncovered until the project was installed as a result of poor testing? In this case, the person should be given a poor review for generating poor quality results.

In some companies, the direction of performance reviews is to evaluate performance based upon the entire team. The team result is the individual result. One reason for this trend is the belief that team members will support each other and "force" everyone to participate and carry their own weight. The verdict is still out on this. One concern in this type of review is that sometimes one individual's performance outshines all others. It is not always fair to that individual when others do not carry their weight on the team. Another concern is the uneven distribution of individual talent among teams. Until these concerns are addressed and a standard in place, there is the potential risk of unfairness when solely using team reviews.

Future Career Opportunities

Technology in the computer arena is reshaping the workplace and is giving data processing professionals, long a mysterious priesthood, new power and prominence. Computer scientists and systems analysts will be among the fastest growing occupations through the year 2005. Employment of programmers is expected to grow faster than the average for all occupations through the year 2005 as computer usage expands.[7]

This presents a good news/bad news scenario. The good news is that there will be greater opportunity and better jobs for IT professionals. The bad news is that IT retains the image of a "mysterious priesthood." IT cannot become part of strategic planning if viewed as a necessary but alien function. The IT professional must embrace the language of business, and businesspeople must learn to communicate with the IT professional. The success of IT, total quality, process engineering, or any business/technology plan is heavily dependent on the success of this cross-communication.

IT professionals, who for years experienced a certain job security, are now beginning to fear for their jobs. Many companies are shrinking IT functions by outsourcing them to external companies in order to save money. The external company has the option of hiring existing staff, but many IT management positions disappear. Technology, hardware, and software have also changed, and many firms replace older individuals, who have outdated technical skills, with younger individuals who have learned newer technologies, do not require retraining, and are lower salaried. The dilemma is: *Will the company want young, up-to-date technical professionals or will it train the older, experienced IT personnel in the newer technology?* No one can predict what companies will do in this situation; every company will respond differently.

Another concern is the career path for IT professionals. Initially, the only way to climb the corporate ladder or advance was to go into management.

Fortunately, this is changing; now excellent technicians who would be ineffective managers can receive the same status and remuneration as managers and still remain technicians.

Information Technology Cross-Functional Roles

The IT organization traditionally has been hierarchical and consisted of different specialized areas. These special areas are necessary because technological advances are ongoing and no one person can be an expert in everything. Examples are applications programmers and telecommunication analysts. Each area of expertise requires its own unique language, has its own skill set, and is continually changing. Each functional area has its own unique hardware and software. *It is important that individuals within IT gain a basic knowledge about other IT functional units to support one another and work as a team.* The applications support area should not implement a new project unless the data center (and in today's world, the telecommunications area) is involved from the beginning.

INFORMATION TECHNOLOGY INFRASTRUCTURE

The IT organization should be customized based on how a firm conducts business and how processes are used to meet business goals and objectives. The intention of this section is to stress that the IT organization consists of multiple functional units configured to support overall business goals and objectives. There is no "right" or "wrong" IT structure; what is right is what works for your company.

Why an Infrastructure?

Every organization needs leadership and communication. They are a means to direct and coordinate activities and a way to monitor and evaluate performance.

Total quality stresses teamwork, customer service, service reliability, efficiency, and innovation. Without an infrastructure, the different functional areas within a company (or within IT) would be unable to effectively communicate with one another.

Structuring an Information Technology Organization

When structuring or restructuring the IT organization, the same considerations must be followed as when structuring the overall organization:

1. Decide what type of organization (centralized, decentralized, or combined) best fits the goals and objectives of the company.
2. Establish the goals and objectives of the IT organization.
3. Prioritize the goals and objectives.
4. Determine the precepts that apply.
5. Define the services to be offered.
6. Determine functions and job families.
7. Decide on a location.

The IT organization should be in a position to handle continual and rapid change. This not only preserves a competitive edge in the market but also promotes internal business support. When company management turnover occurs, IT is affected, as business processes usually change and the information needed for decision making changes.

The IT organization should be structured in manageable functional pieces in order to monitor budgets and schedules, as well as evaluate performance and provide feedback at the departmental and individual levels.

There is not now, nor will there ever be, a standard organization that fits every firm or even a majority of users. Each organization has its own unique constraints and variables; thus, a single solution cannot possibly work for all.[8]

Types of Organization

There are two key considerations when deciding on the type of organizational structure for IT:

1. To whom will the organization report and be accountable?
2. Where are the computer facilities (equipment and people) to be located *and* will there be multiple locations?

There are many variations and types of organizational structure. The common IT types are:

Centralized—The IT organization's management representation is on the same level as the other business functions reporting to senior management. *All* the IT functions throughout the company are managed through this one central point and location. Equipment, facilities, and personnel are all at a central location. There is no duplication.

Decentralized—The IT organization is spread out over multiple locations, each with its own staff, management, and equipment.

Partial Centralized and Decentralized—IT functions are split throughout the company. The data center and telecommunications support functions are located at one central site, but the applications, management, and equipment are divided throughout the company.

Placing Information Technology in the Company

The IT organization must represent the entire company and all of its entities. IT should be in a position to *fairly* provide support to all business functions. One suggested approach is for IT management to report directly to senior management at the same level as other business managers. IT would then be a provider for the *entire* company. The current business direction is geared toward interorganizational systems that have integrated information and processes that cross corporate entities. The American Airlines SABRE system and American Hospital Supply's ASAP order-entry system are examples of the potential competitive advantage of interorganizational systems.[9] IT can better support the company when reporting to top management and when top management makes a commitment to IT.

When IT reports directly to one functional department, there is sometimes a barrier between supporting the entire company versus supporting one function. As an example, when IT reports to the chief financial officer (CFO), the CFO is interested in saving money (and technology costs money). In such circumstances, IT often feels budget cuts before other departments.

Business integration becomes difficult when everyone is "doing their own thing" with technology without coordination. Without the coordination of a company-wide team to consider all technical needs, funds are spent over and again for the same software and hardware without standards. One way to avoid this is to use cross-functional teams, where representatives from the different units meet and compare notes. Departmental responsibility, control, and budgeting are needed, but no project should be implemented without company-wide IT/business consultation. (For additional information, see Abstract 2.3 at the end of this chapter.)

EXTERNAL SUPPORT CONSIDERATIONS

Defining External Support

IT is an area where a single function or entire functional units could be external to the company or, using today's terminology, "outsourced." There is a fine line between the term "outsourcing" and its use. For our purposes, outsourcing is using a specialized outside company to provide a particular service. Other names are time-share (buying computer time) and insourcing (offering more than temporary staffing but less than full outsourcing). All this adds to the confusion. The bottom line is that a firm seeks outside assistance; the level of services provided can and will vary. It can consist of temporary help, including people and equipment, or printing at a remote location. Multi-sourcing is the term used when a firm outsources multiple functions.

Why Consider Outsourcing?

Each IT functional unit can be considered a separate business. IT functional units could function independently but must remain coordinated and integrated to ensure quality and consistency.

The trend is for organizations to use outside companies to conduct IT activities and support. This is called a value-added or strategic business partnership. A value-adding partnership is a set of independent companies that work closely together to manage the flow of goods and services along the entire value-added chain.[10] The value-adding partnership is becoming popular and gives small firms the opportunity to compete with and work with larger firms. This is one example of teamwork, a key total quality principle.

What Can Be Outsourced?

Any company, large or small, can consider going outside to replace an IT activity and save money on value-added services. Almost every large corporation has used external help in IT at some time or another, especially for software support. The imagination is the limit, but managers must remember to be reasonable and think the situation through. Sending an activity to an outside firm may save dollars, but it necessarily gives up some control.

Many activities take place within IT functional units. When outsourcing, it is recommended that the activities going outside be grouped modularly by function and not divided. This activity can vary from firm to firm as each has its own organization and work functions. There are no set rules. A sampling of IT functions and activities that are candidates for external support are:

Data Center—Facilities management, computer hardware, equipment maintenance, printing, imaging, or remote location IT needs.

Telecommunications—Computer network usage, including voice and data communications support.

Applications Support—Maintenance support for existing systems, programming, design, and new project development.

Information Administration—Help desks, office automation, workstation maintenance, strategic planning, business recovery planning, documentation writing, and training.

Some firms often outsource separate business support computer systems such as:

- Payroll
- Human resources benefit packages (i.e., pensions)
- Sales analysis
- Financial ledgers
- Accounts payable

A firm may already have an in-house IT support organization, but it is sometimes feasible to contract an outside company to provide the IT area with information which can be integrated into the in-house system. Payroll is an excellent example of a process that continually requires mandatory changes and may be more beneficial to outsource.

Another area often outsourced is education and training. Firms often have an outside firm write their procedure manuals and then conduct the business-user and technical training for a project.

Within IT, one area where it might be feasible to outsource is the data center facilities (while retaining in-house programming support) because of costs associated with hardware upgrades. A company should analyze the cost–benefits of new technology to determine whether outsourcing IT functions is appropriate. This analysis is usually done by experienced outside advisors. By going outside, a company ensures an objective study, without internal, emotional, or political considerations. The main criterion is what will be best for the firm.

Without knowing all the facts and conducting a feasibility study, it is impossible to know whether or not a company should outsource.

Why Go External?

Most companies decide to go outside to reduce the full-time employee head count and to obtain quick savings. In the past, financially unstable firms were the main users of outsourcing, but current trends indicate that healthy companies are now following suit. Xerox (considered a "healthy" firm) is outsourcing IT functions. A Xerox spokesman indicated that although the company expects to achieve considerable savings, "it was motivated to outsource by other reasons as well: to speed the rate that it can move to new technologies and to free management to focus on strategic information management issues instead of on day-to-day concerns."[11]

There are risks in outsourcing entire IT functions, and the bottom-line dollars and cents should not be the sole determining factor. Reasons a company might consider outsourcing include:

Pace of Technical Change—Technology is constantly changing; by outsourcing, a firm does not need to continually invest in hardware that becomes outdated almost before a project is implemented. The outside company would assume the expense of upgrading hardware and software.

Free Up IT Management and Personnel—One difficulty may be that the IT staff is too busy supporting antiquated, day-to-day business systems and unable to devote effort to new development. By outsourcing, existing management and staff would be able to devote time to focusing on strategies, learning new tools and techniques, and becoming active participants in business reengineering efforts. The existing staff, who understand the business, would be better qualified to assist with new development efforts than would outside new development experts.

Reduce Workforce—When a firm outsources, it does not require additional support staff and can sometimes eliminate employees. The outside firm may even hire part or all of the company's staff.

Eliminate Layoffs—At times, additional support staff may be needed temporarily. There are many specialized skills within the IT function, and it is often advantageous to obtain outside help. Outsiders, usually referred to as contractors or consultants, perform temporary tasks for a limited duration of time. This saves a firm from having to hire additional employees and release them when a project is completed.

Risks of Going External

In addition to bottom-line costs and savings, there are other factors a company should consider before deciding whether or not to go outside. Risks include:

- Legal ramifications
- Employee loyalty and morale
- Customer service impacts
- Quality standards
- Security and confidentiality
- Turnaround time and costs
- Stability of outsource firm

A price must be put on all the above factors when considering the feasibility and risks of outsourcing.

Legal Ramifications—Before outsourcing, a firm must consider any legal implications. Considerations include liability for inaccurate information, not meeting mandatory schedules, licensing agreements, and existing contractual agreements.

Employee Loyalty and Morale—Employees may take an "I don't care" attitude and feel that their jobs will be eliminated no matter what. This attitude ripples from unhappy employees to customers, adversely affecting customer service and quality. A firm should also consider security, since an unhappy employee will sometimes join the competition. The loss of key IS employees can have a devastating effect on an organization's ability to use IS to support in-house activities.[12]

Customer Service Impacts—Consideration should be given to how customer service will be affected by having an outside firm provide a service. This includes outside analysts interfacing directly with both business users and customers.

Quality Standards—It is important that standards and measurements be established and strictly enforced. When dealing with an outside firm, a company (client) encounters multiple risks. Sometimes, especially when contracting programming, the outside firm assigns inexperienced personnel. This lack of experience affects the overall quality and usually extends the completion time. Another risk is that the employees of the outside firm may be temporary or may have minimal loyalty to the client and, in some instances, the outside firm. This generates an added risk in that those employees may leave the outside firm during the project. The client company must ensure that the outside firm follows the agreed upon standards and measurements. The results should be continuously monitored. It is suggested that the client company have at least one employee act as a liaison with the outside firm.

Security and Confidentiality—When a company uses outsourcing, someone outside the company becomes responsible for the security of company information. Outside individuals have access to information which some competitors may want. When going outside, the hiring company *must* be certain that it does not give up control of its information. A firm also does not want an outsider to be responsible for generating information used for decision making.

Turnaround Time and Costs—When a company outsources all or a portion of its IT function, it becomes additionally important that technology considerations be part of overall business planning. It is no longer possible to "go down the hall and ask Joe Tech for a report." Users must formally go outside the company for requests and pay for each request. While many companies have internal charge-backs for technical services, this money is transferred from one budget to another but remains within the company. When outsourcing, the firm pays *another* company for technical support services. The funds then leave the corporate entity, which can result in lower profits.

Outsource Firm Stability—Firms must examine performance records and potential longevity of potential outsourcers; without proper planning, IS performance is likely to be diminished if the outsourcer goes out of business.[13] It is important to make certain the outside firm can and will deliver what the company needs.

Whether outsourcing or not, someone must lead or facilitate. When going outside, it is even more important to have a technology plan that is integrated into the business strategic plan. A company must have someone in house to represent its best interests and coordinate the technology activities. A formalized sign-off process should be in place before accepting any changes an outside firm makes. Without this extra monitoring, a firm could well lose control of its business. (For additional information, see Abstract 2.4 at the end of this chapter.)

ENDNOTES

1. Daniels, N. Caroline (1994). *Information Technology. The Management Challenge*. Wokingham, England: Addison-Wesley and The Economist Intelligence Unit, p. 36.
2. Frates, Jeffrey and Moldrup, William (1984). *Introduction to the Computer*. Englewood Cliffs, NJ: Prentice-Hall, p. 535.
3. Tapscott, Don and Caston, Art (1993). "Information Technology Enters a Second Era." *Business Week*. October 25 (special supplement).
4. Drucker, Peter F. (1966). "What the Computer Will Be Telling You." *Nation's Business*. August, p. 84.
5. McGee, James V. and Prusak, Laurence (1993). *Managing Information Strategically*, The Ernst & Young Information Management Series. New York: John Wiley & Sons, p. 180.
6. O'Reilly, Brian (1994). "What Companies and Employees Owe One Another." *Fortune*. June 13, p. 47.
7. Occupational Outlook Handbook, 1994–95 Edition. Bulletin 2450. Washington, D.C.: Bureau of Labor Statistics, U.S. Department of Labor, p. 226.
8. Hoyt, Douglas B. (1978). *Computer Handbook for Senior Management*. New York: MacMillan Information, p. 31.
9. McGee, James and Prusak, Laurence (1993). *Managing Information Strategically*, The Ernst and Young Information Management Series. New York: John Wiley & Sons, p. 76.

10. Johnson, Russel and Lawrence, Paul (1988). "Beyond Vertical Integration—The Rise of the Value-Adding Partnership." Reprinted in *Revolution in Real Time Managing: Information Technology in the 1990's*. Boston: Harvard Business School, 1991, p. 17.

11. Halper, Mark (1994). "Xerox Signs-Up EDS." *Computerworld*. March 28, p. 8.

12. Arnett, K. and Jones, Mary C. (1994). "Firms that Choose Outsourcing: A Profile." *Journal of Information Systems Applications*. April, p. 182.

13. Arnett, K. and Jones, Mary C. (1994). "Firms that Choose Outsourcing: A Profile." *Journal of Information Systems Applications*. April, pp. 179–188.

EXHIBITS

EXHIBIT 2.1 INFORMATION TECHNOLOGY MANAGER SKILL DESCRIPTION

Job Title: Information Technology Manager

Department: Information Technology

Duties and Responsibilities:
1. Coach and lead IT personnel
2. Plan and maximize IT resources (people, equipment, time, costs) to the fullest
3. Establish measurements and monitor IT performance within IT and business support group(s)
4. Perform routine administrative tasks such as planning, scheduling, budgeting, and leading
5. Interface with business management and provide superior technical solutions for the business direction
6. Prepare and monitor IT budget
7. Develop salary structures, training plans, and career paths for staff
8. Maintain IT disaster contingency plan; ensure security for information and the data center
9. Foster a cooperative, friendly working relationship between IT personnel and all IT customers (i.e., business users, suppliers)
10. Provide the company's technical services at all levels
11. Confirm that the technical strategic plan complements the company's vision, mission, goals, and objectives

Desirable Qualifications:
1. Minimum ten years of strong management experience
2. College graduate with degree in business administration
3. Excellent oral and written communication skills
4. Gregarious; able to interact with all levels of business and management
5. Technical exposure, with hands-on technical background a plus
6. Capable of selling senior management on technology by working with business processing teams and communicating technical data in plain language
7. Politically "savvy"
8. A visionary and leader

EXHIBIT 2.2 PROJECT TEAM MANAGER SKILL DESCRIPTION

Job Title: Project Team Manager

Department: Information Technology

Duties and Responsibilities:
1. Coach and lead IT projects and personnel
2. Plan and maximize IT resources (people, equipment, time, costs) to the fullest for assigned projects
3. Establish measurements and monitor IT performance within IT and business support group(s) for assigned projects
4. Perform routine administrative tasks such as planning, scheduling, budgeting, and leading
5. Interface with business and provide superior technical solutions for the business direction
6. Prepare and monitor IT budget for assigned projects
7. Interview and hire IT team individuals for assigned projects
8. Prepare performance evaluations and feedback for team members
9. Foster a cooperative, friendly working relationship between IT personnel and all IT customers (i.e., business users, suppliers)

Desirable Qualifications:
1. Minimum five years of technical and team leadership experience
2. College graduate with degree in business administration or computer science
3. Excellent oral and written communication skills
4. Able to interact with all levels of business and management
5. Technical exposure, with hands-on technical background a plus
6. Capable of selling business management on technology by working with business processing teams and communicating technical data in plain language
7. A visionary, coach, and leader
8. Knowledge of existing IT systems, tools, procedures, and standards
9. Responsible, with a "can do" attitude

EXHIBIT 2.3 SYSTEMS ANALYST
SKILL DESCRIPTION

Job Title: Systems Analyst–Project Lead

Department: Information Technology/Applications Support

Duties and Responsibilities:

1. Coach and lead IT project team on assigned projects
2. Participate as team member on the business cross-functional team representing technology
3. Plan resources and schedule IT tasks for assigned projects
4. Establish measurement norms and monitor IT performance on assigned projects
5. Offer innovative solutions to existing systems and business processes
6. Verify standards are being met
7. Design systems and write specifications based upon business needs and what is best for the business
8. Liaison with all IT functional areas for projects (i.e., programming, data center, telecommunications, and administrative information)
9. Assist with testing of assigned projects
10. Coordinate with IT customers on assigned projects
11. Measure work progress and report status to management
12. Coordinate training and education requirements for new projects
13. Assist project group members in overcoming difficulties with their work
14. Monitor conversion and final installation of assigned projects
15. Prepare contingency plan for projects being installed in case installation cannot proceed
16. Obtain and analyze feedback on newly installed projects
17. Develop and maintain a business disaster recovery plan and coordinate with other IT functional areas

Desirable Qualifications:

1. Over five years of working experience in technical and business analysis
2. College graduate; preferably a degree in business administration or computer science
3. Excellent oral and written communication skills
4. Enjoy working with others and able to interact with all levels of business support and management
5. Ability to lead, organize, and gather information
6. Previous programming background a plus
7. Capable of communicating as a business analyst and computer analyst
8. Understanding of the company and its business
9. Creative, innovative problem solver
10. Knowledge of existing IT systems, tools, procedures, and standards
11. Responsible, with a "can do" attitude

EXHIBIT 2.4 PROGRAMMER SKILL DESCRIPTION

Job Title: Programmer

Department: Information Technology/Applications Support

Duties and Responsibilities:
1. Receive system specifications from systems analyst lead
2. Determine effort and time needed for programs and testing with the systems analyst lead
3. Prepare test data
4. Conduct and participate in all testing
5. Check testing results and review with systems analyst lead
6. Design and code programs in a modular fashion with maintainability in mind
7. Prepare documentation and ensure it meets IT standards
8. Report progress to lead programmer or systems analyst lead
9. Conduct program walk-throughs with others on the IT project programming team
10. Interface with business users and other IT customers as needed for clarification, testing, and installation support on assigned projects
11. Meet agreed-upon project delivery dates based on quality and time
12. Evaluate software and hardware and make recommendations
13. Maintain existing programs

Desirable Qualifications:
1. Minimum two years of programming experience, preferably on the same type hardware as in the organization
2. High school graduate, technical programming school or college a plus
3. Above average oral and written communication skills
4. Enjoy working with others and able to interact with all levels of business users
5. Logical approach to solving problems
6. Detail-oriented individual
7. Responsible and motivated
8. Willing to work odd hours, as needed
9. General knowledge of the company and its business
10. Function as a team player and offer technical solutions

EXHIBIT 2.5 COMPUTER OPERATOR SKILL DESCRIPTION

Job Title: Computer Operator

Department: Information Technology/Data Center

Duties and Responsibilities:

1. Receive and review work schedules from operations manager
2. Ensure that security procedures for the data center are being met
3. Verify that scheduled work is completed and distributed to all internal and external customers on time
4. Monitor the computer equipment and report any interruptions of service to IT management immediately
5. Participate in conducting the business recovery plan testing at off-site locations, verify its results, and document any procedural changes

Desirable Qualifications:

1. Minimum two years of computer operations experience, preferably on the same type of hardware as in the organization
2. High school graduate
3. Team player who can interact with all levels of users
4. Follow directions and procedures
5. Responsible, with a sense of schedule
6. Basic knowledge of the company and its business

EXHIBIT 2.6 STRATEGIC PLANNER
SKILL DESCRIPTION

Job Title: Strategic Planner

Department: Information Technology/Administrative

Duties and Responsibilities:

1. Develop and maintain a technical strategic plan which ensures that the IT organization and company are working toward the same vision, mission, goals, and objectives

2. Verify that resources allocated to IT meet company plans for competitive positioning and growth

3. Review IT proposals to ensure they meet company goals and objectives and do not adversely affect existing technical strategic plans

4. Participate with the company strategic planning team to offer state-of-the-art technical data

5. Optimize the return on investment for the IT resources and systems

6. Develop and maintain a business disaster recovery plan that covers the business functional units in addition to the IT functional units

Desirable Qualifications:

1. Minimum five years of planning experience

2. College graduate with a degree in business administration

3. Work well with others and able to interact with all levels of business users and top management

4. Innovative and creative

5. Responsible and highly motivated

6. Strong knowledge of the company and its business

7. Technical expertise, preferably as a systems analyst

EXHIBIT 2.7 TELECOMMUNICATIONS ANALYST SKILL DESCRIPTION

Job Title: Telecommunications Analyst

Department: Information Technology/Telecommunications

Duties and Responsibilities:
1. Support the telephone and data communications functions within the company
2. Keep abreast of new technical communications in the marketplace
3. Ensure security and business recovery for existing communication networks
4. Coordinate activities with the other IT functional areas and business processes
5. Provide technical advice and solutions pertaining to communications
6. Optimize the return on investment for IT communications (voice and data)
7. Develop and maintain a business disaster recovery plan covering the telecommunications function and coordinate with other IT functional areas and business departments

Desirable Qualifications:
1. Minimum four years of telecommunications experience with the IT platform the company uses
2. College graduate with a degree in computer science or engineering
3. Get along well with others and able to interact with all levels of business users and management
4. Innovative, dedicated, and self-motivated
5. Responsible; do what is needed without direction
6. Basic knowledge of the company and its business
7. Understand data requirements for developing networks
8. Strong knowledge of LANs (local area networks), WANs (wide area networks), voice response, and video conferencing

EXHIBIT 2.8 DATA ANALYST
SKILL DESCRIPTION

Job Title: Data Analyst

Department: Information Technology/Administration

Duties and Responsibilities:
1. Document the data and the structure used throughout the entire company
2. Analyze data requirements for new projects and determine whether the data are new or existing
3. Regulate data access by system and security
4. Coordinate activities with the other IT functional areas and business departments
5. Provide data recovery
6. Ensure data are integrated for the entire company and easily accessible to the business processes and top management
7. Confirm standards are being met and each data element is given a definition, owner, and a list of users by business process, function, and IT system
8. Develop and maintain a business disaster recovery plan covering the data recovery function and coordinate with other IT functional areas and the business areas

Desirable Qualifications:
1. Minimum four years of data analyst experience with the IT platform the company uses
2. College graduate with a degree in computer science
3. Interface well with others and able to interact with all levels of business users and management
4. Innovative, dedicated team player
5. Know the job and do it efficiently
6. Good knowledge of the company and its business
7. Superior analytical skills

EXERCISE

EXERCISE 2.1   CAREER PATH: PERSONAL VISION AND MISSION

Each IT associate must have a vision and mission in order to create a career path that provides personal growth and development. The following are questions to ask yourself and examples for various positions within the IT organization.

- What career path do I want to take (i.e., remain technical hands-on or pursue a management position)?

- Do I want some management responsibility and some hands-on?

- Do I want to remain in IT management, possibly with a larger company, or do I want to progress to company top management?

- Do I have the aptitude, education, and patience for the position?

INFORMATION TECHNOLOGY MANAGER
John, 47 years old, started in computers 25 years ago. He obtained a four-year college degree in business administration while attending college nights and working full-time days. He began his career as a computer operator, advanced to programmer, progressed into systems analysis, and within ten years was the IT manager for a mid-sized company. He has worked for the same company for five years and has functioned in the same role while the company has increased its use of technology. Over the years, he was oriented toward technical management, but when he became a manager, his management knowledge was acquired on the job.

    Five-Year Vision: John reevaluated his career direction choices and decided he could: (1) remain in IT management and move to a larger company, (2) progress to a business management top position, (3) remain where he was and continue growing the company, or (4) go back to a hands-on position, possibly telecommunications. John decided to remain with the company and progress to a business top management position, where he felt his technical expertise would bring down communication barriers associated with technology. He will take additional MBA executive training to enhance his business management knowledge.

SYSTEMS ANALYST
Cathy is 28 and a 4-year college graduate with a B.S. in computer science. She started as a programmer trainee and advanced into systems analysis after four years with the same large corporation. Her responsibilities have become more oriented toward administrative management.

    Five-Year Vision: Cathy is at the stage where she must decide whether to pursue a full-time management position or continue to function in her current role. She is young and aggressive, and her career ambition is to become an IT manager, where her technical skills can be used to a company's advantage. To move in this direction, she will need to expand her business management skills and continue to stay current with technical developments to provide technical solutions to business problems.

PROGRAMMER

Joe is 23 and has been a programmer with the same company for two years. He enjoys the technical aspect, hates talking with people, but loves a challenge. Joe is an excellent programmer, logical and detail oriented.

Three-Year Vision: Joe analyzed his strengths and weaknesses. A possible three-year career path for a programmer would be lead programmer/analyst, systems analyst, data analyst, or telecommunications analyst (any of which would be a specialty change). He decided to remain in the programming arena since he dislikes interviewing business users and solving business problems. In the future, however, he may need to change professions, as the company direction is for programmers to become more involved with the business. The IT organization has a career path for people who are not management material and want to remain technically focused. Joe decided to remain with the company another two years and then determine whether he would be interested in management. He will learn the newest technology tools and techniques and remain abreast of advancements in technology.

COMPUTER OPERATOR

Linda is 20 and has been a computer operator for one year. She is a high school graduate and has not attended college. Linda is at the point where she must determine what career direction she wishes to pursue.

Five-Year Vision: Linda decided to remain in the IT organization. She is not certain what she wants and has decided to remain hands-on and reconsider management in five years. Her logical career path would be as a telecommunications analyst, data center manager, programmer, or data analyst. The opportunities within IT are many. Linda decided to become a telecommunications analyst.

ABSTRACTS

ABSTRACT 2.1
BETTER INFORMATION MEANS BETTER QUALITY

Ashmore, G. Michael
Journal of Business Strategy, January–February 1992, pp. 57–60

What role can information systems play in achieving total quality? This article examines three main areas where information technology can play a very important role.

1. *Process monitoring*—This takes many forms: collecting performance data, modeling possible scenarios, or tracking the results of quality efforts. By monitoring a process closely, it is possible to detect and fix problems early.

2. *Customer service*—The author gives the example of a software company whose goal was "to make it as easy as possible for the customer to do business with it and to work with its product." A 50 percent share of a very competitive market was the result of the company's efforts. Quality in customer service refers to every interaction that might take place between the customer and the company, from the moment of purchase, to delivery, maintenance, etc. Quality is solving your customers' problems. "Information systems," says the author, "can play a critical role in providing answers quickly and accurately, in every aspect of the service strategy." He then enumerates many ways in which this can be done.

3. *Production*—Production systems can contribute to quality in two ways: (1) production support, which includes yield, productivity, and cost control, and (2) cross-functional information exchange between production and other basic business functions.

Information systems can have a great impact in making total quality a reality. Applying the total quality philosophy to the information systems themselves increases their capacity to be more responsive to the needs of "customers (both internal and external) and the quality needs of the business."

ABSTRACT 2.2
IS THIS WORKPLACE HEAVEN? NO, IT'S QUAD/GRAPHICS

Simmons, John
Journal for Quality and Participation, July–August 1992, pp. 6–10

Quad/Graphics has become large by thinking small, according to CEO Harry Quadracci, subject of this interview. The essence of thinking small, he believes, is fostering close personal relationships—with one another and with clients. This is encouraged by "Think Small Dinners" and "Think Small Activities" to promote communication. Quad/Graphics also emphasizes an egalitarian organization. Managers wear the same uniform as other employees; employees share in the company by owning 70 percent of the company stock. Employee ownership, says Quadracci, allows the company to think more long term than short term. Another key is beginning with inexperienced new hires (who haven't learned bad habits elsewhere) and immersing them in a culture which is proud of its high quality and builds self-esteem. Quadracci sees Quad/Graphics as a value-based company. While peers communicate the culture to new hires these days, Quadracci remembers when he had to implant the culture forcibly: either you do this or you're fired. Since then, he has nurtured the culture by communicating values to employees in ways which might seem a little corny. "The typical American executive is too sophisticated to do it," he says. Quadracci sees money as a demotivator; rather, adequate pay with proper recognition of each employee's contribution produces motivated workers. Quad/Graphics does not benchmark. They have a saying, "keep your eye on the customer, not the competition," and they empower employees to go to extraordinary lengths to satisfy the needs of the customer. (©*Quality Abstracts*)

ABSTRACT 2.3
MAKING TOTAL QUALITY WORK: ALIGNING ORGANIZATIONAL PROCESSES, PERFORMANCE MEASURES, AND STAKEHOLDERS

Olian, Judy D. and Rynes, Sara L.
Human Resources Management, Vol. 30 Issue 3, Fall 1991, pp. 303–333

Throughout this article, four survey sources are used: the KPMG survey of 62 companies, two Conference Board surveys of 149 firms and 158 Fortune 1000 companies, and the AQF/Ernst & Young study of 500 international organizations. The cornerstone of this 30-page article revolves around the authors' statement: "The goals of total quality can be achieved only if organizations entirely reform their cultures. Total quality (TQ) is increasingly used by companies as an organization-wide system to achieve fully satisfied customers through the delivery of the highest quality in products and services. In fact, TQ is the most important single strategic tool available to leaders to effect the transformation of their organizations. Traditional management, operations, finance and accounting systems are reviewed against changes that are needed in organizational processes, measurement systems, and the values and behaviors of key stakeholders to transform the status quo and shift to a total quality culture that permeates every facet of the organization."

Total quality must reflect a system-wide commitment to the goal of serving the strategic needs of the organization's customer bases, through internal and external measurement systems, information and authority sharing, and committed leadership. In this sense, the objectives are very similar to ISO 9000 readiness for registration. Therefore, the concepts presented by the authors are also valid for those TQM organizations that are seeking ISO 9000 certification. The article contains the following pertinent data: (1) organizational synergies critical to achieving a pervasive culture, whether it be for TQM, ISO 9000, or other types of quality assurance; (2) the essentials of TQ; (3) organizational processes that support TQ; (4) establishing quality goals, including a look at Six Sigma and benchmarking; (5) training for TQ; (6) recognition and rewards; (7) measuring customer reactions and satisfaction; (8) developing four areas of measurement: operation, financial, breakthrough, and employee contributions; and (9) getting stakeholder support. Of significant added value are over 60 references on the subjects discussed, which are reason enough to obtain a copy of this extremely worthwhile article, in spite of its formidable length. This is highly recommended reading for IS/IT organizations seeking to implement total quality.

ABSTRACT 2.4
ALIGNING VALUES WITH VISION: ENHANCING THE TOTAL QUALITY PROCESS

Witmer, Neil T. and Sherwood, Stephen
Continuous Journey, October–November 1992, pp. 30–35

Values, say the authors, are deep-seated pervasive standards that influence all aspects of our behavior—our personal bottom line. Values are especially critical in times of change, when normal policies and habits no longer apply. After discussing how personal values are formed and changed, the authors turn to the importance of corporate values. They present a hierarchy-of-values graphic which shows a *vision of desired values* at the top of a pyramid, below which are *shared corporate values*, then *group values* of various groups in the corporation, followed by *personal operating values and behavior.* "Ultimately," the authors contend, "shared corporate values can unify the efforts of disparate groups and the behavior of employees." After discussing a three-step methodology for assessing values, the authors offer suggestions on how to align company values. Then they identify four types of employees which emerge in a TQM process: (a) those who already possess the desired values and behave accordingly (20 percent), (b) those who easily learn desired values as part of the TQM process (40 percent), (c) those who successfully shift their values with considerable effort and hands-on leadership (20 percent), and (d) those who cannot change their values (20 percent). The last group "will probably have to be outplaced or moved to a more appropriate assignment before they cause costly damage," say the authors. Finally, they discuss some specific strategies to maximize value shifts in a TQM effort:

- Top leaders must keep their fingers on the pulse of the changing norms and culture, identify informal leaders and "gatekeepers" to create a "critical mass" of change, and "walk the talk."

- The company vision, mission, and values must be kept visible through constant communication and storytelling by key leaders.

- Goals and objectives must be clearly specified and understood by all employees.

- Customers must have an open channel of communication and feedback to the organization.

- A well-designed management process should be used to give recalcitrant managers an honest look at their versatility, maturity, confidence, self-awareness, and attitudes.

- People's competencies should be matched to their jobs and career expectations.

- A continuous improvement strategy should continue to develop and reexamine desired values, corporate values, and personal operating values, while the CEO meets regularly to seek input and discuss problems. (©*Quality Abstracts*)

CHAPTER 3

ROLE OF INFORMATION TECHNOLOGY

IDENTIFYING TECHNOLOGY GROUND RULES

New technical innovations are giving small and large companies the opportunity to grow and improve profits. The following are a set of "ground rules" that have grown out of the ever-evolving use and evolution of technology:

1. Information technology (IT) is necessary to gain and maintain a competitive edge.

2. IT personnel must be both business analysts, who provide business solutions, *and* computer analysts, who provide computer solutions.

3. Information planning must be part of all business plans, and not simply the province of the IT department. IT functions must be supportive corporate-wide.

4. Integrating various IT functions, such as personal computers (PCs), E-mail, communications, programming, analysis, etc., is a responsibility of business management, as well as the responsibility of IT management.

5. Hardware and software are becoming more affordable and are of advantage to areas where heretofore automation was not cost effective.

6. High technology plays a significant role in almost every product life cycle. This includes education, healthcare, food production, publishing, and related services.

7. From the time a product or software/hardware is off the drawing board until it is available, a new and improved technology has been introduced.

Understanding these "ground rules" helps eliminate the "black hole" label often associated with IT. Integrating total quality with IT is difficult because IT is rapidly changing and difficult to quantify. Software or hardware recommended today may not be the best tomorrow. The number of lines of program code produced per day should not be used to determine programmer productivity; the quality of the results of the code is what is important, as well as how the programmer interacts with the business.

Technology gains are being achieved every day. Without a vision and plan to provide a systematic method for business improvement which includes managing change and training, a company is only "spinning its technology wheels" and not improving its information flow to become more competitive and profitable. New technical breakthroughs are inevitable. Everyone should learn to accept change and work with technology as a team.

The bottom line is that IT should not be used solely to save money or for convenience. It can, and should, be used to make money *and* expand the business. Just because technology is installed and works does not mean it is optimal. A business can have the newest and best technology, but what good is it if it does not improve the company's quality and service?

It is human nature to treat knowledge "like a jewel," hiding it, protecting it, and keeping it to ourselves. Individuals must stop hoarding knowledge and not sharing it with others, as we have in the past. *All* business functional departments must work together and determine what is best for the company instead of just a particular department or area. Each business department must work to eliminate emotional, selfish concerns. The aim is to function as a corporate team and eliminate the mindset of "my department is bigger than yours and I'm only concerned about my functional area." Obviously, one does want to be concerned about one's own department, but *responsibilities must be shared when sharing improves company-wide quality*. One of the primary rules of total quality is *teamwork*, and without it, the quality process will fail, no matter how great the information or technology.

The following statement was made by Jacques Maisonrouge, a former IBM executive:

> But technology is not an end in itself; its essential function is to permit the manufacture of better products that allow us to find a quicker and more satisfactory solution to the problems encountered by men and women in every profession.[1]

COMMON INFORMATION TECHNOLOGY ROLES

IT personnel wear many different hats, and based on a company's industry and size, the processes and type of technology vary. Companies must consider IT a valuable partner and stop thinking of IT as a support function that costs money. IT plays many common roles in business:[2]

- Automates existing processes
- Builds communication infrastructures both within the company and externally
- Links a company to its customers and suppliers
- Supplies decision support
- Quickly calculates large quantities of information

The above IT roles should be found in any company, regardless of size or type of industry. Another important role of IT is gathering information that gives a firm a competitive edge. Peoples Express Airline, which is now defunct, is an example of a company that failed to use IT for business information in order to stay ahead of its competition. Its competitors (such as American Airlines) were changing their information systems, but Peoples Express opted to remain unchanged.

IT offers advantages to small businesses as it gives them an opportunity to compete with larger companies. A small business can be made to look larger by forming strategic alliances with other firms when completing certain technical functions. Hardware prices have dropped considerably over the past years, and as the PC has become as powerful as older mainframes, small businesses are able to compete. *The key is proper business and technology planning before getting into the "nuts and bolts" of the process.*

Another small business advantage is that larger companies have antiquated computer systems which will take years to replace due to corporate and geographic barriers. This gives the smaller firm a chance to outshine a larger company by offering customers more modern technology, as small firms need not stay tied to older systems.

IDENTIFYING INFORMATION TECHNOLOGY CUSTOMERS

IT has many "customers." The generic definition of a customer is "one who buys." A customer, per our definition, is defined as anyone, whether a company, individual, or business process, that uses or interfaces with technology. The IT customer is not necessarily "buying" something but nevertheless expects the highest quality product, service, or support to be delivered.

Customers can be categorized according to four perspectives:

1. Internal within the IT organization
2. Internal within the company
3. Direct external
4. Indirect external

Internal Customers

Internally within a company, IT customers are the individuals, business departments, processes, or entities that represent the same company IT supports. Figure 3.1 presents an example of the interaction between IT and its internal customers. Basically every functional department and individual

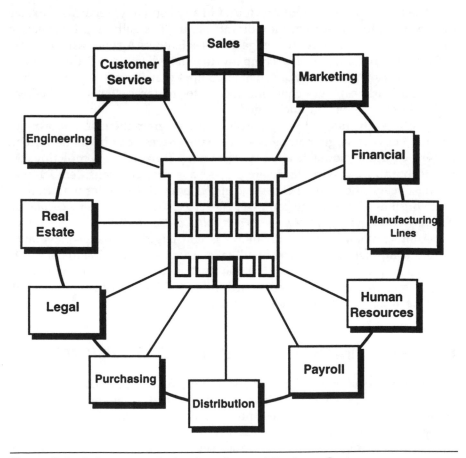

Figure 3.1 Information Technology Internal Business Customers.

within the company is a customer of IT and should be treated in the same manner as an external customer. IT provides a product (automated systems) and service supporting that product. For example, telephone support is usually a responsibility of the telecommunications IT function.

When an outside firm is used to deliver any IT organizational function, as in outsourcing, it is expected to deliver quality products and service or risk losing its reputation and future business. Why should an IT organization within a company be treated or respond any differently?

Internally within the IT organization, customers are the various IT functions and individuals who support each other (Figure 3.2). IT has many specialized functional areas that interact with each other. For example, a programmer who needs additional computer time becomes a customer of the scheduler in the data center. The programmer requests additional time from the scheduler, and the scheduler responds to the customer (programmer) as

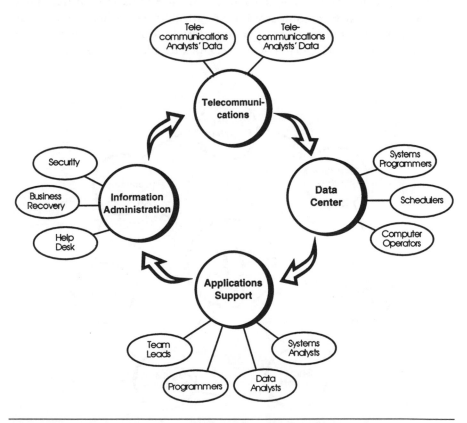

Figure 3.2 Information Technology Internal Customers.

to when the service can be provided. Unless a company is small and has a one-person IT organization, there is always interaction between the functions as services are provided. Each IT functional area and its staff must interact with and support one another if quality service is to be provided. This internal IT customer service is also a key to helping achieve overall company goals.

External Customers

External customers are interests or individuals outside of the company. Figure 3.3 displays an example of IT external customer interaction. Direct external customers are outside recipients who are provided information or service as a result of the products and services provided by IT. For example, when a supplier inquires about an invoice, availability of information, timeliness, and accuracy are the result of IT.

Indirect external customers are firms and individuals who may never directly interact with a company but are affected by the information provided by IT. Shareholders would be considered indirect external customers who are affected by IT since they expect stock dividends. This is basically a

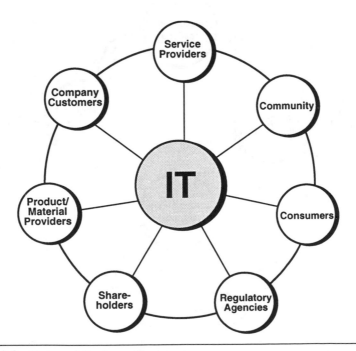

Figure 3.3 External Business Customers.

ripple effect; when the buying customers are happy, sales go up, which increases profits, which are distributed as dividends. IT does not interface directly with shareholders but indirectly affects them. The community and regulatory agencies are also indirect external customers. For example, a firm might decide to expand, based upon information received from IT. The community would benefit, since new jobs would be created, which would generate revenue to the local economy. IT must satisfy regulatory and government agencies (local, state, federal, and international), which indirectly are "customers" in that their information needs must comply with regulations or requirements.

Customer Needs

Customer-identified needs play a vital role in corporate strategic planning, which in turn affects the direction of technology. Table 3.1 displays various IT customers and their needs. IT should team with "internal users," which consist of the business functional departments and the processes responsible for providing services or products to external customers (i.e., marketing, sales, field engineering, customer service, etc.). The role of IT is to support the team by offering its technical input so that the company can consider options which will support customer needs. Automated processes are designed based on customer needs analysis; it is helpful for IT to understand how business processes interface with and support customer needs.

Reduced product-to-market cycles and increasing competition demand that IT functions keep pace with internal and external customer needs and provide processes that are responsive to ever-changing market needs.

TECHNICAL STRATEGIC PLANNING

What Is a Technical Strategic Plan?

A technical strategic plan defines a vision, mission, and goals for technology efforts within a company. This plan is a "road map"; it takes a company from where it is to where it wants to be by using technology. The technical strategic plan should be developed and maintained corporate-wide. The basic objective is to provide a means for technology to establish an efficient return on investment using its resources: human, hardware, and software.

Why a Technical Strategic Plan?

Every business that utilizes technology should have a technical strategic plan. However, unless there is a separate technical budget, this does not

Table 3.1 Information Technology Customer Needs

Type of customer	Needs
Internal customers	
IT employees	Knowledge, skills, and abilities to pursue professional goals; enjoy working with others, sharing knowledge, and learning
IT management	Leadership, continuous personal growth, providing knowledge to and coaching others
IT functional units	Continuous improvement, cooperation, and information exchange
Internal customers within the business	
Business employees	Services provided when needed or requested, questions answered and support given; personal growth and training
Business functions and processes	Continuous improvement, information exchange, teamwork, and cooperation
External customers—direct	
Customers/clients	Quality service and products, dealing with knowledgeable individuals
Suppliers/vendors	Capable, informative individuals with whom to interface
Competitors	United effort to establish industry guidelines and standards
External customers—indirect	
Shareholders	Ethical, profitable firm
Regulatory agencies	Compliance with government regulations/requirements
Community	Competent and reliable involvement with area services

occur. A business, no matter how large or small, will only have a plan for IT if it represents a substantial part of its budget.[3] *Every* technology organization needs a vision, mission, and direction, or funds will continually be wasted. The plan does not need to be lengthy or involved, but the technology direction must be well designed. Decisions about whether outside expertise or additional resources are needed for anticipated projects are based on the business strategic plan. The results are then used when preparing the technical budget.

The technical strategic plan assists IT by defining objectives and responsibilities more explicitly and helping IT personnel to understand their roles. Without knowing its objectives and vision, IT is functioning in a vacuum and cannot be a full contributor. IT must play a role in a firm's strategic and tactical planning. After developing company goals, senior management must prioritize them. Then company management must determine how to assist IT in meeting any priority tasks. Just like any other business unit, IT must have a direction and develop priorities in order to function efficiently. It is difficult for the IT area to effectively plan and budget for growth without knowing the business direction.

A corporation cannot afford "islands of technology" within the business; all resources must be combined into an integrated network. Without integrated information, a company has fractured information at multiple locations. This causes inconsistencies and makes accurate change–response difficult for IT. Isolated information "sandboxes" have multiple "business owners"; this forces IT to respond individually and interface with each entity before making any change. (For additional information, see Abstract 3.1 at the end of this chapter.)

There is also an audit/security concern which could bring on disastrous results. When information is located at multiple locations and no one location claims "ownership," an arbiter is needed to determine access or who can alter information. Auditors abhor separate, redundant information for which no manager is responsible. On the security side, an irate employee may decide to internally sabotage a company. When information is not integrated and secure, such an employee can destroy or contaminate data and cause crippling damage. Information can also be illegally pirated from company computers and confidential information sold to a competitor for someone's personal gain. Another concern is software "viruses," which can completely destroy information.

BUSINESS MANAGEMENT AND INFORMATION TECHNOLOGY INTERACTION

Why Business Management Support?

When top management endorses and uses technology, lower levels will follow. For example, when senior managers use electronic mail (E-mail), others are forced to use it when communicating with the top (the ripple effect). When top management does not use or support IT functions, then the system is doomed to fail, as the lower levels feel they do not have to use it or make a commitment to support IT. A considerable number of systems have languished or failed because of this.[4] Top management support and teamwork from all levels and departments are important in order for IT efforts to truly succeed and meet total quality requirements.

Business management must start thinking of IT as a means to make money and gain a competitive edge. *Everyone in the company, both IT and business staff, should be a contributor in finding new ways to improve the process.* Business users (customers) too often presume that the IT area knows what is needed. On the other hand, IT assumes that because a user did not ask for something, he or she does not want it. Business management and IT management must endorse the concept of IT and business functions working together in supporting the business processes. Each must stop thinking of functional boundaries, look at the business process, and involve all functional units.

Well-known management consultant Peter Drucker had the following to say about management's role in IT:

> Executives and professional specialists need to think through what information is for them, what data they need: first, to know what they are doing; then, to be able to decide what they should be doing; and finally to appraise how well they are doing. Until this happens MIS departments are likely to remain cost centers, rather than become the result centers they should be.[5]

Products and systems are increasingly more dependent on software and hardware. Every department must be computer literate. Engineering resources in the manufacturing process must become software dependent. Companies must provide cross-functional business/computer usage training to improve employee productivity. IT must solicit input from users when developing or enhancing automated systems, because it is the departmental personnel who utilize these systems to serve the company's customers. When users participate in developing systems, they have pride of ownership, are less resistant to change, and welcome rather than resist new technology.

Why It Helps Information Technology to Understand the Business

When a company practices total quality, the needs of the customer drive decisions. IT employees must know who the outside customers are and understand the functions of all the internal processes as well as the departments they support. IT must learn the business "whys" in order to become a member of the business cross-functional team and an accepted partner in the organizational strategy.

Most businesspeople do not understand the technologies available, either now or in the near future. In some cases, they may know just enough to be dangerous! Many simply consider the computer a means to "crunch numbers" and do not look for improved ways to conduct business. Some business users do not understand the time and cost ramifications of automating an entire process around an exception that happens once a year. IT can assist by sharing its technical knowledge and by working with the business user to find a better solution. Each can learn from the other. Compare a lawyer writing a contract and a technician designing a system for business needs; both should offer advice for making improvements and avoiding potential pitfalls. When developing new systems, the technician must review the existing computer systems that support the business, However, it is important to remember that there may be a better way to conduct business—by changing the processing flow of the existing system.

Business Involvement

IT can be thought of as a business in itself. As such, it requires the same disciplines as a company. When a company uses an outside firm for technical support functions, it is even more important that technology be considered. The company is now spending money to purchase technical services; without proper planning, procedures, and controls, the company will lose control, which will cost more money due to miscommunication and rework. IT should be an active participant in the following key activities since technology considerations are usually involved:

- Corporate business planning
- Change management
- Continual improvement
- Business reengineering

Corporate Business Planning

IT can usually respond to changing business demands by becoming part of the overall business planning process. Suppose a firm is planning a merger but does not inform the IT organization until the press is notified. Management then expects IT to implement all changes due to the merger within a month, even though it took two years for the merger to become final. Had IT been informed earlier, IT management could have planned for the merger and responded quicker.

When IT is not included in the planning process, then those in IT management should take it upon themselves to alert senior management about the potential IT has to offer the business. When senior management realizes the value-added benefit of involving IT, it will be more likely to include IT in the planning process, but *IT will need to prove its worth to the company before it is considered part of the business team.*

The corporate vision can be be expanded to include new business opportunities when top management is made aware of technical advancements available. CEOs have various "extreme" attitudes toward IT, which range from completely ignoring technology to believing they know all about it. Somewhere between the extremes is the CEO who knows enough to be involved by setting an appropriate direction for information systems (IS) and involving IT management because the CEO has sufficient confidence in the IS manager's abilities to contribute to the firm's strategic direction.[6] Simply put, IT must earn the respect and trust of the business.

IT should incorporate its technical strategic plan into the overall corporate plan, which is based upon company strategic and tactical plans. This eliminates any potential confusions about the growth and direction of IT and ensures that the business and technical worlds are working together and using the same blueprint. (For additional information, see Abstract 3.2 at the end of this chapter.)

Change Management

Changes impact IT personnel as well as business users. IT personnel often must learn a new tool or technique that alters the way they perform a task, such as new programming languages, revised project development tools, and computer hardware. Both business users and IT staff handle change in similar ways; after all, people are people. Although technical people should be used to change, they have also been known to resist new methods and techniques. IT personnel, like business users who have always performed a task a certain way, also build a comfort factor when using a certain technology. They usually dislike dealing with change, especially when deadlines do not allow for learning the new technology. IT staff can compare themselves to business users who receives a new computer system without education or involvement before installation. IT personnel should remember that they themselves usually resist change when proper training and communication do not take place before implementing new technical tools and techniques. Think of the reverse situation. Can you blame business users for resisting technical change when they were not involved?

Ways to Overcome Change

Change is inevitable. It is human nature for individuals to become comfortable with methods they use every day, but these "comfort zones" must be changed if only to keep up with competition. No human advancement would have occurred if everyone had accepted things as they were.

Suggested approaches for overcoming resistance to change include:

• Keep everyone informed and communication lines open
• Make certain all staff are involved from start to finish

- Receive, and be receptive to, feedback
- Conduct thorough training sessions before a change is implemented
- Explain the reasons for a change
- Refrain from "changing a change"—one thing at a time

The above suggestions pertain to technology modifications or any type of change.

How to Handle Change

The following suggestion is offered as a means to handle fear of change:[7]

> The best way to deal with fearful employees is to address these fears openly at the outset. Make it clear that the computer applications you will ask them to use do not require advanced mathematics or technical abilities. All employees will be given the opportunity to learn the programs, at their own pace, and from their own level, without negative performance appraisals if it should take them longer to learn.

Introducing new technology causes fear because of a management perception that more technology means less staff. People are not receptive when they believe a change can cost them their jobs. But technology can be used to create new positions. The people using the old processes should welcome the opportunity to learn new skills and to become more valuable as a result. By using this "carrot," the company expands its market, retains the same staff, and improves both employee skills and company morale, resulting in higher productivity and profits.

IT personnel are also concerned about job security because many firms outsource IT functions. They fear that new user-friendly languages and end-user systems will eliminate their functions and place information access directly in the hands of the end users.

Technology is rapidly and continually changing. People (even those in IT) have difficulty keeping up with all the new leading-edge technologies and are not receptive to the continuous changes. IT is more a matter of culture than machines. If great gains seem possible, IT might choose to risk trying new technology, but the risk must be carefully considered and a contingency plan prepared in the event of failure. All too often, a vendor sells a company "vaporware" (a product as yet unavailable but promised for a specific date). Then, when the company needs the technology on the promised date, the vendor says that it is not available yet. In such cases, the business and its schedule are held hostage by the vendor.

Information Technology Resources Change Control Process

IT needs to have a formalized change control process when implementing technical resource (i.e., software and hardware) changes, in addition to handling people concerns. The objectives of the change control process are to plan, coordinate, monitor, and provide a consistent means to control modifications involving IT resources. A formal change process will enable IT to have a visible means to measure system change activity and results, such as maintenance versus new project development, nature of the changes, systems affected, business risks, successes versus failures, and how many changes are made.

A change control process can be an aid when IT prioritizes its workload. For instance, two major stand-alone projects, which happen to overlap business processes and were assigned to different project team leaders, were being scheduled for implementation the same weekend. The change control process caused the project managers to realize that the same date had been chosen to implement both projects, but neither manager was in a position to change the date. Management then became involved to decide which project was to be given higher priority and implemented on the original date. In this example, a potential conflict was resolved before customer-deliverable commitments were made, allowing IT to save face and provide quality customer service.

One suggested approach is to form a team with a minimum of one representative from each IT functional area to enhance the communication between functions. This helps ensure that all parties are aware of planned changes. The change control process can be as simple or complex as the team feels is needed. Some larger companies have a weekly change review meeting where representatives from each IT functional area discuss any planned change activity affecting IT resources. Every company currently has some type of change process, but it should become formalized. When a change will impact a particular business process, it is important that the customer be involved and made aware of the change.

It is also strongly recommended that a testing environment be built separate from the production environment. It is risky to make modifications directly to the existing production systems until new change requests have been thoroughly tested and their implementation has been carefully planned. For example, suppose a programmer is changing program code that is currently being used in a production environment. A test environment does not exist and no back-up version of the program is made before the programmer starts making changes and testing the program. A production problem occurs that affects the program being modified. How does the programmer distinguish the original program code from the changes he or she has made? Basically, the programmer has two choices: (1) try to remember the changes and temporarily delete them from the program or (2) take a chance and implement the program with the untested changes. Let's take this example one step further. Programmer A is making changes to a program and programmer B is also making changes to the same program, unaware of programmer A's changes. This situation can be pretty scary when you consider the potential business impacts when program coding is inadvertently overlaid. A formal change process and test environment would help overcome such difficulties.

Commitment from IT and business management is a must before implementing a formal IT change control process. Benefits of this process are hidden. Until a major error occurs, there is no visible monetary payback. The only return on investment is determining the cost of having a set change process by asking, "If an error occurred, how much would this impact customer service and our company's quality indicators?" Similar to a disaster recovery plan, there is no payback until a disaster occurs, but without such a plan, an organization could be destroyed or suffer a severe setback.

Our purpose is not to try to outline how a change control process should be implemented. It is suggested that the change control process be assigned as an IT total quality project and a formalized team created to define a vision, goals, and deliverables which support improving the change control process. To be successful, it must be aligned with the business strategy. An outside advisor may be consulted to assist in implementing a formalized change control process. Each company is unique, and there is no one right or wrong approach, as long as quality is being maintained; however, as a firm grows, a standard change process will provide a common direction and means of competitive cost benchmarking. (For additional information, see Abstract 3.3 at the end of this chapter.)

Continuous Improvement

The automated systems that IT creates and operates become an integral part of all business work processes. This is viewed as a plus in the beginning, but difficulties arise as IT's company-wide responsibilities grow and the time needed to make changes to the systems increases. Continuous improvements drive the organization toward constant change. IT may receive an avalanche of change requests, become backlogged, and be slow to respond. IT is then perceived as a barrier and not part of the company team. When IT personnel are part of a management planning effort, they often overcome this perception through creative and/or innovative methods. However, even if IT cannot handle all requests as fast as others might like, being in contact with all levels of management involves everyone in developing a solution.

IT pressures and backlogs can be understood and managed by various means, such as cross-functional management priority committees, joint business planning, user funding of suggestions, and downloading information to

PCs. All are useful. Thus, IT can relieve pressure for requests by interacting with user departments. The obvious benefit is that business users become guardians and advocates of their systems and IT becomes a valuable friend.

Business Reengineering

What Is Reengineering?

Reengineering is reviewing existing business processes and finding more efficient ways to handle them. It may radically change the way a company operates. Reengineering really is moving to a process-managed organization as opposed to simply improving performance.[8] Authoritative management and rigid organizational structure become teams and shared responsibility. Reengineering technology solutions should not be thrown at problems. Applying IT to business reengineering demands *inductive* thinking—the ability to first recognize a powerful solution and then seek the problems it might solve, problems a company probably does not even know it has.[9]

Total quality and reengineering go hand in hand, continually improving processes, seeking innovation, building teams, and finding new business solutions.

Who Is Reengineering?

Basically, all types of companies are reengineering. Refer to Figure 3.4 for additional information about the types of industries that are reengineering. Approximately 25 percent of the larger companies are reengineering. Their efforts usually involve one or two projects and are not widespread implementations. Japan, the nation that used the "made in America" concept of total quality management to rebuild its war-shattered economy, is now eyeing another American notion: business reengineering.[10] The Japanese have realized that a business must be looked at by process versus function and are including technology to maximize any business reengineering effort.

Business areas considered prime reengineering targets are the back-office processes, sales support, marketing, and accounting.

Implementing Reengineering

IT, in some companies, must modify its thought processes and change itself. This section provides the information and steps that should be followed when reengineering a business.

Two important reengineering rules IT **must** remember are:

1. Reengineering a business process is **not** rewriting the existing computer systems using a new and improved technology *or* designing a new computer system using the existing business processes.

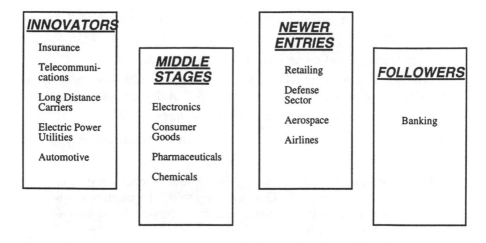

INNOVATORS	MIDDLE STAGES	NEWER ENTRIES	FOLLOWERS
Insurance			
Telecommunications		Retailing	
Long Distance Carriers	Electronics	Defense Sector	Banking
Electric Power Utilities	Consumer Goods	Aerospace	
Automotive	Pharmaceuticals	Airlines	
	Chemicals		

Figure 3.4 Reengineering Status by Industry. (Source: Maglitta, Joseph (1994). "One on One with Michael Hammer." *Computerworld*, January 24, p. 84.)

2. The business process changes should be implemented gradually using a modular and pilot plan approach. This decreases the risk of failure by thinking the process through in pieces and lessens user resistance to change.

Technology and customer demands have changed over the years. What is needed to support a business and how this will be accomplished usually differ from the original systems implemented years ago. Too many people still think the answer is computer-aided software engineering (CASE) tools or other such Band-Aids.[11] A company can have the best tools and techniques, but if IT and the business processes and their functional units are not working together, there can be no great success story.

IT cannot be the leader in driving any reengineering effort; it is merely a helper. A firm's senior management must take the initiative, or IT management must persuade senior management to recognize the business problem and take steps to resolve it. IT personnel have important roles to play in the reengineering activity itself because they understand processes, they are accustomed to change, and they are oriented to new technology.[12] Some business managers envision IT personnel as the reengineering leaders and expect them to intuitively know the customer needs. IT personnel are there to help but should not make any business decisions alone. The business reengineering effort involves IT and the business working together as a team. IT is there to support the business and help it improve, but it should not take responsibility for determining how the business should be run.

In a *Computerworld* interview, Michael Hammer, one of the authors of

Reengineering the Corporation, states that reengineering projects fail due to three major reasons:[13]

1. Lack of management commitment to push it through.
2. A firm says it is going to reengineer, doesn't get results, and then says it failed at reengineering when it never tried it in the first place.
3. People do not know how to go about it and improvise.

To quote Michael Hammer when asked about how reengineering affects an organization:

> Re-engineering is basically taking an ax and a machine gun to your existing organization. One company said, "Through re-engineering we have saved the business and destroyed the organization." That just puts it perfectly.

Implementing Business Involvement and Information Technology

Strategic planning is the building block used for determining the company's policy management. The definition of policy management for our purpose is directing an organization to identify, solve, maintain, and improve its corporate priorities. This provides a way to accomplish corporate short- and long-term strategies and "achieve the vision."

Policy management, commonly referred to as the company steering or priority committee, plays a key role in achieving total quality and continuous improvement. Policy management is a blueprint for a company using continuous improvement techniques. Other total quality processes help achieve the goals of the company. Policy management provides a forum to instruct the entire firm as to what is important to customers, stockholders, regulators, management, and employees. The IT organization benefits from this since it is given a direction in terms of what the business is doing and is able to plan for future technical activities. The policy also assists IT in knowing what should be worked on, monitoring the number of requests, and prioritizing tasks, since everyone wants their requests completed now.

INFORMATION ARCHITECTURE

What Is Information Architecture?

An information architecture is a set of models and plans that represents the flow of information throughout the business.[14]

Before defining the architecture, a company must identify the information and consider:

- *Value*—How important is it or is it needed?
- *Usage*—Who will use it and where?
- *Storage*—What way will it be accessed and when?

Value

Companies are realizing that information (or data) is a valuable resource and should be treated as a useful ally. The value of any information system for top management depends on the quality of the data—its timeliness, accessibility, accuracy, and completeness.[15] This holds true not only for top management, but for anyone using the information, whether to make internal decisions or to provide customer support. According to a popular saying, information is only as accurate as what is entered into the computer system. When a customer's name is spelled incorrectly or an address is inaccurate, it was usually entered into the system incorrectly. Customers become irritated when their names are spelled wrong or they receive late payment telephone calls for bills they never received. A company can have all the information in the world, but if it is untimely or inaccurate, customer service and quality will be affected.

In order to be effective, there should never be an overabundance of information that is not used. The costs of gathering and retaining information must be considered. The cost of obtaining information must not exceed the value of that information.[16] Sometimes the expense of capturing, processing, and storing information far exceeds the benefits gained in using the information for decision-making analysis. The information should be given to people who can use it and react.

When IT functions are outsourced, it becomes even more critical to define information needs and the value of information. The outsource firm must have a clear, concise understanding of who can access information and when the information will be accessed in order to meet customer requirements. A company that hires an outsource firm should keep control of its information. After all, it is the company's information base that is used for decision making.

Usage

Access to and the use of information ought to be standardized, integrated, process driven, and "user owned." Information should never be redundant or processed or stored without a clear, concise idea of its use—even between vendors, suppliers, and internal customers. Each piece of information, called a data element, must be clearly defined and a "business owner" identified. A determination must be made for each data element as to who is allowed to create, view, or alter it for integrity and audit/security reasons. An internal individual or business process must accept responsibility for the ownership, accuracy, and security of information.

Information use has changed dramatically over the years, but the data elements remain the same. Defining the base requirements, standardizing data elements, and providing user-oriented definitions for elements help in the planning of future systems. The business user should be involved in establishing data element definitions. Data, properly identified and tied to other tools, makes new IT development faster and more accurate. Examples of other tools include data dictionaries, repositories, and productivity programming languages (report writers). These shorten IT's response time for system changes and reporting requests. It is much easier to make changes or issue reports, and there is less risk of error, when the data is documented with such information as where it is used throughout the IT systems, what business processes use it, and a definition.

Measurement

The measurement of IT and technology planning is required for the proper budgeting of computer investment. However, there has been an inability to measure effectiveness and accurately quantify benefits. This leads to problems in productivity measurement, because you can't measure what you can't define. Many experts feel that conventional ratio analysis and critical success factor methods only yield partial answers. The value-added approach seems to offer better ways to measure quality and productivity, as discussed in Abstract 3.4. For a discussion on measurement, see the article at the end of this chapter.

Storage

Keeping data in a central location will expedite IT's response time in delivering business requests. The following quote is based on a company's complaint about IT service and what could have been done to improve it:

> If the company had maintained all its computer-readable data in a single pool or bank—in a so called "data base"—and if the company had structured this base of data so that a program for virtually any feasible use could have been run from this data base, then it would have been a matter of sheer expertise and flair for a good, experienced programmer to concoct a program that pulled the desired information together.[17]

Many business departments start their own user information base, which causes a mish-mash of information inaccuracy and redundancy. IT has the capability, thanks to PCs and computer networks, to distribute data to business departments or processes which will allow them to generate additional information or models. A central base is the key to adding and maintaining consistency. An example showing how the same information is fragmented is a customer address. Sales and marketing has the address in its system and the order department has the same address in its separate system. A customer informs the company of her address change, but only the sales/marketing area receives the change. Since only one department changes the address, the frustrated customer, who knows she sent the company an address change, must notify the company again.

Data can be stored and easily accessed in various ways, but to be readily accessible for IT, data should be stored via some type of electronic medium, such as disk or tape. Many a businessperson has requested information and become upset when the IT organization informs him or her that the data are not being captured or there is no way to automatically access the information. This relates back to the importance of determining the information a company needs when defining system requirements. It is difficult for IT to respond to customer requests unless it has the data.

Databases or files can be designed in modular segments that can be woven into new applications and processes. The data should be tied to customer needs, have key measure indicators, and allow for future usage. Having a readily available source with a clear data element definition and knowing who uses the data helps the IT professional solve business problems in a dependable and timely manner and at a reasonable cost.

COMMUNICATION

Understanding a company's organizational structure is important, but it is just as vital to understand the functional interactions that make the structure work. When interacting with customers and reviewing business processes, business users and IT professionals should follow a few simple communication rules:

- Don't become insulted or defensive when suggestions are made about a type of technology or a revised business process.

- Speak in understandable terms (technicians should not use technical jargon). In the same vein, businesspeople such as accountants and lawyers should also explain their jargon in simpler terms.

• Follow the Keep It Simple (KIS) philosophy—Don't make something more complex than it has to be.

Timothy Edwards, chief operating officer of Matewan National Bank, had the following to say about the interaction between IT and the business:

> Operations and IS must be looking at the total picture together, as a team. Turf battles are non-productive. There's no time for internal conflict; it'll drag down the whole organization and kill you in today's market.[17]

Before the communication barriers can come down, IT management *and* business management must understand each other and work together. Table 3.2 shows typical business and technical managers' thinking roles. When they realize they must cooperate and work as a team, the effect ripples throughout the organization. When business management and IT management become allies, they can approach top management, as a team, to obtain the support they may need to improve the process.

Other ways to keep everyone in the company informed about new technologies or projects are to:

• Distribute a newsletter

• Provide project updates

• Circulate information for everyone to review and provide feedback to the project team

Table 3.2 Why Information Technology and Business Management Disconnect

The chief operations officer (COO) and chief information officer (CIO) usually have different approaches to their roles:	
COOs	CIOs
Short-term oriented	Long-term oriented
Dislike having technology forced upon them	Must introduce new technologies
Fear encroachment of IT into their territory	Fear involvement by COOs threatens their jobs
Underestimate strategic role of IT	Most adopt business-oriented strategies

Source: Menagh, Melanie (1994). *Computerworld.* February 28, p. 87.

These techniques can be used for IT internal coordination, but it is recommended that they be introduced company-wide. There is no such thing as too much communication or too much awareness of changes that are taking place.

SUMMARY

The IT organization must become part of the business planning process to effectively support the corporate goals and objectives. In large companies, IT should provide support based on the entire corporate business process and not just by business functional unit. Change is inevitable, and a formalized process should be introduced to aid in improving controls and eliminating resistance.

IT should be viewed as the creator and maintainer of information systems and technology. Business users should claim ownership of information and be responsible for its usage and integrity. IT should become part of the overall business cross-functional team and offer technical solutions that will benefit the business. IT personnel must project an image that indicates they really care about business-user requests and when they will be completed. The driving force behind reengineering should be the business and not IT, whose role is to contribute technical expertise. When reengineering any existing process or system, it should not be rewritten simply by using a newer technology. This defeats the purpose of reengineering, which is re-evaluating and improving the business process.

Communication barriers between the business and technical worlds must come down. If this means bringing in outside help, then that must be done.

ENDNOTES

1. Maisonrouge, Jacques (1985). *Inside IBM, A Personal Story*. New York: McGraw-Hill, pp. 283–284.
2. Daniels, Caroline N. (1994). *Information Technology—The Management Challenge*. Wokingham, England: Addison-Wesley and The Economist Intelligence Unit, p. 20.
3. Winfield, Ian (1991). *Organisations and Information Technology Systems, Power and Job Design*. Oxford: Blackwell Scientific, p. 157.
4. Eliot, Levinson (1984). "The Implementation of Executive Support Systems." Working Paper No. 119. Cambridge, MA: Center for Information Systems Research, Sloan School of Management, MIT, October, p. 68.
5. Drucker, Peter (1988). "The Coming of the New Organization." Reprinted

in *Revolution in Real Time, Managing Information in the 1990's.* Boston: Harvard Business School, 1991, p. 9.

6. Arnett, Kirk P. and Jones Mary C. (1994). "Firms that Choose Outsourcing: A Profile." *Information and Management Journal.* April, p. 180.

7. Shore, Joel (1989). *Using Computers in Business.* Carmel, IN: Que Corporation, pp. 35–36.

8. Maglitta, Joseph (1994). "One on One with Michael Hammer." *Computerworld.* January 24, p. 85.

9. Champy, James and Hammer, Michael (1993). *Reengineering the Corporation.* New York: Harper Business, p. 84.

10. Alter, Allan (1994). "Japan, Inc. Embraces Change." *Computerworld.* March 7, pp. 24–25.

11. Maglitta, Joseph (1994). "One on One with Michael Hammer." *Computerworld.* January 24, p. 84.

12. Ibid., p. 85.

13. Ibid.

14. Daniels, Caroline N. (1994). *Information Technology—The Management Challenge.* Wokingham, England: Addison-Wesley and The Economist Intelligence Unit, p. 44.

15. DeLong, David W. and Rockart, John F. (1988). *Executive Support Systems: The Emergence of Top Management Computer Use.* Homewood, IL: Dow Jones-Irwin, p. 189.

16. Shore, Joel (1989). *Using Computers in Business.* Carmel, IN: Que Corporation, p. 32.

17. Brandon, Dick (1970). *Management Planning for Data Processing.* Princeton, NJ: Brandon/Systems Press, p. 228.

18. Menagh, Melanie (1994). "Crossfire." *Computerworld.* February 28, p. 87.

ARTICLE

BUILDING THE MEASUREMENT SYSTEM FOR INFORMATION SYSTEMS AND TECHNOLOGY

If you can't measure it, you can't manage it.

Peter Drucker

While many IS/IT organizations are embarking on some form of a total quality program, few have implemented a measurement system which can be used to figure out how good of a job is being done. Because so few have done this well enough to be examples for industries to follow, it is difficult to do any real benchmarking in this area. From the studies conducted on the practices of excellent IS/IT operations, however, some operating models have resulted. One of the most useful is a variation of the Corporate Measurement System (CMS) approach, based upon the work of Jack Rockart of MIT and others.* This model suggests the use of a vital few critical success factors (CSFs), which are linked to the business objectives and processes, around which the corporate indicator system is built.

What formerly took three years or more to accomplish can now be done in six to nine months using available software programs such as COMSHARE or PILOT. In addition to implementation speed and economy, the CMS approach is extremely flexible in terms of environment, future needs, and changes.

What IS organizations need is a measurement system that is simple and flexible in design, easy to use and modify, and integrated into key functions and processes. The information provided needs to be timely and accurate and must be perceived by the employees as truly useful and not just another "Big Brother is watching" type of system. Instead, what is needed is a

---

*The work of Rockart and others is detailed in a technical report titled "Building the Corporate Measurement System," published by Strategy Associates, Miami, Florida, 1992. The basic premise is that an effective measurement must not only be comprehensive and screen input from many constituencies, but it must also be selective in considering only the critical information. Without this, the system may become so cumbersome that it will not be effectively utilized to make IS decisions.

measurement system that IS professionals can use to manage their efforts better and to link all areas of the company, from the computer in the field or office to the corporate vision.

The following attributes are needed in an IS/IT measurement system:

- Simple system that is easy to understand
- Analyst/programmer commitment and motivation
- Specific objectives, procedures, and guidelines for use
- Consistent, continuous monitoring
- Assignment of specific responsibility and accountability
- Top management interest and support
- Timeliness
- Good lines of communication
- Good monitoring staff who provide competent analysis
- Periodic reports
- Useful and relevant information
- Accurate, reliable information linked to strategy and business objectives

PRINCIPLES AND OBJECTIVES

There are two guiding principles to follow when developing an IS/IT measurement system: (1) people on the information lines of the organization respond best to information relevant to their piece of the world and (2) when people have relevant information about things they deem important and can influence, they become very committed to using the information.

The following is a summary of the objectives of an IS/IT measurement system:

- Translate the vision to measurable outcomes all staff can understand
- Focus and align the direction of staff based on measurable results
- Track systems-related breakthrough and continuous improvement results
- Foster accountability and commitment
- Integrate strategic plans, business plans, quality, and benchmarking
- Provide standards for benchmarking
- Problem-solve IS business problems
- Provide basis for reward and recognition
- Create individual and shared views of performance

IMPLEMENTATION OVERVIEW

There are three types of measures that must be considered when implementing an IS/IT measurement system: outcome (or macro) measures, just-in-time process (or micro) measures, and upstream control (predictive) measures.

Outcome measures are often called macro due to their broad nature which generally reflects an after-the-fact type of indicator. Examples are return on investment, or equity, overall customer satisfaction, program/project savings, etc. Micro, or process, measures represent work-in-process types of situations and are often used to stop the project or program when bugs and/or rejects occur. Predictive measures are used for "upstream control" or prevention of problem situations. Most effective measurement systems have an effective combination of macro, micro, and predictive indicators.

Micro measures act as trip wires by enabling us to look at programs and see if we can increase speed of actions and decrease time, cycle, and steps. Whereas macro measures help us to focus on measuring the results of leadership on the corporate outcomes and to work the vision to see if the message is getting out there, micro measures help focus on the day-to-day routines. Conversation needs to be created among technicians in the field to help determine if the programming attribute corresponding to a particular corporate function enhances or inhibits the ability to create external customer satisfaction. In other words, do the programs, functions, routines and processes enhance or inhibit the journey along the path of total quality?

CATEGORIES OF IS/IT MEASURES

There are seven general or broad categories into which most measures can be classified or rolled up: accuracy or reliability, responsiveness, timeliness, customer satisfaction, cost, maintainability, and implementation responsibility.

The first three—accuracy or reliability, responsiveness, and timeliness—refer to the manner in which and the speed with which the IS organization conducts its business transactions and the way its programs and services perform. The fourth category—customer satisfaction—can also include employee satisfaction when IS employees are viewed as internal customers. The fifth and sixth categories—cost and maintainability—can be broken down into a wide variety of subcategories. The final category—implementation responsibility—is often replaced in larger organizations with a more relevant category relating to the competition, such as competitive marketing intelligence.

Templates, or flowcharts, are used to first link all existing measures to the corporate vision and objectives. Once existing indices are linked, then gaps and missing indices are identified and added to the system where appropriate. Decisions are also made about modifying or eliminating existing indices as new ones are added. Overall, there are generally between 25 to 100 detailed indicators that roll up into the seven broad categories.

GENERAL SYSTEM DESIGN

The IS/IT measurement system model consists of 26 major milestones which are used for the successful implementation of most measurement systems. These 26 milestones can be compared to running a marathon, which consists of 26 miles. These milestones are organized into three phases.

Phase 1: Linking to Business Objectives/CSFs

Activity/milestone	Estimated man-hours
1. Prepare getting started plan and obtain approvals	5
2. Communicate the plan to corporate executives	1
3. Meet with design team and do initial training	9
4. Management workshop	4
5. Follow-up design team and consolidate documentation	6
6. Assemble CSF rollout plan using available templates	3
7. Hold CSF workshop and work with design team on gathering CSF data	21
8. Coordinate with design team and conduct second round of CSF interviews	21
9. Coordinate with design team and finalize corporate data profiles	3
10. Hold focusing workshop with management	8
11. Complete preliminary system design	10
Total man-hours	91

Phase 2: Decision Scenarios

Activity/milestone	Estimated man-hours
12. Plan and hold key indicators workshop for design team rollout	19
13. Design team discusses indices with key user areas and assists with format indices, screens, and data	14
14. Plan and conduct decision scenario workshop and help design "what if" scenarios	21
15. Help finalize general design	20
Total man-hours	74

Phase 3: Prototyping The System

Activity/milestone	Estimated man-hours
16. Define prototype in terms of info templates	10
17. Define in which areas to pilot the prototype and which IS measurement systems functions to include	20
18. Complete draft of detailed specs	25
19. Investigate application software alternatives	20
20. Review and document coding structure required to implement CMS	2
21. Conduct interviews to resolve open points	12
22. Select a software package for CMS	12
23. Perform programming coordination and also perform unit testing	10
24. Complete prototype system testing using test data	3
25. Load/convert live data, finalize testing, and go live with system prototype	15
26. Project management and coordination	64
Total man-hours	193

SUMMARY OF BENEFITS

The following ten benefits can be realized by using well-defined measures which are part of an IS measurement system:

1. Identify the current capabilities of the IS/IT organization
2. Highlight opportunities for process improvement and reengineering
3. Facilitate goal-setting
4. Mark progress toward goal attainment
5. Benchmarking comparisons with other organizations
6. Improve job satisfaction and morale by enabling staff to work more effectively
7. Strong emphasis on employee technical involvement
8. Emphasis on process, not people
9. Produce higher quality products and enhance pride in delivering them
10. Lower cost and increase productivity by harnessing the intelligence of everyone in the organization

Overall, the effective use of a well-designed corporate measurement system should yield a payback ratio of four to one or greater over a one-year period following implementation.

ABSTRACTS

ABSTRACT 3.1
ELM: A HOLISTIC APPROACH

Teresko, John
Industry Week, June 20, 1994

The author is a well-known business writer who presents a concise look at one of the key features of how to use information technology to more successfully coordinate logistics throughout the organization in order to more reliably deliver goods and services to customers. ELM stands for Enterprise-Logistics Management, which is an important new step in the passage of manufacturing from art form to science. The author often quotes author Thomas Gunn, using excerpts from his book *Age of the Real-Time Enterprise: Managing for Winning Business Performance Through Enterprise Logistics Management* (Oliver Wight Publications). Gunn defines ELM as a holistic approach to managing operations and the value-added pipeline (total supply chain), from suppliers to end-use customers.

The author discusses three drivers to achieve competitive position: (1) a relentless quest for customer satisfaction, (2) recognition of the need for real-time management, and (3) ability to perform in a world-class manner. Additionally, superior logistics management is increasingly being cited as the new strength of the Japanese manufacturers, instead of just-in-time (JIT) alone. The post-JIT environment places an emphasis on information systems and technology, including electronic production-control systems. According to Professor Jichiro Nakane of the Systems Science Institute, Tokyo, the key is to achieve superior management of the flow of information, from customer order to the delivered product or service, with an integrated enterprise-wide system.

The shortcomings in today's software solutions are discussed in terms of the inability of MRP products/vendors to execute distribution resource planning at the front end and a lack of procurement applications at the back end. The inability to track material through the entire manufacturing process results in poorly tracked plans and schedules. When computing is diffused throughout the entire organization, it is difficult to collect and understand cost allocation trends attributed to open, distributed architecture. The author concludes with the premise that there is ample evidence that the total cost of spending on information systems in a typical company may represent 30 to 40 percent of its capital spending. And a company may be surprised to learn that in the catch-up mode, it is not spending nearly enough. This article is worthwhile reading in spite of the absence of references.

ABSTRACT 3.2
IS DATA SCATTER SUBVERTING YOUR STRATEGY?

Lingle, John H. and Schiemann, William A.
Management Review, May 1994

The main premise of this article is that lots of organizations have information available from many sources to let them know how they are doing. The authors argue that the problem is the poor coordination of this data and its frequently nebulous connection with the organization's purpose. The solution lies in systems and processes for overcoming "data-scatter."

When viewed from the perspective of information systems, most organizations are Balkanized environments—bits and pieces scattered in often conflicting jurisdictions such as MIS, marketing, finance, sales, human resources, and so forth. They have a 21st century computing capacity and a 1960s approach to transforming data into useful information. Data-scatter results from the poor job that organizations do in managing and transforming data into integrated information needed to drive success.

The symptoms of data-scatter that signal possible trouble are:

- *Strategy silos*—Each executive defines the future in terms of his or her own self-image, which is suboptimized to the overall detriment. The authors pose five useful questions to test for symptoms.
- *Data wars*—Knowledge is power and weapons pointed at colleagues often start a family feud. Bootleg databases abound.
- *Decision jerk*—Occurs when management zigs and zags with each piece of data, continually shifting priorities or piling on new initiatives. Chunks of data are used to make decisions resulting in multiple misguided efforts.

The authors offer five measures of success with the key word as "focus":

1. Strategically anchor gauges
2. Reflect the outcomes, not the activities
3. Create a counterbalance
4. Ensure responsiveness to change
5. Exhibit strong signal-to-noise characteristics

They point out that winning organizations focus their measures around a balanced scorecard type of system in a family of measures approach. To maintain focus, it is important that organizations track a limited number of gauges, which are updated regularly and available to all the people in the work force. To the extent they can avoid data-scatter, organizations will be able to tap into that storehouse of information and convert it to new knowledge for serving customers in a more innovative way than the competition. This is a thought-provoking piece for the business community. No references are provided.

ABSTRACT 3.3
HOW TO IMPLEMENT COMPETITIVE-COST BENCHMARKING

Markin, Alex
Journal of Business Strategy, May–June 1992, pp. 14–20

"Competitive-cost benchmarking," says the author, "is a powerful bottom-line tool that uses and assimilates quantitative and financial information on competitor performance to upgrade production capabilities, set measurable targets for process improvement, identify markets where competitors are vulnerable, and improve the realism of strategic decision making." This article begins with several case studies of chemical producers (resin, caustic, soda/chlorine, and polymer) that conducted competitive-cost benchmarking against significant competitors and then used the information gained to make strategic decisions. The author gives tips on how to carry out this type of benchmarking:

- *Multifunctional team*—The benchmarking process should be carried out by a coordinated multifunctional team composed of business analysts and managers from the various functions, as well as outside consultants.

- *Quantitative thrust*—The author gives a list of nine areas of questions to research concerning competitors, such as: "How are products, coproducts, and byproducts integrated with other company business?"

- *Quantitative thrust*—He suggests ways to show detailed cost stacks for each competitor using spreadsheets. In addition, he gives sources for learning about competitors.

- *Refinement of data*—"As the analysis progresses and input is reviewed and assimilated," the author says, "care should be taken to validate key assumptions and findings and understand the reasons for cost differences."

- *Action plan preparation*—He observes that research may show points of vulnerability, or it may lead a company to consider joint ventures, or even to phase out an operation.

- *Presentation of findings*—Information and recommendations are now distilled into a simple format. (©*Quality Abstracts*)

ABSTRACT 3.4
PARADIGM SHIFT: THE NEW PROMISE OF INFORMATION TECHNOLOGY

Tapscott, Don and Caston, Art
McGraw-Hill, New York, 1993, 337 pp.

This is an exhaustive and highly recommended work, based upon investigations of more than 4,500 business and government organizations. The authors offer profiles of organizations such as Toys 'R' Us and Fedex to illustrate how new information technology can be of assistance and help leaders and business managers take action to gain and maintain competitive advantage. Throughout, the authors focus on how organizations achieve long-term success with IS/IT. The major breakthrough areas covered are enterprise computing, interenterprise computing, and team/work cell computing. It can be used as an effective companion piece to *The New Paradigm in Business: Emerging Strategies for Leadership and Organizational Change* (Ray and Rinzger, World Business Academy, Tarcher/Perigee, 1993), which is a collection of essays by leading-edge business managers and thinkers on business in the new age of connectivity and vision. Contributors include Warren Bennis, Peter Senge, Willis Harman, and others. Both volumes can be purchased for $39 total.

CHAPTER 4

OVERVIEW OF TOTAL QUALITY

Frank Voehl

WHAT IS TOTAL QUALITY?

Introduction

During the past five years, there has been an explosion of books in the field of total quality. Yet in all of the thousands of books and billions of words written on the subject, there is an absence of three essential ingredients: a good working definition, a comprehensive yet concise history, and a clear and simple systems model of total quality. This overview of total quality is intended to fill that void and provide some interesting reading at the same time.

Understanding the Concept of Total

Total quality is total in three senses: it covers every process, every job, and every person. First, it covers *every process*, rather than just manufacturing or production. Design, construction, R&D, accounting, marketing, repair, and every other function must also be involved in quality improvement. Second, total quality is total in that it covers *every job*, as opposed to only those involved in making a product. Secretaries are expected not to make typing errors, accountants not to make posting errors, and presidents not to make strategic errors. Third, total quality recognizes that *each person* is responsible for the quality of his or her work and for the work of the group.

Total quality also goes beyond the traditional idea of quality, which has been expressed as the degree of conformance to a standard or the product of workmanship. Enlightened organizations accept and apply the concept that quality is the degree of user satisfaction or the fitness of the product for use. In other words, *the customer determines whether or not quality has been achieved in its totality.*

This same measure—total customer satisfaction—applies throughout the entire operation of an organization. Only the outer edges of a company actually have contact with customers in the traditional sense, but each department can treat the other departments as its customers. The main judge of the quality of work is the customer, for if the customer is not satisfied, the work does not have quality. This, coupled with the achievement of corporate objectives, is the bottom line of total quality.

In that regard, it is important, as the Japanese say, to "talk with facts and data." Total quality emphasizes the use of fact-oriented discussions and statistical quality control techniques by everyone in the company. Everyone in the company is exposed to basic quality control ideas and techniques and is expected to use them. Thus, total quality becomes a common language and improves "objective" communication.

Total quality also radically alters the nature and basic operating philosophy of organizations. The specialized, separated system developed early in the 20th century is replaced by a system of *mutual feedback and close interaction of departments.* Engineers, for example, work closely with construction crews and storekeepers to ensure that their knowledge is passed on to workers. Workers, in turn, feed their practical experience directly back to the engineers. The information interchange and shared commitment to product quality are what make total quality work. Teaching all employees how to apply process control and improvement techniques makes them party to their own destiny and enables them to achieve their fullest potential.

However, total quality is more than an attempt to make better products; it is also a search for better ways to make better products. Adopting the total quality philosophy commits a company to the belief that there is always a better way of doing things, a way to make better use of the company's resources, and a way to be more productive. In this sense, total quality relies heavily upon value analysis as a method to develop better products and operations in order to maximize value to the stakeholder, whether customers, employees, or shareholders.

Total quality also implies a different type of worker and a different attitude toward the worker from management. Under total quality, workers are generalists rather than specialists. *Both workers and managers are expected to move from job to job, gaining experience in many areas of the company.*

Defining Total Quality

First and foremost, total quality is a set of philosophies by which management systems can direct the efficient achievement of the objectives of an organization to ensure customer satisfaction and maximize stakeholder value. This is accomplished through the continuous improvement of the quality system, which consists of the social system, the technical system, and the management system. Thus, it becomes a way of life for doing business for the entire organization.

Central to the concept is the idea that a company should *design quality into its products*, rather than inspect for it afterward. Only by a devotion to quality throughout the organization can the best possible products be made. Or, as stated by Noriaki Kano, "Quality is too important to be left to inspectors."[1]

Total quality is too important to take second place to any other company goals. Specifically, it should not be subsidiary to profit or productivity. Concentrating on quality will ultimately build and improve both profitability and productivity. Failure to concentrate on quality will quickly erode profits, as customers resent paying for products they perceive as low quality.

The main focus of total quality is on *why*. It goes beyond the *how to* to include the *why to*. It is an attempt to identify the causes of defects in order to eliminate them. It is a continuous cycle of detecting defects, identifying their causes, and improving processes so as to totally eliminate the causes of defects.

Accepting the idea that the customer of a process can be defined as the next process is essential to the real practice of total quality. According to total quality, control charts should be developed for each process, and any errors identified within a process should be disclosed to those involved in the next process in order to raise quality. However, it has been said that it seems contrary to human nature to seek out one's own mistakes. People tend to find the errors caused by others and to neglect their own. Unfortunately, exactly that kind of self-disclosure is what is really needed.[2]

Instead, management too often tends to blame and then take punitive action. This attitude prevails from front-line supervisors all the way up to top management. In effect, we are encouraged to hide the real problems we cause; instead of looking for the real causes of problems, as required by total quality, we look the other way.

The Concept of Control

The Japanese notion of *control* differs radically from the American; that difference in meaning does much to explain the failure of U.S. management to adopt total quality. In the United States, control connotes someone or something that limits an operation, process, or person. It has overtones of a "police force" in the industrial engineering setting and is often resented.

In Japan, as pointed out by Union of Japanese Scientists and Engineers counselor and Japanese quality control scholar Noriaki Kano, *control* means "all necessary activities for achieving objectives in the long-term, efficiently and economically. Control, therefore, is doing whatever is needed to accomplish what we want to do as an organization."[1]

The difference can be seen very graphically in the Plan-Do-Check-Act (PDCA) continuous improvement chart, which is widely used in Japan to describe the cycle of control (Figure 4.1). Proper control starts with planning, does what is planned, checks the results, and then applies any necessary corrective action. The cycle represents these four stages—Plan-Do-Check-Act—arranged in a circular fashion to show that they are continuous.

In the United States, where specialization and division of labor are emphasized, the cycle is more likely to look like Fight-Plan-Do-Check. Instead of working together to solve any deviations from the plan, time is spent arguing about who is responsible for the deviations.

This sectionalism, as the Japanese refer to it, in the United States hinders collective efforts to improve the way things are done and lowers national productivity and the standard of living. *There need be nothing threatening about control if it is perceived as exercised in order to gather the facts necessary to make plans and take action toward making improvements.*

Total quality includes the control principle as part of the set of philosophies directed toward the efficient achievement of the objectives of an orga-

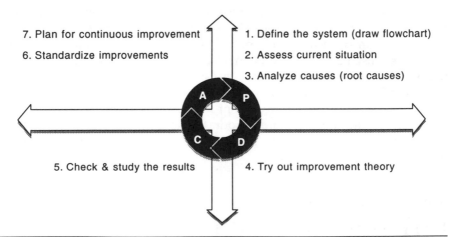

Figure 4.1 PDCA Chart. System improvement is the application of the Plan-Do-Check-Act cycle to an improvement project.

nization. Many of the individual components of total quality are practiced by American companies, but few practice total quality as a whole.

TOTAL QUALITY AS A SYSTEM

Introduction

Total quality begins with the redefinition of management, inspired by W. Edwards Deming:

> *The people work in a system. The job of the manager is to work on the system, to improve it continuously, with their help.*

One of the most frequent reasons for failed total quality efforts is that many managers are unable to carry out their responsibilities because they have not been trained in how to improve the quality system. They do not have a well-defined process to follow—a process founded on the principles of customer satisfaction, respect for people, continuous improvement, and speaking with facts. Deming's teachings, as amplified by Tribus,[3] focus on the following ten management actions:

1. Recognize quality improvement as a system.
2. Define it so that others can recognize it too.
3. Analyze its behavior.
4. Work with subordinates in improving the system.
5. Measure the quality of the system.
6. Develop improvements in the quality of the system.
7. Measure the gains in quality, if any, and link them to customer delight and quality improvement.
8. Take steps to guarantee holding the gains.
9. Attempt to replicate the improvements in other areas of the system.
10. Tell others about the lessons learned.

Discussions with Tribus to cross-examine these points have revealed that the manager must deal with total quality as *three* separate systems: a social system, a technical system, and a management system. These systems are depicted as three interlocking circles of a ballantine,[4] as shown in Figure 4.2.

Overview of the Social System

Management is solely responsible for the transformation of the social system, which is basically the culture of the organization. It is the social system that

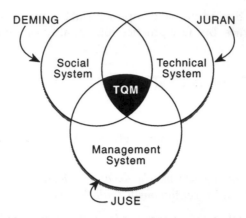

Figure 4.2 Implementing Total Quality Management—System Model.

has the greatest impact on teamwork, motivation, creativity, and risk taking. How people react to one another and to the work depends on how they are managed. If they enter the organization with poor attitudes, managers have to reeducate, redirect, or remove them. The social system includes the reward structure, the symbols of power, the relationships between people and among groups, the privileges, the skills and style, the politics, the power structure, the shaping of the norms and values, and the "human side of enterprise," as defined by Douglas McGregor.

If a lasting culture is to be achieved, where continuous improvement and customer focus are a natural pattern, the social system must be redesigned so as to be consistent with the vision and values of the organization. Unfortunately, the social system is always in a state of flux due to pressure from ever-changing influences from the external political and technological environments. The situation in most organizations is that the impact of total quality is not thought through in any organized manner. Change occurs when the pain of remaining as the same dysfunctional unit becomes too great and a remedy for relief is sought.

As shown in Figure 4.3, six areas of strategy must be addressed in order to change and transform the culture to that of a quality organization:

- Environment
- Product/service
- Methods
- People
- Organizational structure
- Total quality management mindset

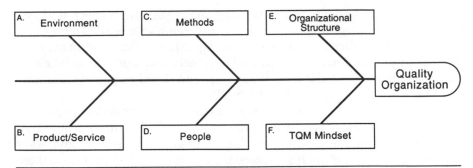

Figure 4.3 Strategic Areas for Cultural Transformation.

Each of these areas will be covered in some detail in the chapters in this book. Of the six, however, structure is key in that total quality is about empowerment and making decisions at lower levels in the organization. Self-managing teams are a way to bring this about quickly.

The Technical System

According to Tribus,[5] "The technical system includes all the tools and machinery, the practice of quality science and the quantitative aspects of quality. If you can measure it, you can probably describe and perhaps improve it using the technical systems approach." The technical system thus is concerned with the flow of work through the organization to the ultimate customer. Included are all the work steps performed, whether by equipment, computers, or people; whether manual labor or decision making; or whether factory worker or office worker.

The technical system in most organizations contains the following core elements:

- Scientific accumulation of technology
- Pursuit of standardization
- Work flow, materials, and specifications
- Job definitions and responsibilities
- Machine/person interface
- Number and type of work steps
- Availability and use of information
- Decision-making processes
- Problem-solving tools and process
- Physical arrangement of equipment, tools, and people

The expected benefits from analyzing and improving the technical system are to (1) improve customer satisfaction, (2) eliminate waste and rework, (3) eliminate variation, (4) increase learning, (5) save time and money, (6) increase employee control, (7) reduce bottlenecks and frustration, (8) eliminate interruptions and idle time, (9) increase speed and responsiveness, and (10) improve safety and quality of work life.

The three basic elements of every system are (1) suppliers who provide input, (2) work processes which add value, and (3) output to the customer. High-performing units and teams eliminate the barriers and walls between these three elements. A standard problem-solving process is often used by teams, such as the quality control story, business process analysis, etc.[6]

The Management System

The third system is the managerial system, which becomes the integrator. Only senior managers can authorize changes to this system. This is the system by which the other two systems are influenced. It is the way that practices, procedures, protocols, and policies are established and maintained. It is the leadership system of the organization, and it is the measurement system of indicators that tell management and the employees how things are going.

The actual deployment of the management system can be visualized in the shape of a pyramid. As shown in Figure 4.4, there are four aspects or intervention points of deployment: strategy management, process management, project management, and individual activity management. A brief overview of these four aspects is as follows:

- *Strategy management*—Purpose is to establish the mission, vision, guiding principles, and deployment infrastructure which encourage all employees to focus on and move in a common direction. Objectives, strategies, and actions are considered on a three- to five-year time line.

- *Process management*—Purpose is to assure that all key processes are working in harmony to guarantee customer satisfaction and maximize operational effectiveness. Continuous improvement/problem-solving efforts are often cross-functional, so that process owners and indicator owners need to be assigned.

- *Project management*—Purpose is to establish a system to effectively plan, organize, implement, and control all the resources and activities needed for successful completion of the project. Various types of project teams are often formed to solve and implement both process-related as well as

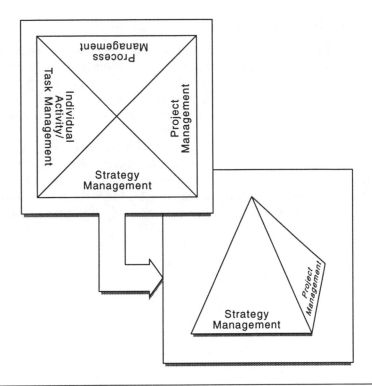

Figure 4.4 Management System Pyramid.

policy-related initiatives. Team activities should be linked to business objectives and improvement targets.

- *Individual activity management*—Purpose is to provide all employees with a method of implementing continuous improvement of processes and systems within each employee's work function and control. Flow-charting key processes and individual mission statements are important linkages with which all employees can identify. A quality journal is often used to identify and document improvements.

Various types of assessment surveys are used to "audit" the quality management system. Examples include the Malcolm Baldrige assessment, the Deming Prize audit, and the ISO 9000 audit, among others. Basic core elements are common to all of these assessments. Their usefulness is as a yardstick and benchmark by which to measure improvement and focus the problem-solving effort. Recent efforts using integrated quality and productivity systems have met with some success.[7]

The House of Total Quality

The House of Total Quality (Figure 4.5) is a model which depicts the integration of all of these concepts in a logical fashion. Supporting the three systems of total quality described in the preceding section are the four principles of total quality: customer satisfaction, continuous improvement, speaking with facts, and respect for people. These four principles are interrelated, with customer satisfaction at the core or the hub.

As with any house, the model and plans must first be drawn, usually with some outside help. Once the design has been approved, construction can begin. It usually begins with the mission, vision, values, and objectives which form the cornerstones upon which to build for the future. The pillars representing the four principles must be carefully constructed, well posi-

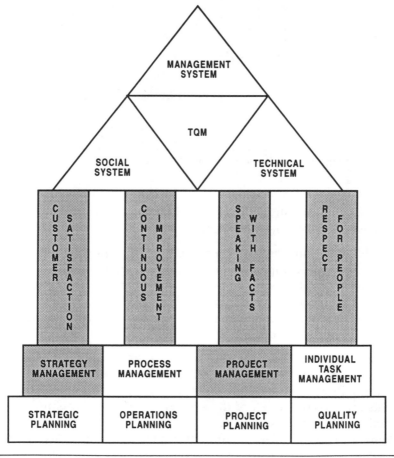

Figure 4.5 House of Total Quality.

tioned, and thoroughly understood, because the success of the total quality system is in the balance. As previously mentioned, many of the individual components of total quality are practiced by American companies, but few practice total quality as a whole.

HISTORY OF TOTAL QUALITY

In the Beginning

About the year one million B.C., give or take a few centuries, man first began to fashion stone tools for hunting and survival.[8] Up until 8000 B.C., however, very little progress was made in the quality control of these tools. It was at this time that man began assembling instruments with fitting holes, which suggests the use of interchangeable parts on a very limited basis. Throughout this long period, each man made his own tools. The evidence of quality control was measured to some extent by how long he stayed alive. If the tools were well made, his chances of survival increased. A broken axe handle usually spelled doom.

Introduction of Interchangeable Parts and Division of Labor

A little over 200 years ago, in 1787, the concepts of interchangeable parts and division of labor were first introduced in the United States. Eli Whitney, inventor of the cotton gin, applied these concepts to the production of 10,000 flintlock rifles for the U.S. military arsenal. However, Whitney had considerable difficulty in making all the parts exactly the same. It took him ten years to complete the 10,000 muskets that he promised to deliver in two years.

Three factors impacted Whitney's inability to deliver the 10,000 muskets in two years as promised. First, there was a dramatic shortage of qualified craftsmen needed to build the muskets. Consequently, Whitney correctly identified the solution to the problem—machines must do what men previously did. If individual machines were assembled to create each individual part needed, then men could be taught to operate these machines. Thus, Whitney's application of division of labor to a highly technical process was born. Whitney called this a *manufactory*.

Next, it took almost one full year to build the manufactory, rather than two months as Whitney originally thought. Not only did the weather inflict havoc on the schedule, but epidemics of yellow fever slowed progress considerably.

Third, obtaining the raw materials in a timely, usable manner was a hit-or-miss proposition. The metal ore used was often defective, flawed, and pitted. In addition, training the workers to perform the actual assembly took much longer than Whitney imagined and required a considerable amount of his personal attention, often 15 to 20 hours a day. Also, once the men were trained, some left to work for competing armories.[9]

To compound these factors, his ongoing cotton gin patent lawsuits consumed a considerable amount of his highly leveraged attention and time. Fortunately for Whitney, his credibility in Washington granted him considerable laxity in letting target dates slip. War with France was no longer imminent. Thus, a quality product and the associated manufacturing expertise were deemed more important than schedule. What was promised in 28 months took almost 120 months to deliver.

Luckily for Whitney, the requirement of "on time and within budget" was not yet in vogue. What happened to Whitney was a classic study in the problems of trying to achieve a real breakthrough in operations. Out of this experience, Whitney and others realized that creating parts exactly the same was not possible and, if tried, would prove to be very expensive. This concept of interchangeable parts would eventually lead to statistical methods of control, while division of labor would lead to the factory assembly line.

The First Control Limits

The experiences of Whitney and others who followed led to a relaxation of the requirements for exactness and the use of tolerances. This allowed for a less-than-perfect fit between two (or more) parts, and the concept of "go–no-go" tolerance was introduced between 1840 and 1870.[10]

This idea was a major advancement in that it created the concept of upper and lower tolerance limits, thus allowing the production worker more freedom to do his job with an accompanying lowering of cost. All he had to do was stay within the tolerance limits, instead of trying to achieve unnecessary or unattainable perfection.

Defective Parts Inspection

The next advancement centered around expanding the notion of tolerance and using specifications, where variation is classified as either meeting or not meeting requirements. For those pieces of product that every now and then fell outside the specified tolerance range (or limits), the question arose as to what to do with them. To discard or modify these pieces added significantly to the cost of production. However, to search for the unknown causes of defects and then eliminate them also cost money. The heart of the problem was as follows: how to reduce the percentage of defects to the point where (1) the rate of increase in the *cost of control* equals the rate of *increase* in *savings*, which is (2) brought about by *decreasing the number of parts rejected*.

In other words, inspection/prevention had to be cost effective. Minimizing the percent of defects in a cost-effective manner was not the only problem to be solved. Tests for many quality characteristics require destructive testing, such as tests for strength, chemical composition, fuse blowing time, etc. Because not every piece can be tested, use of the statistical sample was initiated around the turn of the century.

Statistical Theory

During the early part of the 20th century, a tremendous increase in quality consciousness occurred. What were the forces at work that caused this sudden acceleration of interest in the application of statistical quality control? There were at least three key factors.

The first was a rapid growth in standardization, beginning in 1900. Until 1915, Great Britain was the only country in the world with some type of national standardization movement. The rate of growth in the number of industrial standardization organizations throughout the world, especially between 1916 and 1932, rose dramatically.[11] During that 15-year period, the movement grew from one country (Great Britain) to 25, with the United States coming on line about 1917, just at the time of World War I.

The second major factor ushering in the new era was a radical shift in ideology which occurred in about 1900. This ideological shift was away from the notion of exactness of science (which existed in 1787 when interchangeability of parts was introduced) to probability and statistical concepts, which developed in almost every field of science around 1900.

The third factor was the evolution of division of labor into the factory system and the first assembly-line systems of the early 20th century. These systems proved to be ideal for employing an immigrant work force quickly.

Scientific Management and Taylorism

Frederick Winslow Taylor was born in 1856 and entered industry as an apprentice in the Enterprise Hydraulics Shop in 1874. According to popular legend, the old-timers in the shop told him: "Now young man, here's about how much work you should do each morning and each afternoon. Don't do any more than that—that's the limit."[12]

It was obvious to Taylor that the men were producing below their capacity, and he soon found out why. The short-sighted management of that day would set standards, often paying per-piece rates for the work. Then, when a worker discovered how to produce more, management cut the rate. In turn, management realized that the workers were deliberately restricting output but could not do anything about it.

It was Taylor's viewpoint that the whole system was wrong. Having studied the writings and innovations of Whitney, he came to realize that the concept of division of labor had to be revamped if greater productivity and efficiency were to be realized. His vision included a super-efficient assembly line as part of a management system of operations. He, more than anyone at the time, understood the inability of management to increase individual productivity, and he understood the reluctance of the workers to produce at a high rate. Because he had been a working man, it was apparent to him that there was a tremendous difference between *actual* output and *potential* output. Taylor thought that if such practices applied throughout the world and throughout all industry, the potential production capacity was at least three or four times what was actually being produced. When he became a foreman, Taylor set out to find ways to eliminate this waste and increase production.

For more than 25 years, Taylor and his associates explored ways to increase productivity and build the model factory of the future. The techniques they developed were finally formalized in writing and communicated to other people. During the early years of this experimentation, most who knew about it were associated with Taylor at the Midvale Steel Company and Bethlehem Steel.

Other famous names began to enter the picture and contribute to the body of science of the new management thinking. Among them were Carl G.L. Barth, a mathematician and statistician who assisted Taylor in analytical work, and Henry L. Gantt (famous for the Gantt chart), who invented the slide rule. Another associate of Taylor's, Sanford E. Thompson, developed the first decimal stopwatch.[12] Finally, there was young Walter Shewhart, who was to transform industry with his statistical concepts and thinking and his ability to bridge technical tools with a management system.

At the turn of the century, Taylor wrote a collection of reports and papers that were published by the American Society of Mechanical Engineers. One of the most famous was *On the Art of Cutting Metals*, which had worldwide impact. With Maunsel White, Taylor developed the first high-speed steel. Taylor was also instrumental in the development of one of the first industrial cost-accounting systems, even though, according to legend, he previously knew nothing about accounting.

Frank G. and Lillian Gilbreth, aware of Taylor's work in measurement and analysis, turned their attention to mechanizing and commercializing Taylorism. For their experimental model, they chose the ancient craft of bricklaying. It had been assumed that production in bricklaying certainly should have reached its zenith thousands of years ago, with nothing more to be done to increase production. Yet Frank Gilbreth was able to show that by following his techniques and with proper management planning, production could be raised from an average of 120 bricks per hour to 350 bricks per hour, and the worker would be less tired than he had been under the old system.

The Gilbreths refined some of the studies and techniques developed by Taylor. They used the motion picture camera to record work steps for analyses and broke them down into minute elements called "therbligs" (Gilbreth spelled backwards). Their results were eventually codified into the use of predetermined motion–time measures which were used by industrial engineers and efficiency experts of the day.

By 1912, the efficiency movement was gaining momentum. Taylor was called before a special committee of the House of Representatives which was investigating scientific management and its impact on the railroad industry. He tried to explain scientific management to the somewhat hostile railroad hearings committee, whose members regarded it as "speeding up" work. He said:

> Scientific management involves a complete mental revolution on the part of the *working man* engaged in any particular establishment or industry…a complete mental revolution on the part of these men as to their duties toward their work, toward their fellow man, and toward their employers.
>
> And scientific management involves an equally complete mental revolution on the part of those on *management's side*…the foreman, the superintendent, the owner of the business, and the board of directors. Here we must have a mental revolution on their part as to their duties toward their fellow workers in management, toward their workmen, and toward all of their daily problems. Without this complete mental revolution on both sides, scientific management does not exist!
>
> I want to sweep the deck, sweep away a good deal of the rubbish first by pointing out what scientific management is not— it is not an efficiency device, nor is it any bunch or group of efficiency devices. It is not a new system of figuring costs. It is not a new scheme of paying men. It is not holding a stopwatch on a man and writing things down about him. It is not time study. It is not motion study, nor an analysis of the movements of a man. Nor is scientific management the printing and ruling and unloading of a ton or two of blank forms on a set of men and saying, "Here's your system—go to it."
>
> It is not divided foremanship, nor functional foremanship. It is not any of these devices which the average man calls to mind when he hears the words "scientific management." I am not sneering at cost-keeping systems—at time-study, at functional foremanship, nor at any of the new and improved schemes of paying men. Nor am I sneering at efficiency devices, if they are really devices which make for efficiency. I believe in them. What I am emphasizing is that these devices in whole or part are *not* scien-

tific management; they are useful adjuncts to scientific management, but they are also useful adjuncts to other systems of management.[12]

Taylor found out, the hard way, the importance of the cooperative spirit. He was strictly the engineer at first. Only after painful experiences did he realize that the human factor, the social system, and mental attitude of people in both management and labor had to be adjusted and changed completely before greater productivity could result.

Referring to his early experiences in seeking greater output, Taylor described the strained feelings between himself and his workmen as "miserable." Yet he was determined to improve production. He continued his experiments until three years before his death in 1915, when he found that human motivation, not just engineered improvements, could alone increase output.

Unfortunately, the human factor was ignored by many. Shortly after the railroad hearings, self-proclaimed "efficiency experts" did untold damage to scientific management. Time studies and the new efficiency techniques were used by incompetent "consultants" who sold managers on the idea of increasing profit by "speeding up" employees. Consequently, many labor unions, just beginning to feel their strength, worked against the new science and all efficiency approaches. With the passing of Taylor in 1915, the scientific management movement lost, for the moment, any chance of reaching its true potential as the catalyst for the future total quality management system. Still, the foundation was laid for the management system that was soon to become a key ingredient of organizations of the future.

Walter Shewhart—The Founding Father

Walter Shewhart was an engineer, scientist, and philosopher. He was a very deep thinker, and his ideas, although profound and technically perfect, were difficult to fathom. His style of writing followed his style of thinking—very obtuse. Still, he was brilliant, and his works on variation and sampling, coupled with his teachings on the need for documentation, influenced forever the course of industrial history.

Shewhart was familiar with the scientific management movement and its evolution from Whitney's innovation of division of labor. Although he was concerned about its evolution into sweatshop factory environments, his major focus was on the other of Whitney's great innovations—interchangeable parts—for this encompassed variation, rejects, and waste.

To deal with the issue of variation, Shewhart developed the control chart in 1924. He realized that the traditional use of tolerance limits was shortsighted, because they only provided a method for judging the quality of a product that had already been made.[13]

The control limits on Shewhart's control charts, however, provided a ready guide for acting on a process in order to eliminate what he called *assignable causes*[8] of variation, thus preventing inferior products from being produced in the future. This allowed management to focus on the future, through the use of statistical probability—a prediction of future production based upon historical data. Thus, the emphasis shifted from costly correction of problems to prevention of problems and improvement of processes.[14]

Like Taylor, Shewhart's focus shifted from individual parts to a systems approach. The notion of zero defects of individual parts was replaced with zero variability of system operations.

Shewhart's Control System

Shewhart identified the traditional act of control as consisting of three elements: the act of specifying what is required, the act of producing what is specified, and the act of judging whether the requirements have been met. This simple picture of the control of quality would work well if production could be viewed in the context of an exact science, where all products are made exactly the same. Shewhart knew, however, that because variation is pervasive, the control of quality characteristics must be a matter of probability. He envisioned a statistician helping an engineer to understanding variation and arriving at the economic control of quality.[15]

Shewhart's Concept of Variation

Determining the *state of statistical control* in terms of degree of variation is the first step in the Shewhart control system. Rather than specifying what is required in terms of tolerance requirements, Shewhart viewed variation as being present in everything and identified two types of variation: *controlled* and *uncontrolled*.

This is fundamentally different from the traditional way of classifying variation as either acceptable or unacceptable (go–no-go tolerance). Viewing variation as controlled or uncontrolled enables one to focus on the causes of variation in order to improve a process (before the fact) as opposed to focusing on the output of a process in order to judge whether or not the product is acceptable (after the fact).

Shewhart taught that controlled variation is a consistent pattern of variation over time that is due to random or *chance causes*. He recognized that there may be many chance causes of variation, but the effect of any one of these is relatively small; therefore, which cause or causes are responsible for observed variation is a matter of chance. Shewhart stated that a process that is being affected only by *chance* causes of variation is said to be *in a state of statistical control*.

All processes contain chance causes of variation, and Shewhart taught that it is possible to reduce the chance causes of variation, but it is not realistic or cost effective to try to remove them all. The control limits on Shewhart's control charts represent the boundaries of the occurrence of chance causes of variation operating within the system.

The second type of variation—uncontrolled variation—is an inconsistent or changing pattern of variation that occurs over time and is due to what Shewhart classified as *assignable causes*. Because the effects of assignable causes of variation are relatively major compared to chance causes, they can and must be identified and removed.[16] According to Shewhart, a process is *out of statistical control* when it is being affected by assignable causes.

One of Shewhart's main problems was how to communicate this newfound theory without overwhelming the average businessman or engineer. The answer came in the form of staged experiments using models which demonstrated variation. His *Ideal Bowl Experiment*[17] with poker chips was modeled by his protege, W. Edwards Deming, some 20 years later with his famous *Red Bead Experiment*.

Another major contribution of Shewhart's first principle of control was recognition of the need for operational definitions that can be communicated to operators, inspectors, and scientists alike. He was fond of asking, "How can an operator carry out his job tasks if he does not understand what the job is? And how can he know what the job is if what was produced yesterday was O.K., but today the same product is wrong?" He believed that inspection, whether the operator inspects his own work or relies on someone else to do it for him, must have operational definitions. Extending specifications beyond product and into the realm of operator performance was the first attempt to define the "extended system of operations" which would greatly facilitate the production process.

The Shewhart System of Production

Shewhart's second principle—the act of producing what is specified—consists of five important steps (Shewhart's teachings are in italics):

1. **Outline the data collection framework**—*Specify in a general way how an observed sequence of data is to be examined for clues as to the existence of assignable causes of variability.*

2. **Develop the sampling plan**—*Specify how the original data are to be taken and how they are to be broken up into subsamples upon the basis of human judgments about whether the conditions under which the data were taken were essentially the same or not.*

3. **Identify the formulas and control limits for each sample**—*Specify the criterion of control that is to be used, indicating what statistics are to be com-*

puted for each subsample and how these are to be used in computing action or control limits for each statistic for which the control criterion is to be constructed.

4. **Outline the corrective actions/improvement thesis**—*Specify the action that is to be taken when an observed statistic falls outside its control limits.*

5. **Determine the size of the database**—*Specify the quantity of data that must be available and found to satisfy the criterion of control before the engineer is to act as though he had attained a state of statistical control.*[8]

The Shewhart system became a key component of the technical system of total quality. The works of Deming, Juran, Feigenbaum, Sarasohn, Ishikawa, and others who followed would amplify Shewhart's concept of quality as a *technical system* into its many dimensions, which eventually led to the body of knowledge known as total quality.

The Shewhart Cycle: When Control Meets Scientific Management

From the "exact science" days of the 1800s to the 1920s, *specification, production,* and *inspection* were considered to be independent of each other when viewed in a straight-line manner. They take on an entirely different picture in an inexact science. When the production process is viewed from the standpoint of the control of quality as a matter of probability, then specification, production, and inspection are linked together as represented in a circular diagram or wheel. *Specification and production* are linked because it is important to know how well the tolerance limits are being satisfied by the existing process and what improvements are necessary. Shewhart compared this process (which he called the Scientific Method) to the dynamic process of acquiring knowledge, which is similar to an experiment. Step 1 was formulating the hypothesis. Step 2 was conducting the experiment. Step 3 was testing the hypothesis.[18] In the Shewhart Wheel, the successful completion of each interlocking component led to a cycle of continuous improvement. (Years later, Deming was to popularize this cycle of improvement in his famous Deming Wheel.)

Shewhart Meets Deming

It was at the Bell Laboratories in New Jersey where Shewhart, who was leading the telephone reliability efforts during the 1930s, first met Deming. Shewhart, as discussed earlier, was developing his system for improving worker performance and productivity by measuring variation using control charts and statistical methods. Deming was impressed and liked what he saw, especially Shewhart's intellect and the *wheel*—the Shewhart cycle of control. He realized that with training, workers could retain control over their work processes by monitoring the quality of the items produced. Deming also believed that once workers were trained and educated and were empowered to manage their work processes, quality would be increased and costly inspections could once and for all be eliminated. He presented the idea that higher quality would cost less, not more. Deming studied Shewhart's teachings and techniques and learned well, even if at times he was lost and said that his genius was in knowing when to act and when to leave a process alone. At times he was frustrated by Shewhart's obtuse style of thinking and writing.[19]

In 1938, Shewhart delivered four lectures to the U.S. Department of Agriculture (USDA) Graduate School at the invitation of Deming. In addition to being in charge of the mathematics and statistics courses at the USDA Graduate School, Deming was responsible for inviting guest lecturers. He invited Shewhart to present a series of lectures on how statistical methods of control were being used in industry to economically control the quality of manufactured products. Shewhart spent an entire year developing the lectures, titled them *Statistical Method from the Viewpoint of Quality Control*, and delivered them in March of 1938. They were subsequently edited into book format by Deming and published in 1939.

In a couple of years, both Deming and Shewhart were called upon by the U.S. government to aid the war effort. As David Halberstam recounted, the War Department, impressed by Shewhart's theories and work, brought together a small group of experts on statistical process control (SPC) to establish better quality guidelines for defense contractors.[20] Deming was a member of that group and he came to love the work.

Origins of Deming

Who was Dr. W. Edwards Deming, the man who was to take Shewhart's teachings, popularize them, and even go beyond? He was born on October 14, 1900 and earned his Ph.D. in physics at Yale University in the summer of 1927, which is where he learned to use statistical theory. As a graduate student in the late 1920s, he did part-time summer work at the famous Western Electric Hawthorne Plant in Chicago. It was at this plant that Elton Mayo some ten years later would perform his experiments later known as the Hawthorne Experiments. While working at Hawthorne, Deming could not help noticing the poor working conditions of this sweatshop environment, which employed predominantly female laborers to produce telephones. Deming was both fascinated and appalled by what he saw and learned. It was at Hawthorne that he saw the full effects of the abuses of the Taylor system of scientific management. He also saw the full effect of Whitney's second great innovation—division of labor—when carried to extreme by ivory tower management uncaring about the state of the social system of the organization. So what if the work environment was a sweatshop—the workers were paid well enough! "The women should be happy just to have a job" seemed to be the unspoken attitude.

When Deming Met Taylor(ism)

A couple of years before meeting Shewhart, when Deming encountered Taylorism at Hawthorne, he found a scientific management system with the following objectives:

- Develop a science for each element of work.
- Scientifically select a workman and train and develop him.
- Secure wholehearted cooperation between management and labor to ensure that all work is done in accordance with the principles developed.
- Divide the work between management and labor. The manager takes over all work for which he is better suited than the workman.

It was the fourth point, which evolved out of the division of labor concept, that Deming found to be the real villain. In practice, this meant removing from the worker basic responsibility for the quality of the work. What Deming disliked was that workers should not be hired to think about their work. That was management's job. Errors will occur, but the worker need not worry—the inspector will catch any mistakes *before* they leave the plant. In addition, management could always reduce the per-piece pay to reflect scrap and rework. Any worker who produced too many inferior quality pieces would be fired.

The problem with Taylorism is that it views the production process mechanistically instead of holistically, as a system which includes the human elements of motivation and respect. Taylorism taught American industry to view the worker as "a cog in the giant industrial machine, whose job could be defined and directed by educated managers administering a set of rules."[21] Work on the assembly lines of America and at Hawthorne was simple, repetitive, and boring. Management was top-down. Pay per piece meant that higher output equals higher take-home pay. Quality of work for the most part was not a factor for the average, everyday worker.

This system found a friend in the assembly-line process developed by Henry Ford and was widely incorporated into America's private and public sectors. Taylor's management system made it possible for waves of immigrants, many of whom could not read, write, or speak English (and at times not even communicate with one another), to find employment in American factories. Taylor's ideas were even introduced into the nation's schools.[22]

Edwards Deming had various colleagues at the time, one of whom was Joseph Juran, another famous quality "guru." They rebelled at the scientific management movement. They felt that the authoritarian Taylorism method of management was degrading to the human spirit and counterproductive to the interests of employees, management, the company, and society as a whole.[23] Mayo and his Hawthorne research team confirmed these feelings with their findings: good leadership leads to high morale and motivation, which in turn leads to higher production. Good leadership was defined as democratic, rather than autocratic, and people centered, as opposed to production centered. Thus began the human relations era.

Post-World War II

When the war ended, American industry converted to peacetime production of goods and services. People were hungry for possessions and an appetite developed worldwide for products "made in the U.S.A." The focus in the United States returned to quantity over quality, and a gradual deterioration of market share occurred, with billions of dollars in international business lost to Japanese and European competitors. These were the modern-day phoenixes rising from the ashes of war. America became preoccupied with the mechanics of mass production and its role as world provider to a hungry people. What followed was an imbalance between satisfying the needs of the worker and a lack of appreciation for and recognition of the external customer. America moved away from what had made it great!

The Japanese Resurrection

Japan first began to apply statistical control concepts in the early 1920s, but moved away from them when the war began.[24] In 1946, under General Douglas MacArthur's leadership, the Supreme Command for the Allied Powers (SCAP) established quality control tools and techniques as the approach to effect the turnaround of Japanese industry. Japan had sacrificed its industry, and eventually its food supply, to support its war effort. Subsequently, there was little left in post-war Japan to occupy. The country was a shambles. Only one major city, Kyoto, had escaped wide-scale destruction; food was scarce and industry was negligible.[24]

Against a backdrop of devastation and military defeat, a group of Japanese scientists and engineers—organized appropriately as the Union of Japanese Scientists and Engineers (JUSE)—dedicated themselves to working with American and Allied experts to help rebuild the country. Reconstruction was a daunting and monumental task. With few natural resources available or any immediate means of producing them, export of manufactured goods was essential. However, Japanese industry—or what was left of it—was producing inferior goods, a fact which was recognized worldwide. JUSE was faced with the task of drastically improving the quality of Japan's industrial output as an essential exchange commodity for survival.

W.S. Magill and Homer Sarasohn, among others, assisted with the dramatic transformation of the electronics industry and telecommunications. Magill is regarded by some as the father of statistical quality control in Japan. He was the first to advocate its use in a 1945 lecture series and successfully applied SPC techniques to vacuum tube production in 1946 at NEC.[25]

Sarasohn worked with supervisors and managers to improve reliability and yields in the electronics field from 40 percent in 1946 to 80 to 90 percent in 1949; he documented his findings for SCAP, and MacArthur took notice. He ordered Sarasohn to instruct Japanese businessmen how to get things done. The Japanese listened, but the Americans forgot. In 1950, Sarasohn's attention was directed toward Korea, and Walter Shewhart was asked to come to Japan. He was unable to at the time, and Deming was eventually tapped to direct the transformation.

In July 1950, Deming began a series of day-long lectures to Japanese management in which he taught the basic "Elementary Principles of Statistical Control of Quality." The Japanese embraced the man and his principles and named their most prestigious award for quality the Deming Prize. During the 1970s, Deming turned his attention back to the United States. He died at the age of 93, still going strong. His 14 Points go far beyond statistical methods and address the management system as well as the social system or culture of the organization. In many ways, he began to sound more and more like Frederick Taylor, whose major emphasis in later years was on the need for a *mental revolution*—a transformation. Deming's Theory of Profound Knowledge brings together all three systems of total quality.

The Other "Gurus" Arrive

What began in Japan in the 1950s became a worldwide quality movement, albeit on a limited basis, within 20 years. During this period, the era of the "gurus" evolved (Deming, Juran, Ishikawa, Feigenbaum, and Crosby). Beginning with Deming in 1948 and Juran in 1954, the movement was eventually carried back to the United States by Feigenbaum in the 1960s and Crosby in the 1970s. Meanwhile, Ishikawa and his associates at JUSE kept the movement alive in Japan. By 1980, the bell began to toll loud and clear in the West with the NBC White Paper entitled "If Japan Can Do It, Why Can't We?" The following are thumbnail sketches of the teachings of the other gurus.

Joseph Juran

Joseph Juran was the son of an immigrant shoemaker from Romania and began his industrial career at Western Electric's Hawthorne Plant before World War II. He later worked at Bell Laboratories in the area of quality assurance. He worked as a government administrator, university professor, labor arbitrator, and corporate director before establishing his own consulting firm, the Juran Institute, in Wilton, Connecticut. In the 1950s, he was invited to Japan by JUSE to help rebuilding Japanese corporations develop management concepts. Juran based some of his principles on the work of Walter Shewhart and, like Deming and the other quality gurus, believed that management and the system are responsible for quality. Juran is the creator of statistical quality control and the author of *The Quality Control Handbook*, which has become an international standard reference for the quality movement.

Juran's definition of quality is described as "fitness for use as perceived by the customer." If a product is produced and the customer perceives it as fit for use, then the quality mission has been accomplished. Juran also believed that every person in the organization must be involved in the effort to make products or services that are fit for use.

Juran described a perpetual spiral of progress or continuous striving toward quality. Steps on this spiral are, in ascending order, research, development, design, specification, planning, purchasing, instrumentation, production, process control, inspection, testing, sale, service, and then back to research again. The idea behind the spiral is that each time the steps are completed, products or services would increase in quality. Juran explained that chronic problems should be solved by following this spiral; he formulated a breakthrough sequence to increase the standard of performance so that problems are eliminated. To alleviate sporadic problems, which he finds are often solved with temporary solutions, he suggests carefully examining the system causing the problem and adjusting it to solve the difficulty. Once operating at this improved standard of performance, with the sporadic problem solved, the process of analyzing chronic and sporadic problems should start over again.

Juran pointed out that companies often overlook the cost of producing low-quality products. He suggested that by implementing his theories of quality improvement, not only would higher quality products be produced, but the actual costs would be lower. His Cost of Quality principle was known as "Gold in the Mine."

Juran is known for his work with statistics, and he relied on the quantification of standards and statistical quality control techniques. He is credited with implementing use of the Pareto diagram to improve business systems as well.

Juran's concept of quality included the managerial dimensions of planning, organizing, and controlling (known as the Juran Trilogy) and focused on the responsibility of management to achieve quality and the need to set goals. His ten steps to quality are as follows:

1. Build awareness of opportunities to improve.
2. Set goals for improvement.
3. Organize to reach goals.
4. Provide training.
5. Carry out projects to solve problems.
6. Report progress.
7. Give recognition.
8. Communicate results.
9. Keep score.
10. Maintain momentum by making annual improvement part of the regular systems and processes of the company.

Ishikawa and the Japanese Experts

Kaoru Ishikawa studied under both Homer Sarasohn and Edwards Deming during the late 1940s and early 1950s. As president of JUSE, he was instrumental in developing a unique Japanese strategy for total quality: the broad involvement of the entire organization in its *total* sense—every worker, every process, and every job. This also included the complete life cycle of the product, from start to finish.

Some of his accomplishments include the success of the quality circle in Japan, in part due to innovative tools such as the cause-and-effect diagram (often called the Ishikawa fishbone diagram because it resembles a fish skeleton). His approach was to provide easy-to-use analytical tools that could be used by all workers, including those on the line, to analyze and solve problems.

Ishikawa identified seven critical success factors that were essential for the success of total quality control in Japan:

1. Company-wide total quality control and participation by *all* members of the organization
2. Education and training in all aspects of total quality, which often amounts to 30 days per year per employee
3. Use of quality circles to update standards and regulations, which are in constant need of improvement
4. Quality audits by the president and quality council members (senior executives) twice a year
5. Widespread use of statistical methods and a focus on problem prevention
6. Nationwide quality control promotion activities, with the national imperative of keeping Japanese quality number one in the world

7. Revolutionary *mental* attitude on the part of both management and workers toward one another and toward the customer, including welcoming complaints, encouraging risk, and a wider span of control

Ishikawa believed that Japanese management practices should be democratic, with management providing the guidelines. Mission statements were used extensively and operating policies derived from them. Top management, he taught, must assume a leadership position to implement the policies so that they are followed by all.

The impact on Japanese industry was startling. In seven to ten years, the electronics and telecommunications industries were transformed, with the entire nation revitalized by the end of the 1960s.

Armand Feigenbaum

Unlike Deming and Juran, Feigenbaum did not work with the Japanese. He was vice president of worldwide quality for General Electric until the late 1960s, when he set up his own consulting firm, General Systems, Inc. He is best known for coining the term *total quality control* and for his 850-page book on the subject. His teachings center around the integration of people–machine–information structures in order to economically and effectively control quality and achieve full customer satisfaction.

Feigenbaum taught that there are two requirements to establishing quality as a business strategy: establishing customer satisfaction must be central and quality/cost objectives must drive the total quality system. His systems theory of total quality control includes four fundamental principles:

- Total quality is a continuous work process, starting with customer requirements and ending with customer satisfaction.
- Documentation allows visualization and communication of work assignments.
- The quality system provides for greater flexibility because of a greater use of alternatives provided.
- Systematic reengineering of major quality activities leads to greater levels of continuous improvement.

Like Juran and Deming, Feigenbaum used a visual concept to capture the idea of waste and rework—the so-called Hidden Plant. Based upon studies, he taught that this "Hidden Plant" can account for between 15 and 40 percent of the production capacity of a company. In his book, he used the concept of the "9 M's" to describe the factors which affect quality: (1) markets, (2) money, (3) management, (4) men, (5) motivation, (6) materials, (7) machines and mechanization, (8) modern information methods, and (9) mounting product requirements.

According to Andrea Gabor in "The Man Who Discovered Quality," Feigenbaum took a nuts-and-bolts approach to quality, while Deming is often viewed as a visionary. Nuts and bolts led him to focus on the benefits and outcomes of total quality, rather than only the process to follow. His methods led to increased quantification of total quality program improvements during the 1970s and 1980s.

Philip Crosby

Unlike the other quality gurus, who were scientists, engineers, and statisticians, Philip Crosby is known for his motivational talks and style of presentation. His emergence began in 1961, when he first developed the concept of zero defects while working as a quality manager at Martin Marietta Corporation in Orlando, Florida. He believed that "zero defects" motivated line workers to turn out perfect products. He soon joined ITT, where he quickly moved up the ranks to vice president of quality control operations, covering 192 manufacturing facilities in 46 countries. He held the position until 1979, when he opened his own consulting company, which became one of the largest of its kind with over 250 people worldwide.

He established the Quality College in 1980 and used that concept to promote his teachings and writings in 18 languages. It has been estimated that over five million people have attended its courses, and his trilogy of books are popular and easy to read. It is in these works where he introduces the four absolutes of his total quality management philosophy:

1. The definition of quality is conformance to requirements.
2. The system of quality is prevention of problems.
3. The performance standard of quality is zero defects.
4. The measurement of quality is the price of nonconformance, or the Cost of Quality.

The fourth principle, the Cost of Quality, is similar to Feigenbaum's Hidden Plant and Juran's Gold in the Mine. Like Deming, he has 14 steps to quality improvement. Also like Deming, he has been very critical of the Malcolm Baldrige National Quality Award, although his influence (like Deming's) can be seen in virtually all seven categories.

He departs from the other gurus in his emphasis on performance standards instead of statistical data to achieve zero defects. He believes that identifying goals to be achieved, setting standards for the final product, removing all error-causing situations, and complete organizational commitment comprise the foundation for excellence.

ISO 9000 and the Quality Movement

At the turn of the century, England was the most advanced nation in the world in terms of quality standards. During World War I, England led the charge and during World War II was at least the equal of the United States— with one exception. England did not have Shewhart, Deming, and the other American quality gurus. It was not until the Common Market accepted the firm touch of Prime Minister Margaret Thatcher that the European movement was galvanized in 1979 with the forerunner of ISO 9000. It was Thatcher who orchestrated the transformance of the British ISO 9000 series for the European community. In less than 20 years, it has become the worldwide quality standard.

ENDNOTES

1. During the course of the Deming Prize examination at Florida Power & Light in 1988 and 1989, Dr. Kano consistently emphasized this point during site visits to various power plants and district customer service operations. The concept of worker self-inspection, while new in the United States, has been a practiced art in Japan over the past 20 years.
2. Whethan, C.D. (1980). *A History of Science*, 4th edition. New York: Macmillan.
3. Tribus, Myron (1990). *The Systems of Total Quality*, published by the author.
4. The total quality ballantine was developed by Frank Voehl to illustrate the three-dimensional and interlocking aspects of the quality system. It is loosely based on the military concept of three interlocking bullet holes representing a perfect hit.
5. Tribus, Myron (1990). *The Three Systems of Total Quality*, published by the author; referenced in Voehl, Frank (1992). *Total Quality: Principles and Practices within Organizations*. Coral Springs, FL: Strategy Associates, pp. IV, 20.
6. The use of a storyboard to document the various phases of project development was introduced by Dr. Kume in his work on total quality control and was pioneered in the United States by Disney Studios, where it was used to bring new movies to production sooner.
7. For details, see Voehl, F.W. (1992). *The Integrated Quality System*. Coral Springs, FL: Strategy Associates.
8. Shewhart, W.A. (1931). *Economic Control of Quality of Manufactured Product*. New York: Van Nostrand.
9. Olmstead, Denison (1972). *Memoir of Eli Whitney, Esq.* New York: Arno Press.
10. Walter Shewhart on the "go–no-go" concept: If, for example, a design involving the use of a cylindrical shaft in a bearing is examined, inter-

changeability might be ensured simply by using a suitable "go" plug gauge on the bearing and a suitable "go" ring gauge on the shaft. In this case, the difference between the dimensions of the two "go" gauges gives the minimum clearance. Such a method of gauging, however, does not fix the maximum clearance. The production worker soon realized that a slack fit between a part and its "go" gauge might result in enough play between the shaft and its bearing to cause the product to be rejected; therefore, he tried to keep the fit between the part and its "go" gauge as close as possible, thus encountering some of the difficulties that had been experienced in trying to make the parts exactly alike.

11.   Walter Shewhart was the first to realize that, with the development of the atomic structure of matter and electricity, it became necessary to regard laws as being statistical in nature. According to Shewhart, the importance of the law of large numbers in the interpretation of physical phenomena will become apparent to anyone who even hastily surveys any one or more of the following works: Darrow, K.K. (1992). "Statistical Theories of Matter, Radiation, and Electricity." *The Physical Review Supplement.* Vol. I, No. I (also published in the series of Bell Telephone Laboratories reprints, No. 435); Rice, J. (1930). *Introduction to Statistical Mechanics for Students of Physics and Physical Chemistry.* London: Constable & Company; Tolman, R.E. (1927). *Statistical Mechanics with Applications to Physics and Chemistry.* New York: Chemical Catalog Company; Loeb, L.B. (1927). *Kinetic Theory of Gases.* New York: McGraw-Hill; Bloch, E. (1924). *The Kinetic Theory of Bases.* London: Methuen & Company; Richtmeyer, F.K. (1928). *Introduction to Modern Physics.* New York: McGraw-Hill; Wilson, H.A. (1928). *Modern Physics.* London: Blackie & Son; Darrow, K.K. (1926). *Introduction to Contemporary Physics.* New York: D. Van Nostrand; Ruark, A.E. and Urey, H.C. (1930). *Atoms, Molecules and Quanta.* New York: McGraw-Hill.

12.   Matthies, Leslie (1960). "The Beginning of Modern Scientific Management." *The Office.* April.

13.   Walter Shewhart on the use of the control chart: Whereas the concept of mass production of 1787 was born of an *exact* science, the concept underlying the quality control chart technique of 1924 was born of a *probable* science, which has empirically derived control limits. These limits are to be set so that when the observed quality of a piece of product falls outside of them, even though the observation is still within the limits L_1 and L_2 (tolerance limits), it is desirable to look at the manufacturing process in order to discover and remove, if possible, one or more causes of variation that need not be left to chance.

14.   Shewhart noted that it is essential, however, in industry and in science to understand the distinction between a stable system and an unstable system and how to plot points and conclude by rational methods whether they indicate a stable system. To quote Shewhart, "This conclusion is consistent with that so admirably presented in a recent paper by S.L. Andrew in the *Bell Telephone Quarterly*, Jan., 1931, and also with conclu-

sions set forth in the recent book *Business Adrift,* by W.B. Donham, Dean of the Harvard Business School. Such reading cannot do other than strengthen our belief in the fact that control of quality will come only through the weeding out of assignable causes of variation—particularly those that introduce lack of constancy in the chance cause system."

15. As the statistician enters the scene, the three traditional elements of control take on a new meaning, as Shewhart summarized: "Corresponding to these three steps there are three senses in which statistical control may play an important part in attaining uniformity in the quality of a manufactured product: (a) as a concept of a statistical state constituting a limit to which one may hope to go in improving the uniformity of quality; (b) as an operation or technique of attaining uniformity; and (c) as a judgment."

16. Deming refers to assignable causes as being "specific to some ephemeral (brief) event that can usually be discovered to the satisfaction of the expert on the job, and removed."

17. Shewhart used what he called the *Ideal Bowl Experiment* to physically characterize a state of statistical control. A number of physically similar poker chips with numbers written on them are placed in a bowl. Successive samples (Shewhart seems to prefer a sample size of four) are taken from the bowl, each time mixing the remaining chips. The chips removed from the bowl are drawn by chance—there are only chance causes of variation. In speaking of chance causes of variation, Shewhart proves, contrary to popular belief, that the statistician can have a sense of humor. "If someone were shooting at a mark and failed to hit the bull's-eye and was then asked why, the answer would likely be *chance.* Had someone asked the same question of one of man's earliest known ancestors, he might have attributed his lack of success to the dictates of fate or to the will of the gods. I am inclined to think that in many ways one of these excuses is about as good as another. The Ideal Bowl Experiment is an abstract means of characterizing the physical state of statistical control." A sequence of samples of any process can be compared mathematically to the bowl experiment and, if found similar, the process can be said to be affected only by random or chance causes of variation or can be characterized as being in a *state of statistical control.* Shewhart states: "It seems to me that it is far safer to take some one physical operation such as drawing from a bowl as a physical model for an act that may be repeated at random, and then to require that any other repetitive operation believed to be random shall in addition produce results similar in certain respects to the results of drawing from a bowl before we act as though the operation in question were random."

18. It may be helpful to think of the three steps in the mass production process as steps in the Scientific Method. In this sense, specification, production, and inspection correspond, respectively, to formulating a hypothesis,

conducting an experiment, and testing the hypothesis. The three steps constitute the dynamic scientific process of acquiring knowledge.

19.　The following story was related at one of Deming's now-famous four-day quality seminars: I remember him [Shewhart] pacing the floor in his room at the Hotel Washington before the third lecture. He was explaining something to me. I remarked that these great thoughts should be in his lectures. He said that they were already written up in his third and fourth lectures. I remarked that if he wrote up these lectures in the same way that he had just explained them to me, they would be clearer. He said that his writing had to be foolproof. I thereupon remarked that he had written his thoughts to be so darn foolproof that no one could understand them.

20.　Halberstam, David (1960). "The War Effort during WWII." Lectures, Articles and Interview Notes.

21.　This is a general consensus feeling among many historians and writers as to the inherent "evil" of Taylorism—machine over man. Walter Shewhart, to his credit and genius, tries to marry quality control and scientific management. In the foreword to his 1931 master work referred to in Endnote 8, he writes, "Broadly speaking, the object of industry is to set up economic ways and means of satisfying human wants and in so doing to reduce everything possible to routines requiring a minimum amount of human effort. Through the use of the Scientific Method, extended to take account of modern statistical concepts, it has been found possible to set up limits within which the results of routine efforts must lie if they are to be economical. Deviations in the results of a routine process outside such limits indicate that the routine has broken down and will no longer be economical until the cause of trouble is removed."

22.　Bonstingal, John Jay (1992). *Schools of Quality*. New York: Free Press.

23.　The Hawthorne Experiments, Elton Mayo, 1938.

24.　Voehl, F.W. (1990). "The Deming Prize." *South Carolina Business Journal*. pp. 33–38.

25.　This was first pointed out by Robert Chadman Wood in an article about Homer Sarasohn, published in *Forbes* in 1990.

26.　Figure 4.2 ©1991 F.W. Voehl. Figure 4.3 ©1992 Strategy Associates, Inc.

ARTICLE

THE DEMING PRIZE VS. THE BALDRIGE AWARD*

Joseph F. Duffy

The Deming Prize and the Baldrige Award. They're both named after Americans, both very prestigious to win, both standing for a cry for quality in business, both engaged by their share of critics. One is 40 years old; the other a mere four. One resides in an alluring, foreign land; the other on American soil. One is awarded to the paradigm of Japanese business, individuals and international companies; the other to the best of U.S. business. One has grown in what a psychologist might call a mostly safe, nurturing environment; the other amongst a sometimes sour, sometimes sweet, bipolar parental image of government officials, academia and business gurus who seem to critically tug every way possible. One represents a country hailed as the world leader in quality; the other is trying to catch up—trying very hard.

A battle between Japan's Deming Prize and the Malcolm Baldrige National Quality Award would be as good a making for a movie as *Rocky* ever was: You have the older, wiser Japanese, who emanates a wisdom that withstands time, against the younger, quickly maturing American who has an outstanding reputation for being a victorious underdog. Who would win? We took the two awards to center ring, made them don their gloves and have a go.

ROUND 1: HISTORY

Although residing almost half a world apart, the Deming Prize and the Malcolm Baldrige National Quality Award are bonded by influence. After the ravages unleashed during World War II took a ruinous toll on Japan, W. Edwards Deming came to aid this seemingly hopeless land. With his expertise in statistical quality control (SQC), Deming helped lift Japan out of the rubble and into the limelight by having Japanese businesses apply SQC techniques.

* This article is reproduced from *Quality Digest*, August 1991, pp. 33–53. In it, the author interviewed four individuals representing organizations with a reputation for being involved in the formation of the Baldrige Award. While no conclusions are drawn, the topics are central to total quality and worthy of debate.

In 1951, the Union of Japanese Scientists and Engineers (JUSE) created an accolade to award companies that successfully apply companywide quality control (CWQC) based on statistical quality control. In honor of their American quality champion, JUSE named the award the Deming Prize.

Not until 31 years later did a similar prize take root in the United States, mainly due to the efforts of Frank C. Collins, who served as executive director of quality assurance for the Defense Logistics Agency and has formed Frank Collins Associates, Survival Twenty-One—a quality consulting firm; he also serves on the board of directors of the Malcolm Baldrige National Quality Award Consortium.

Collins, after many trips to Japan, based his U.S. quality award idea on the Deming Prize. "That's where I got the idea for the Malcolm Baldrige Award," he explains, "although I never in my wildest dreams expected it to be connected to Malcolm Baldrige."

Malcolm Baldrige, Secretary of Commerce in the Reagan administration, was killed in a rodeo accident in 1987. Reagan chose to honor Baldrige by naming the newly created award after him.

"The original concept was that it would be the National Quality Award," says Collins. "It would be strictly a private sector affair. The government would have no part in it other than the President being the awarder of the recognition."

ROUND 2: PROCESS

The Deming Prize has several categories: the Deming Prize for Individual Person, the Deming Application Prize and the Quality Control Award for Factory. Under the Deming Application Prize are the Deming Application Prize for Small Enterprise and the Deming Application Prize for Division. In 1984, another category was added: The Deming Application Prize to Oversea Companies, which is awarded to non-Japanese companies.

The Deming Application Prize has 10 examination items and is based on CWQC—the Prize's main objective.

A company or division begins the Deming Prize process by submitting an application form to the Deming Prize Committee, along with other pertinent information. Prospective applicants are advised to hold preliminary consultations with the secretariat of the Deming Prize Committee before completing and submitting the application.

After acceptance and notification, applicants must submit a description of quality control practices and a company business prospectus, *in Japanese.* If successful, the applicant will then be subject to a site visit. If the applicant passes, the Deming Prize is awarded.

Sound easy? Sometimes the applicant's information can fill up to 1,000 pages, and the examination process for U.S. companies is expensive.

The Baldrige Award applicant must first submit an Eligibility Determination Form, supporting documents and $50. Upon approval, the applicant must then submit an application package—running up to 50 pages for small business, 75 pages for a manufacturing or service company—and another fee. Among seven categories, 1,000 points are awarded. No particular score guarantees a site visit.

Each of the three categories—manufacturing, service and small company—are allowed up to two winners only.

ROUND 3: PURPOSE

The American obsession for winning is enormous. From Watergate to Iran-Contra, the American Revolution to Desert Storm, Americans have shown that they love to win no matter what the cost. So it's no wonder that as soon as quality awards and prizes have an impact, they fall under scrutiny. But most critics of these two world-class quality awards think these coveted prizes are mostly pristine in purpose.

Frank Voehl, *Quality Digest* columnist and corporate vice president and general manager of Qualtec Inc., a Florida Power & Light Group company, oversees the implementation of the total quality management programs within Qualtec's client companies. In 1987, Florida Power & Light (FPL) became the first and only U.S. company to win the Deming Prize. Through his work with hundreds of Japanese and U.S. companies, Voehl feels that there are seven reasons why companies quest for the Deming Prize or the Baldrige Award.

"The first general comment that a number of companies that I've talked to in Japan that have applied for the Deming Prize said was, 'We did not apply for the Deming Prize to win but to drive us toward better quality control,'" says Voehl. "Second is applying for and receiving the examination had more meaning than did winning the Prize." Voehl's other five reasons are:

- The audit or the exam itself helped point out many areas of deficiencies and continuous improvement activities that they hadn't noticed.

- Since the Deming Prize dictates a clear goal and time limit, quality control advanced at an extremely rapid rate.

- The company going for the quality award was able to accomplish in one or two years what would normally have taken five or ten years.

- There was a unification of a majority of the employees.

- They were able to communicate with a common language to the whole company. This is where the cultural change takes place.

Robert Peach, who was project manager of the Malcolm Baldrige National Quality Award Consortium for three years and now serves as a senior technical advisor to the administrator, feels the Baldrige Award "is not an award for the sake of the award—it is the 200,000 guidelines and applications that go out that matter, not the handful that actually apply."

And the companies that experiment with and implement the Baldrige criteria, as well as the Deming criteria, can only learn from their endeavor. However, for the companies taking it a step further and committing to win the prize, it isn't Little League, where the profits extracted from learning and having fun are supposed to outweigh the benefits of scoring more points than the other team. The Deming and the Baldrige are the Majors, where going for the award may mean 80-hour work weeks, quick hellos and goodbyes to spouses and missing your child's Little League games.

ROUND 4: GOING TO WAR

So your boss comes up to you and says, "Get ready—we're going for it." How you react may depend on the attitude of your senior-level management and the present quality state of your company. Ken Leach, a senior examiner for the Baldrige Award and founder of Leach Quality Inc., implemented the quality system at Globe Metallurgical—1988 winner of the Baldrige Award's small company category. He says winning the Baldrige was easy because its quality system was in place well before the birth of the Baldrige Award criteria.

"We got into it before Baldrige was even heard of, and we got into it at the impetus of our customers—Ford and General Motors in particular," explains Leach. "So we implemented a number of specific things to satisfy the customer, and you don't have a choice with them—you have to go through their audit system. We did that and did it very well. So that gave us the base to apply for the Baldrige and win it the very first year without trying to redo what we were already doing."

Leach says that because Globe was in such a readied state before the inception of the Baldrige Award, the company did not add any people or spend large sums of money on the implementation of a quality system. In fact, Globe was so advanced in its quality system that Leach claims he took the Baldrige Award application home after work on a Friday and returned it complete by the following Monday.

But even Leach agrees that Globe was exceptional and that not all companies can implement the Baldrige criteria as smoothly as Globe did.

Yokogawa-Hewlett-Packard (YHP) won the Deming Prize in 1982. Unlike Globe and its easy conquest of the Baldrige, YHP claims the quest for the Deming was no Sunday stroll. The company released the following statement in *Measure* magazine:

"Japanese companies compete fiercely to win a Deming Prize. Members of a management team typically work several hundred extra hours each month to organize the statistical charts, reports and exhibits for judging."[1] YHP also says that "audits had all the tension of a championship sports event."[2]

Voehl calls these extra hours and added stresses "pain levels and downside effects" and found that they were typical of most companies going for the Deming Prize. And because the Baldrige Award is a "second generation" of the Deming Prize, Voehl says the Baldrige Award is no exception to possible disruption. He explains that the quest for winning becoming greater than the quest for quality is a "natural thing that occurs within these organizations that you can't really prevent. Senior management focuses in on the journey and the overall effects that will happen as a result of going for the examination and the prize."

Voehl adds, "Getting ready for the examination and the site exams brings a tremendous amount of pressure upon the organizations, whether it's the Deming or the Baldrige, because of the implications that you should be the one department that results in the prize not being brought home."

William Golomski, who is the American Society for Quality Control's representative to JUSE, says deadline time for the award may be a time of pressure.

In the case of the Baldrige, there have been a few companies that hired consultants to help them get ready for a site visit after they've gone through an evaluation by examiners and senior examiners," recalls Golomski. "So I can understand that people who are still being asked to go through role playing for a site visit might get to the point where they'll say, 'Gosh, I don't know if I'm interested as I once was.'"

Collins looks at customers in a dual sense: your internal customers— employees or associates—and your external customers—the people who pay the freight to keep you in business.

"To me," Collins says forcefully, "when you *squeeze* your internal customer to win an award, you're really making a mockery of the whole thing."

But for the companies that take the Baldrige application guidelines and implement them without competing, Peach says the quality goal remains the biggest motivator.

"In my exposure both to applicants and other companies that are using the practice and guidelines independent of applying, I feel that they have the right perspective, that companies identify this as a pretty good practice of what quality practice should be," expounds Peach. "And they're using it that way. That's healthy; that's good."

Deming says it best: "I never said it would be easy; I only said it would work." And this piece of wisdom can pertain to the implementation and competing processes of both the Baldrige Award and the Deming Prize. But although sometimes not easy to pursue, these awards spark many companies to the awareness and benefits of a quality system. But as more companies win the Baldrige, more critics are discussing which accolade—the Baldrige or the Deming—holds more advantages over the other.

ROUND 5: ADVANTAGES VS. DISADVANTAGES

With a U.S. company capturing the Deming Prize, U.S. businesses are no longer without a choice of which world-class quality award to pursue. Motorola, before it went for the Baldrige Award, contemplated which award would improve Motorola's quality best, according to Stewart Clifford, president of Enterprise Media, a documentary film company that specializes in management topics. In a recent interview with Motorola's quality staff, Clifford asked if Motorola was interested in questing for the Deming Prize.

"I asked them the question about if they were looking at applying and going for the Deming," remembers Clifford. "And they said that they felt frankly that while the Deming Prize had some valuable points for them, the reason why they liked the Baldrige Award better was because of its much more intense focus on the customer."

But Voehl claims this is a misconception and that both approaches focus heavily on the customer. "Florida Power & Light really got a lot of negatives from our counselors that we weren't zeroing in on the external and internal customers enough," recalls Voehl. "We had to demonstrate how our quality improvement process was a means of planning and achieving customer satisfaction through TQC."

Section Seven of the Baldrige Award covers total customer satisfaction, and it's worth more points than any other section. In the Deming criteria, total customer satisfaction may seem lost among the need for applicants to document, document, document and use statistical approaches.

One reason Collins says he would compete for the Baldrige instead of the Deming is the Deming's unbending demand to have everything documented. "If you say something, you have to have a piece of paper that covers it," he jokes. "Having worked for the government for 33 years, I see that as a bureaucratic way of doing things. And the Japanese are extremely bureaucratic."

And in an open letter to employees from James L. Broadhead, FPL's chairman and CEO, printed in *Training* magazine, his employees confirm Collins' beliefs: "At the same time, however, the vast majority of the employees with whom I spoke expressed the belief that the mechanics of the QI [quality improvement] process have been overemphasized. They felt that we place too great an emphasis on indicators, charts, graphs, reports and meetings in which documents are presented and indicators reviewed."[3]

However, Collins says that what he likes about the Deming Prize criteria that's missing in the Baldrige Award criteria is the first two examination items of the Deming Prize: policy organization and its operation.

If you want people to understand what you mean by quality, you have to spell it out, you have to define it as policy, explains Collins. As far as objectives go, he remembers asking a Japanese firm what their objectives were. The president of this company said, "First to provide jobs to our company." "How many American firms would say that?" asks Collins. Organization and understanding its operation is extremely important. He says, "Those two criteria are the bedrock foundation of the Deming Prize that makes it somewhat stronger and of greater value than the Malcolm Baldrige National Quality Award."

Another point that may persuade a U.S. company to compete for one of the two awards is cost. All things considered, U.S. companies going for the Deming Application Prize to Oversea Companies seems more costly than U.S. companies competing for the Baldrige Award. Leach describes Globe's venture as very inexpensive: "It doesn't have to cost an arm and a leg for the Baldrige. You don't have to reinvent the wheel of what you're already doing." Peach worked with a small-category company that spent $6,000 on its Baldrige Award venture, and that included the application fee and retaining a technical writer for $1,000.

But these are small companies with 500 employees or fewer. FPL, on the other hand, with about 15,000 employees, spent $1.5 million on its quest for the Deming Prize, according to Neil DeCarlo of FPL's corporate communications. And there are some Baldrige applicants that have spent hundreds of thousands or even millions of dollars on their quality quest, according to *Fortune* magazine.[4]

But no matter how much the Baldrige applicant pays, whether it be $6,000 or millions, it still receives a feedback report as part of the application cost. In comparison, those companies not making it past the first level of the Deming Prize criteria may pay JUSE for counselors, who will come into the company and do a diagnostic evaluation.

Because FPL was a pioneer in the oversea competition, many of the costs that would have otherwise been associated with this award for an overseas company had been waived by JUSE, according to Voehl. But still, FPL dished out $850,000 of that million-and-a-half for counselor fees, says DeCarlo—an amount Voehl claims would be three or four times more if FPL had to hire a U.S. consulting firm.

One of FPL's reasons to go for the Deming award was because in 1986, when it decided to go for a quality award, the Baldrige Award did not yet exist. In fact, what many people, including some FPL critics, don't know is that the company heavily funded the activities leading to the Baldrige Award. FPL agreed not to try for the Baldrige Award for five years to deter any conflict of interest, says Voehl. Also, FPL had an excellent benchmarking company in Japan's Kansai Electric, which had already won the Deming Prize.

The Deming Prize puts no cap on the number of winners; the Baldrige allows a maximum of two winners for each of the three categories. Leach contests that by putting a limit on the winners, you make the Baldrige Award a more precious thing to win. Peach agrees. "I think there should be a limit," he says. "You just don't want scores of winners to dilute this."

Voehl disagrees. "We should take the caps off," he argues. "I think we'd do a lot more for the award, for the process if we didn't have a win–lose mentality toward it."

ROUND 6: CONTROVERSY

"The Baldrige is having such an impact," asserts Peach, "that now people will take a look at it and challenge. That will always happen—that's our American way." And at four years old, the Baldrige Award has already received a fair share of controversy. One of the most disturbing criticisms aimed at the Baldrige Award comes from Deming himself. Deming called the Baldrige Award "a terrible thing, a waste of industry" in a recent issue of *Automotive News*. The article states: "Among the reasons Deming denounces the award is its measurement of performance and the effects of training with numerical goals, which he cites as 'horrible things.'

"'It's a lot of nonsense,' he said. 'The guidelines for 1991 (make that) very obvious.'"[5]

Golomski says that Deming is unhappy with two parts of the Baldrige guidelines. One is the concept of numerical goals, which Deming believes can cause aberrations within companies. "I don't take quite as strong a stand as Deming does," Golomski explains. "He makes another statement about goals and that far too often, goals are set in the absence of any way of knowing how you're going to achieve these goals."

Leach does not know what to think of "Deming's non-supportive or active disregard for the Baldrige Award." He finds it ironic that "a company could very much have a Deming-type philosophy or a Deming-oriented kind of company and could do quite well in the Baldrige application. I'm sure that Cadillac [1990 Baldrige Award winner] must have had a number of Deming philosophies in place."

Even if Deming is trying to be the burr under the saddle and spark U.S. companies into a quality quest, Leach doesn't think that Deming's "serving the pursuit of quality in general or himself very well by making public statements like that."

But Voehl agrees with some of Deming's points. "Cadillac got severely criticized by the board of trustees of the Baldrige because Cadillac took the Baldrige Award and General Motors tried to use it as a marketing tool," he

Deming Prize Application Checklist: Items and Their Particulars

1. Policy

- Policies pursued for management, quality and quality control
- Methods of establishing policies
- Justifiability and consistency of policies
- Utilization of statistical methods
- Transmission and diffusion of policies
- Review of policies and the results achieved
- Relationship between policies and long- and short-term planning

2. Organization and Its Management

- Explicitness of the scopes of authority and responsibility
- Appropriateness of delegations of authority
- Interdivisional cooperation
- Committees and their activities
- Utilization of staff
- Utilization of quality circle activities
- Quality control diagnosis

3. Education and Dissemination

- Education programs and results
- Quality-and-control consciousness, degrees of understanding of quality control
- Teaching of statistical concepts and methods and the extent of their dissemination
- Grasp of the effectiveness of quality control
- Education of related company (particularly those in the same group, subcontractors, consignees and distributors)
- Quality circle activities
- System of suggesting ways of improvements and its actual conditions

4. Collection, Dissemination and Use of Information on Quality

- Collection of external information
- Transmission of information between divisions
- Speed of information transmission (use of computers)
- Data processing, statistical analysis of information and utilization of the results

5. Analysis

- Selection of key problems and themes
- Propriety of the analytical approach
- Utilization of statistical methods
- Linkage with proper technology
- Quality analysis, process analysis
- Utilization of analytical results
- Assertiveness of improvement suggestions

6. Standardization

- Systematization of standards
- Method of establishing, revising and abolishing standards
- Outcome of the establishment, revision or abolition of standards
- Contents of the standards
- Utilization of the statistical methods
- Accumulation of technology
- Utilization of standards

7. Control

- Systems for the control of quality and such related matters as cost and quantity
- Control items and control points
- Utilization of such statistical control methods as control charts and other statistical concepts
- Contribution to performance of quality circle activity
- Actual conditions of control activities
- State of matters under control

8. Quality Assurance

- Procedure for the development of new products and services (analysis and upgrading of quality, checking of design, reliability and other properties)
- Safety and immunity from product liability
- Process design, process analysis and process control and improvement
- Process capability
- Instrumentation, gauging, testing and inspecting
- Equipment maintenance and control of subcontracting, purchasing and services
- Quality assurance system and its audit
- Utilization of statistical methods
- Evaluation and audit of quality
- Actual state of quality assurance

9. Results

- Measurement of results
- Substantive results in quality, services, delivery, time, cost, profits, safety, environment, etc.
- Intangible results
- Measuring for overcoming defects

10. Planning for the Future

- Grasp of the present state of affairs and the concreteness of the plan
- Measures for overcoming defects
- Plans for further advances
- Linkage with long-term plans

says. "And that's not the intention. Those sort of things do not do the Baldrige Award any good because it seems like all you're interested in is public relations."

Cadillac has fallen under scrutiny from many critics for taking home the Baldrige Award.

After returning from consulting in Israel, Collins heard that Cadillac had won the Baldrige Award. "I couldn't believe my eyes," Collins exclaims. "Cadillac has gotten so much bad press over the last decade—transmission problems, difficulty with their diesel engines, their service record—a whole number of things that to me when they said Cadillac won it, I said, 'Impossible. They couldn't win it. Somebody's pulling a cruel joke.'"

Deming is not the only quality guru criticizing the Baldrige Award. Philip Crosby says in *Quality Digest* (February 1991) that customers should nominate the companies that compete for the Baldrige, not the companies themselves.

It is difficult to come by harsh criticism about the Deming Prize since few Americans are familiar with it. However, Collins questions FPL's quest for winning as superseding their quest for quality.

"There's no question in my mind that Florida Power & Light's John Hudiburg was intent on leading Florida Power & Light in a blaze of glory," insists Collins. "And money was absolutely no consideration as far as winning the Deming Prize. I don't know what the final tab on it was, but he bought the prize—there's no question about it."

Collins' comments do not go without backing. A number of articles on FPL's quest contain complaints from disgruntled employees who worked long hours to win the Deming Prize.

"If the goal is to win an award, then the cost of winning the award is not worth the award itself," Voehl admits. "The focus needs to be on the outcomes for the organization." And Voehl feels that FPL's quality outcomes very much outweigh the cost put forth.

ROUND 7: CONSULTANTS

With the two awards, there's a big difference in the use of consultants or counselors, as they're called in Japan. In the case of the Deming Prize, a successful applicant uses counselors trained by JUSE throughout the examination, explains Golomski. "For the Baldrige, you're on your own or you use whomever you wish to help you—if you think it's worth it."

"Considering the tremendous number of brochures I get every day," says Collins, "it appears that everybody and his brother is an expert on the Malcolm Baldrige National Quality Award. And my experience tells me that there *ain't* that many experts on the Malcolm Baldrige National Quality Award."

So, are some consultants or counselors using the Baldrige Award to prey on aspiring companies? Voehl says he sees it happening all over and calls it "absolutely preposterous and absurd and unethical."

Voehl compares it to just like everybody jumping on the TQC bandwagon. "Everybody from a one-man or two-man mom-and-pop consulting company to a 1,000-employee consulting arm of the Big 8 seems to be an expert in TQM," he says. "It's like a dog with a rag: They're shaking it and shaking it, and they won't let it go because they see it can mean money to their bottom line. It's giving the consulting field a terrible black eye. It's giving the people who bring in these consultants the expectations clearly that they are going to win the award. These are false expectations, false hopes and false starts. They shouldn't even be looking at winning the award; they should be looking at implementing a quality system that can ensure customer satisfaction."

But there are good reasons to have consultants help you through the Baldrige quest. Leach points out that if a CEO of a company needs to change his or her approach on something, an employee will probably be intimidated to approach the CEO; instead, a consultant can do this. Also a consultant may carry in an objective view that brings different ideas to the company.

Deming Prize counselors, however, have a reputation to guard. That's why Golomski feels FPL had no chance to "buy the Prize."

"The counselor simply wouldn't agree with them that they [FPL] were ready," Golomski argues. "The counselors help an organization improve itself, but if they don't think the company is ready for the big leagues, they simply won't recommend it."

ROUND 8: MODIFICATIONS

The Baldrige Award criteria are constantly modified to meet changing expectations. This is how it grows stronger, becomes more mature. When awarded the Baldrige Award, recipients must share their knowledge of total quality, but Golomski wants to see better ways of technology transfer.

Collins thinks we will probably have a follow-up award similar to the Japan Quality Control Prize—which is awarded to Deming Prize winners if they have improved their quality standards five years after winning the Deming Prize and pass rigorous examination—but not until the Baldrige Award can be further improved.

Peach feels the Baldrige criteria are at a position where modifications will be in smaller increments. He says cycle time might become important enough to be emphasized more.

The possible modifications of the Deming Prize are hard to predict. However, modifications of the Baldrige Award may be based on the Deming Prize's influence.

ROUND 9: SAVING FACE

Junji Noguchi, executive director of JUSE, was contacted for an interview for this article. When he learned of the subject matter—comparing the two world-class quality awards—he declined to answer. He said, "I am sorry I have to reply that I cannot answer your interviews. That is because the contents were not preferable and that they are not what I was expecting."

Noguchi continued, "Awards or prizes in the country have been established under the most suitable standards and methods considering their own background of industries, societies and cultures. We do not understand the meaning of comparing awards in different countries that have different backgrounds."

Noguchi is displaying some of that ancient wisdom and showing a difference in our cultures that even Americans find difficult to explain. Is this why their award has been going strong for 40 years and why the Baldrige Award is a 4-year-old child growing much too fast thanks to our intrinsic desire to slice it up, examine it and try to put it back together more completely than before? Maybe. But as a result, our U.S. quality award will always remain provocative and exciting and keep the people talking. And this is good.

REFERENCES

1. "YHP Teamwork Takes the Prize," Measure (January–February 1983), 3000 Hanover St., Palo Alto, CA 94304, pg. 6.
2. Measures, pg. 6.
3. James L. Broadhead, "The Post-Deming Diet: Dismantling a Quality Bureaucracy," Training, Lakewood Building, 50 S. Ninth St., Minneapolis, MN 55402, pg. 41.
4. Jeremy Main, "Is the Baldrige Overblown?" Fortune (July 1, 1991), Time & Life Building, Rockefeller Center, New York, NY 10020-1393, pg. 62.
5. Karen Passino, "Deming Calls Baldrige Prize 'Nonsense,'" Automotive News (April 1, 1991), 1400 E. Woodbridge, Detroit, MI 48207.

CHAPTER 5

THE HOUSE
OF QUALITY

The basic concepts and principles associated with total quality are represented by the House of Total Quality (Figure 5.1). As in a well-built house, the major components of the House of Total Quality are (1) the *roof*, or superstructure, consisting of the social, technical, and management systems; (2) the *four pillars* of customer satisfaction, continuous improvement, speaking with facts, and respect for people; (3) the *foundation* of four managerial levels—strategy, process, project, and task management; and (4) the *four cornerstones* of mission, vision, values, and goals and objectives.

As in building any house, the plans must be developed first, usually by experienced individuals working together—a team. Once the plans are approved, construction (implementation) can begin.

Total quality efforts frequently fail because the individuals responsible for the efforts (i.e., management) are unable to carry out their responsibilities. They do not recognize the importance of systems thinking and do not have a well-defined purpose and process to follow. That is why Deming, *kaizen*, and the Baldrige Award focus on the following ten management guidelines[1] as part of the implementation process:

- Recognize quality improvement as a system.
- Define it so others can recognize it, too.
- Analyze its behavior.
- Work with subordinates in improving the system.
- Measure the quality of the system.
- Develop improvements in the quality of the system.

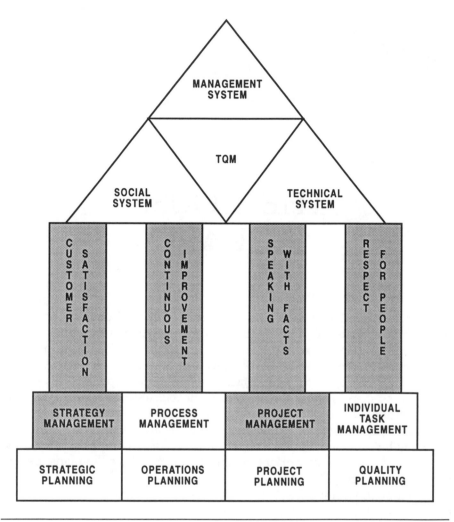

Figure 5.1 House of Total Quality. (Source: ©1992 Strategy Associates, Inc.)

- Measure the gains in the quality, if any, and link these to customer delight and quality improvement.
- Take steps to guarantee holding the gains.
- Attempt to replicate the improvements into other areas of the organization.
- Tell others about the lessons learned.

These guidelines, when implemented, will assure success because of their impact on all aspects of the enterprise. They are also reflected in the House of Total Quality, which illustrates the universality of the basic principles and procedures for carrying out total quality. Use of the House of Total Quality does not negate, but rather supports, the works of Deming and the Baldrige Award. Throughout this chapter, the 14 principles of Deming and the seven categories of the Baldrige Award are presented within the context of the House of Total Quality.

SYSTEMS AND TOTAL QUALITY

The superstructure of the House of Total Quality involves a system composed of three subsystems held together by total quality (Figure 5.2). The three subsystems are social, technical, and management. Their interdependencies are depicted in the three interlocking circles of a ballantine, as shown in Figure 5.2. The successful implementation of total quality and continuous improvement efforts requires the redefinition of management to recognize the importance of the systems. As Deming[2] states, "The people work in a system. The job of the manager is to work on the system, to improve it continuously, with their help." Within the House of Total Quality, the manager must work on the three systems.

The Social System

The social system includes factors associated with the formal and informal characteristics of the organization: (1) organizational culture (the values,

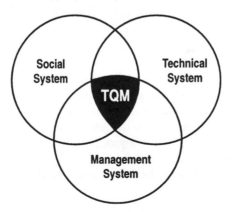

Figure 5.2 Implementing Total Quality Management System Model.

norms, attitudes, role expectations, and differentiation that exist in each organization); (2) quality of social relationships between individual members and among groups, including reward structures and symbols of power; and (3) behavioral patterns between members, including roles and communication. It is the social system that has the greatest impact on such factors as motivation, creativity, innovative behavior, and teamwork. Managers have a major responsibility for the nature and character of the social system.

The social system may or may not have a planned function within the organization. Many managers would like to deny, or at least ignore, the existence of cultures, roles, or organizational values. However, social systems exist, and they exert influence, both positive and negative, on the activities of an organization.

To achieve total quality, a social system must be developed in which constituent or customer satisfaction, continuous improvement, management based on facts, and a genuine respect for people are accepted practices of the enterprise. Frequently this requires a substantial change in the social system, and change does not come easily for most organizations. Change usually occurs when the cost (disadvantages, lost opportunities) of remaining the same becomes greater than the benefit of an alternative condition.

Figure 5.3 represents a fishbone diagram (also known as a causal analysis diagram) of the social system characteristics that help create a total quality organization. As shown in Figure 5.3, six areas of strategy must be addressed in order to change and transform the culture of an organization to a quality-driven organization: (1) the environment, (2) product or service, (3) methods, (4) people, (5) organizational structure, and (6) mindset of total quality improvement. Thus, in organizations driven by total quality, people feel they belong, feel pride in their work, learn continuously, and work to their potential. Each of these major areas will be covered in some detail in the following sections.

The Technical System

According to Tribus,[3] "The technical system includes all the tools and machinery, the practice of quality and the quantitative aspects of quality. If you can measure it, you can probably describe and perhaps improve it using the technical systems approach." The technical system is concerned with the flow of work through the organization. It is driven by two primary guides: fulfillment of its mission and service to the customer. In most organizations, the technical system contains the following core elements:

- Accumulation of technology
- Pursuit of standardization
- Workflow, materials, and specifications

- Job definitions and responsibility
- Machine/person interface
- Number and type of work steps
- Availability and use of information
- Decision-making processes
- Problem-solving tools and processes
- Physical arrangements and equipment, tools, and people

Technology in the information technology (IT) world has even more of an impact. Yesterday's promises are finally being fulfilled through the advances of technology. The following technological advances are making the extended enterprise a reality.

Communication Networks and Associated Technologies—In today's environment, separation of data from text, graphics, images, and voice is not acceptable. Technology is available to integrate all of these components and allow employees to work in the most natural setting possible to achieve greater productivity and customer satisfaction.

Integration of Processes and Systems—The ability to provide timely information to any and all levels of a highly leveraged task team organization, as compared to the hierarchical organization, requires complete integration of many functions. The historical boundaries of organizations are being destroyed. The new organizations are not only crossing functional lines of historical organization, but are also creating strategic alliances with vendors. Partners are acting as strategic partners with their customers. Highly visible teams are assigned tasks that cross all boundaries of an organization, and teams are empowered to solve problems or create solutions. The systems and the organization must be designed to complement, not retard, these types of functions. Data collection, data storage, and data availability must be completely rethought to meet these demands. The old paradigm of control and knowledge by a few is gone. The new paradigm is to provide information to all who need to know in a timely manner. The entire concept of proprietary systems that prohibit the open flow of information within an industry and within an organization is dead!

Open Architecture

Hierarchical organizations controlled information. Command-and-control techniques from the early 1900s influenced the design of the IT industry, and most systems in the industry sector were designed to honor this time-proven methodology. Proprietary software and hardware designed to only comple-

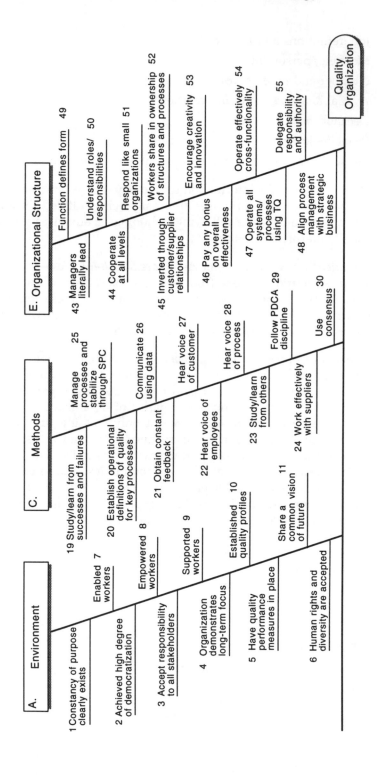

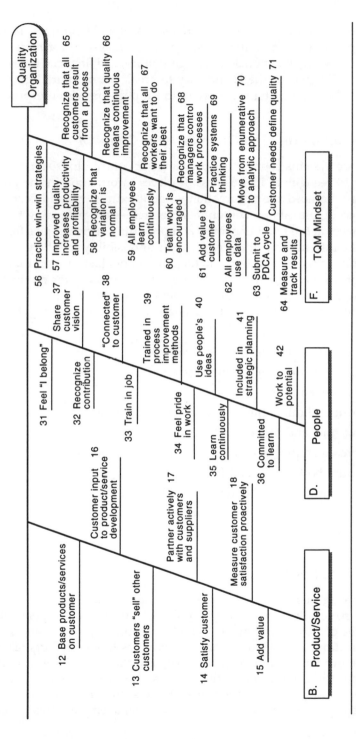

Figure 5.3 Social System Characteristics of a Total Quality Organization (Fishbone Diagram).

ment selected software were the trademark of all IT services. The designers of corporate systems followed suit and made system fortresses out of the smokestack organization. Knowledge, culture, and financial investment have made it difficult for the IT industry to break the old paradigms and move toward the open systems necessary to support today's enterprise.

Client/Server and the Open Systems Concept

The open systems concept has been a major contributor to an organization's ability to reengineer its business. It places information in the hands of the people who need the information without extra steps and cost. Customer-centered organizations without tall hierarchies are providing truly enabled employees at the point of contact and providing enriched jobs for those who have the information, knowledge, and responsibility to satisfy the customer.

Knowledge is distributed to the worker, not just the control points. This promotes a team approach and a greater opportunity for motivated people to provide greater innovation and ideas for improvement.

The expected benefits from analyzing and improving the technical system(s) are to:

- Reduce (eliminate) waste and rework
- Reduce (eliminate) negative variation
- Increase learning
- Reduce (eliminate) interruptions and idle time
- Save time and money
- Increase employee control over the work process
- Reduce bottlenecks and frustration
- Improve safety and quality of work life
- Increase speed and responsiveness
- Improve customer satisfaction

The Managerial System

The managerial system includes factors associated with (1) the organizational structure (formal design, policies, division of responsibilities, and patterns of power and authority); (2) the mission, vision, and goals of the organization; and (3) administrative activities (planning, organizing, directing, coordinating, and controlling organizational activities). Management provides the framework for the policies, procedures, practices, and leadership of the organization. The management system is deployed at four levels: strategy, process, project, and personal management. These comprise the foundation of the House of Total Quality and will be briefly discussed later in this chapter and more thoroughly in Chapter 6.

As stated at the beginning of this chapter, the Deming principles and Baldrige categories are an integral part of the House of Total Quality. Deming's first two principles and the third category of the Baldrige Award address the superstructure and the three systems described above.

Deming Principle 1—Create a constancy of purpose toward improvement. Deming is saying that we need to look to the future in terms of the business for which we are responsible. Items such as training of employees and investment in long-term projects, more often than not, do not yield returns in the short term.

Deming Principle 2—Adopt the new philosophy. This is a difficult area, and changing a culture can take years. Management must have the courage and the vision to understand the new philosophy and live up to the challenge.

Baldrige Category 3—Strategic quality planning examines the planning process of the enterprise and how all key quality requirements are integrated into an overall plan. Also examined are short and longer term plans, as well as how quality and performance requirements are deployed to all work units.

Quality and service are the means, but value for the customer is the end. The final judge of an organization's performance is the customer. As we exercise many means to achieve customer satisfaction, we must not lose sight of the fact that the ultimate goal is that our customer perceive that the product or the service we have rendered provides value. Cost, quality, scheduling, and reliability are all valid items to improve and provide powerful means to achieve our value-added goal.

The effectiveness of an organization is measured by its managerial systems. Most people, however, do not take time to understand the power of their managerial systems. It is here that an organization can gain the most important advantage. Deming states that "80% of the problems with American business is management." Actually, that is a misstatement; the figure is probably closer to 90 percent.

The managerial system consists of three subsystems (Figure 5.4). Each subsystem is divided into other systems. Management systems are composed of three major processes: policy management, quality assurance (ISO 9000), and daily management.

Policy Management

Policy management (Figure 5.5) is a business planning process used to formulate, deploy, and achieve business objectives by concentrating resources

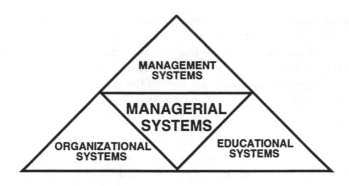

Figure 5.4 Subsystems of the Managerial System.

on high-priority items. This method of management links business activities to the long-term view of the company and provides the system that propels a company toward its vision, while increasing the opportunity for competitive advantage.

It is here that the talkers are separated from the doers. We can talk about principles, give token training to our employees, or say that people are our most important resource. We can even start a few quality circles, but it is only through implementing the systems changes that focus on those items that are critical to the success of the organization and its stakeholders that we start the journey toward improvement.

Policy management is called many things and involves many different functions. True policy management in the total quality management (TQM) arena is the *systematic process needed to direct an organization toward priority issues of the organization*. It provides the vehicle to accomplish the corporate

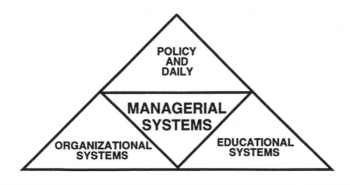

Figure 5.5 Policy and Daily Management.

short- and long-term strategies and achieve customer satisfaction. Policy management provides a blueprint to the organization for how and what is required to achieve its goals.

Policy management also provides a system of indicators, used for tracking progress and results, as well as outlining the strategic plan framework. (For additional information, see Abstract 5.1 at the end of this chapter.)

Improved communication within an organization is also a very important factor and results from the deployment of the policies identified in the policy formulation stage. It provides a clear road map for where the organization is going and what is important to all the stakeholders. This road map is used by teams and individuals to focus their energy on the areas that can best help the organization achieve its goals. The cumulative benefits of the creativity, innovation, and increased productivity of the organization's employees is wonderful, and the cost is recognition, training, and appreciation—a bargain in any business calculation. Managers who listen to their employees and act on their ideas and contributions—what a unique concept! (For additional information, see Abstract 5.2 at the end of this chapter.)

Daily Management

Daily management is a business planning process that provides a systematic focus for day-to-day or repetitive activities not handled by policy management. Examples include processing of sales orders, preparation of certain reports, etc. It involves the aspects of control, promotion of improvement, and review and is founded in the concepts of efficiency and continuous improvement.

Continuous improvement through daily management activities helps accomplish and maintain the gains made through policy management. It also provides the processes and tools to make improvements in our daily activities and builds teamwork within the organization.

Daily management does not receive as much attention as policy management, but it is a very critical part of the TQM journey. Daily management provides a means to improve the daily, routine functions and the gains an organization makes through continuous improvement activities. It also controls the gains made through policy management.

The next important part of the management systems is the organizational systems (Figure 5.6), or how the organization utilizes its personnel to accomplish tasks.

Cross-Functional Management—Management teams formed to carry out company initiatives that cross departmental or functional lines. Key customer concerns are generally cross-functional in nature and require coordination.

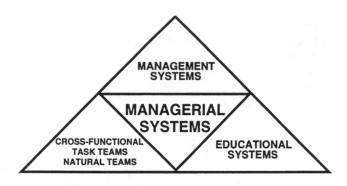

Figure 5.6 Organizational Systems.

Task Teams—Teams formed for a specific purpose, either in the area of policy management or for a major departmental concern. Membership is determined by expertise and organizational background, and individuals are selected by management.

Natural Teams—Similar to quality circles, natural teams have a more homogeneous membership and concentrate their efforts on department production processes. This concept implies that all departmental efforts can be viewed as process and results in the production of something.

The educational system is closely aligned to the social system and must reflect the values and principles of the organization, as shown in Figure 5.7.

Statistical Thought Process—Applying the concepts of priority and variation to the task of management at all levels. Suggested areas for concentration include the seven basic statistical tools (check sheet, Pareto analysis, cause-and-effect diagram, histogram, control chart, scatter diagram, run chart). Additional tools include the graph, process decision program chart, arrow diagram, matrix data analysis, affinity diagram, relations diagram, and systematic diagram) and more advanced techniques such as multivariate analysis, multiple regression, fault tree analysis, etc.

Human Thought Process—The concept of valuing employees and treating them as the most valuable resource encompasses the human thought process. It is in this area that the techniques of team building and consensus are introduced to the organization and the underlying principle of *respect for people* is woven into the fabric of the management system.

The value system or principles of an organization support the managerial, technical, and social systems, which in turn protect the principles and values of the organization.

Figure 5.7   Educational System.

THE PILLARS OF QUALITY

TQM in any organization is supported by four driving forces, or pillars, that move the organization toward the full application of quality service. The four pillars of the House of Total Quality (see Figure 5.1) are customer service, continuous improvement, processes and facts, and respect for people. All are distinct but equal in potential strength. All four must be addressed; minimizing one weakens the others. By not addressing one, the entire House of Total Quality will fall.

Serving the Customer (The First Pillar)

Peter Drucker has said that "The business of business is getting and keeping customers." This philosophy in the House of Total Quality is the first pillar—serving the customer (Figure 5.8). In today's complex business world, it is difficult to clearly identify the "customer." In the world of IT, we must understand the internal customer as well as our ultimate customer. To focus on customer satisfaction places the responsibility for quality in each step of the process and leads us to recognize that the next process is our customer.

While this sounds like an easy philosophy to follow, all too often we take the concept of "product out" instead of considering our customer's needs and evaluating those needs in a "market in" attitude. A "market in" attitude means that we listen to our customers and design the system, product, or service based on their real needs and not our perceived evaluation of their needs.

In order for organizations to be successful, IT must provide systems that are responsive to both the internal and external customers' needs. The sys-

Figure 5.8 Serving the Customer.

tems must be open and allow decisions to be made at any level of the organization, as defined by needs. Today's applications require real-time access by many to critical information.

All too often, management states that the goal is to provide total customer satisfaction but does not have the systems to achieve it. Nor does management take the time to define who its customers are or what quality characteristics are required to meet their needs. This should be a priority of management. By understanding the needs of the customer, management can develop the systems and provide the necessary training and resources to meet those needs.

One of the main issues the technologist faces is how to improve personal service for the customer while applying new technologies.

Why should we take the time to understand our customers and try to satisfy them? A study by the U.S. Office of Consumer Affairs reveals that only 4 percent of unhappy customers complain. The remaining 96 percent never give you a chance to correct the problem; they just tell nine other people about the problem, and 90 percent of the dissatisfied customers never purchase the product or service from the company again. The study goes on to say that 22 percent of the issues that you do not hear about are serious problems.

Continuous Improvement (The Second Pillar)

Continuous improvement (Figure 5.9) is both a commitment (continuous quality improvement) and a process (continuous process improvement). The Japanese word for this second pillar is *kaizen*, and it is, according to Imai,[4] the single most important concept in Japanese management. The commitment to quality is initiated with a statement of dedication to a shared mission and vision and the empowerment of all participants to incrementally move toward the vision. The process of improvement is accomplished through the initiation of small, short-term projects and tasks throughout the organization which collectively are driven by the achievement of the long-term vision and mission. Both are necessary; one cannot be done without the other.

Continuous improvement is dependent on two elements: learning the appropriate processes, tools, and skills and practicing these newfound skills on small achievable projects. The process for continuous improvement, first advanced many years ago by Shewhart and implemented by Deming, is *Plan-Do-Check-Act* (PDCA) (Figure 5.10), a never-ending cycle of improvement that occurs in all phases of the organization. While no rigid rules are required to carry out the process, the general framework of each step can be described.

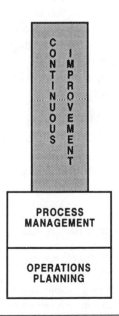

Figure 5.9 Continuous Improvement.

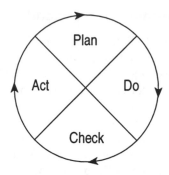

Figure 5.10   Plan-Do-Check-Act.

The first step, *plan*, asks such key questions as what changes are needed, what results are needed, what obstacles need to be overcome, are data available, and what new information is needed. *Do* is the implementation of a small-scale change or pilot test to provide data for answers. *Check* is the assessment and measurement of the effects of the change or test. *Act*, the final step, first asks whether the data confirm the intended plan, whether other variables are influencing the plan, and whether the risks in proceeding are necessary and worthwhile. Then, based on these answers, the project or task is modified and moves into the *plan* stage again, where the iteration continues, expanding knowledge and implementing further improvement. Ideally, this process would continue indefinitely.

Two of Deming's principles and two Baldrige categories address this important aspect of total quality:

Deming Principle 3—Cease dependence on inspection and testing to achieve quality. Reduce the need for inspection by building quality into the programs and services in the first place. Within IT, cease dependence on testing to achieve quality. Provide learning experiences that create quality performance.

Deming Principle 5—Improve constantly and forever the system of program quality and service in order to improve quality performance.

Baldrige Category 5—*Management of process quality* is the key element of how the organization develops and realizes the full potential of the work force to pursue its quality and performance objectives. Also examined are the efforts required to build and maintain an environment for quality excellence that is conducive to full participation and personal organizational growth.

Baldrige Category 6—Quality and operational results examines quality levels and improvement trends in operational performance of IT and supplier quality, as well as the current quality and performance levels of competitors.

In the development of systems, the concepts of continuous improvement come into play in two significant processes. The first is in the development of systems and the second is in the support of systems.

The first part of the *plan* cycle of PDCA in the system development cycle is the requirements phase. This phase, tied to the concepts of customer satisfaction, builds the plan for the product based on customers' valid needs. Focus groups, customer councils, user groups, and partnerships help define the needs of the chain of customers that most systems must serve.

The second part of the *plan* cycle involves the analysis and design phase, where technologies and customer needs are married. This portion of the *plan* phase also requires interface with customers to assure compliance and understanding.

The *do* stage is the development cycle in the system. A clear definition of the quality measurements of the system is required before the development begins. Items include considerations such as:

How to measure customer satisfaction:
- Capability
- Performance
- Availability
- Training
- Reliability
- Changeability
- System documentation
- Flexibility
- Ease of use

Quality of product delivered:
- Timeliness
- Cost
- Ease of installation
- Backlog of errors
- Fit to specification

These are some of the major items that should be understood at the beginning of the development cycle. Measurement processes should be considered and designed prior to beginning the project.

The *check* functions may include:

- A quality system plan
- Performance design points
- Prototyping
- Nine cycle change control systems
- Development of change control systems
- Publications change control systems
- Training
- Documentation
- Quality assurance review
- Unit testing plan
- Integrated testing plan
- Field test

The *act* cycle is the driver for change. It is easy to forget the fact that PDCA is a cycle and that within the individual parts we must PDCA each of the activities with which we are dealing. The metrics of performance must be continually monitored, and these items must be acted upon as opportunities for continuous improvement.

The life cycle system an organization develops with its customers should be its road map to appropriate change and control.

The second significant use of PDCA is the support activity, also known as the maintenance phase of the system. The *kaizen* approach to customer satisfaction means continuing improvement in all aspects of the life of a product or service. (For additional information, see Abstract 5.3 at the end of this chapter.)

Managing with Facts (The Third Pillar)

Deming, paraphrasing the axiom "In God we trust, all others bring cash," noted the central tenet of this third pillar (Figure 5.11): *In God we trust. All others bring facts.* Too often, the management of a program is based on intuition, influence, hunches, or organizational politics. External and internal forces require the elimination of this precarious managerial approach. Stable or diminished funding; the increasing cost of salaries, supplies, and services; the increased number of women and minorities at all levels of the organization; and continuous competition will force *all* organizations to be driven by decisions and actions based on facts, rather than only partial awareness of the issues, reliance on traditional networks, and/or just doing what has always been done. Tom Peters, paraphrasing the axiom "If it isn't broke, don't fix it," repeatedly states, *"If it isn't broke, break it!"*

Figure 5.11 Managing with Facts.

This requires a substantial shift in many areas to a process of carrying out continuous improvement (the second pillar—Plan-Do-Check-Act) and effective process management through the extensive use of a variety of tools designed to gather and analyze data and make decisions based on facts (the third pillar). Seven basic, highly effective tools were identified early in the history of the total quality movement: fishbone diagram (cause-and-effect diagram), check sheet, control chart, histogram, Pareto diagram, run chart, and scatter diagram; the control chart, cause-and-effect diagram, and Pareto diagram are the three tools most commonly used in the total quality process.

None of the Deming principles or Baldrige categories directly apply to this pillar. Managing with facts requires two actions. First, collect objective data so that the information is valid. Second, whenever possible, manage according to this information and not according to instinct, preconceptions, or other nonobjective factors. Managing with facts is important because *people* collect and use the facts, providing a common framework for communication and understanding what is being done and what needs to be done. Thus, not only does it provide a solid base of objective data upon which reliable decisions can be made, but it also contributes to empowerment of and respect for the people within the organization (the fourth pillar of the House of Total Quality).

Respect for People (The Fourth Pillar)

For whom does one work? No one works just for the customers and the company. In the end, each individual works for himself or herself, trying to create a meaningful and satisfying life in the best way possible. Fortunately, quality of output goes hand in hand with quality of work. The only way total quality will be attained is through total commitment and participation.

Every employee must be fully developed and involved. The result will be an empowered individual—a value-added resource, with loyalty to the program, the team, and the entire organization. Respect for people (Figure 5.12) often boils down to such simple things as:

- Creating a sense of purpose in the workplace so that people are motivated to do their best

- Keeping people informed and involved and showing them how they are a part of the bigger picture

- Educating and developing people so that they are the best that they can be at what they do

- Helping people communicate well so that they can perform their jobs with peak effectiveness

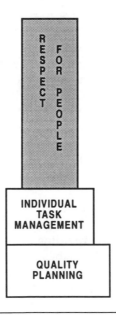

Figure 5.12 Respect for People.

- Delegating responsibility and authority downward so that people are not just doing what they are told, but are taking the initiative to try to make things work better

It is not enough to just go through the motions. These behaviors work well when they are part of a genuine attitude of respect and caring for other people. Managers who do not have this attitude of respect and caring cannot pretend for very long that they do.

It is to this fourth pillar that Deming directed 8 of his 14 principles. It reinforces the reason he retains the opinion that most organizations are unable to truly implement total quality because of their pervasive attitude that people are an expense to be controlled rather than an asset to be developed.

Deming Principle 6—Institute education and training for everyone: management and all employees.

Deming Principle 7—The goal of supervision should be to help people use procedures, techniques, machines, and materials to do a better job. Leadership of management and employees is in need of a general overhaul.

Deming Principle 8—Drive out fear, so that everyone can work effectively for the organization. Create an environment in which people are encouraged to speak freely.

Deming Principle 9—Break down barriers between corporate entitles and all departments. Each area must work as a team (work teams and cross-functional teams). Develop strategies for increasing the cooperation among groups and individuals.

Deming Principle 10—Eliminate slogans, exhortations, and targets that promote perfect performance and new levels of productivity (e.g., write X lines of code, reduce expenses by X percent). Exhortations create adversarial relationships. The bulk of the causes of low quality and low productivity belong to the system and thus lie beyond the control of employees.

Deming Principle 11—Eliminate performance standards (quotas) for employees. Eliminate management by numbers and numerical goals. Substitute leadership.

Deming Principle 12—Remove barriers that rob employees of the right to take pride in and enjoy the satisfaction of personal performance and productivity. This means, among other things, abolishing annual or merit ratings and management by objectives. The focus of responsibility for all managers must be changed from quantity to quality.

Deming Principle 13—Institute a vigorous program of education and self-improvement for everyone.

THE FOUNDATION AND CORNERSTONES

The roof and four pillars rest upon a foundation and cornerstones which consist of four managerial and planning processes. This discussion has evolved from a broad systemic framework, i.e., the three TQM systems (social, technical, and managerial), to the four principles that guide these systems (customer satisfaction, continuous improvement, managing with facts, and respect for people), and now to the procedural functions that make the systems and principles operational. The roof (the systems) is the most theoretical, with the principles providing guides for actualizing the system but still not making it operational. It remains for the managerial and planning processes to be put into action in order to actualize the quality improvement process. Therefore, with the metaphor of the House of Total Quality, it is appropriate that these functions are the foundation and cornerstones of the entire house. It is here where the construction begins. It is also here where you get your hands dirty!

Strategy Management—Quality planning is the broadest of the managerial levels. It establishes the organization-wide TQM strategy and framework. It is a top-down strategy, initiated by senior management but developed with everyone involved through a variety of consensus, team-building, and brainstorming activities. The outcome is a three- to five-year plan that contains the mission, vision, guiding principles or values, and goals and objectives for the organization. "Ownership" of the plan is achieved when everyone acknowledges the focus of the plan and accepts its potential to help the organization move in a common direction.

Process Management—Operations planning assures that all key processes work in harmony with the mission and meet the needs and expectations of the constituents or customers by maximizing operational effectiveness. Its key components are continuous improvement problem-solving methods. Efforts at this managerial stage are often cross-functional, as many functions cross departmental boundaries. This requires interdepartmental collaboration, with process and indicator functions appropriately assigned. The outcome is a common process and language for documenting and communicating activities and decisions and for realizing success in eliminating waste, redundancy, and bottlenecks.

Project Management—Project planning establishes a system to effectively plan, organize, implement, and control all of the resources and activities needed for successful completion of the quality program. It is at this stage that teams are formed to solve and carry out both process- and policy-related initiatives. Team activities are linked to operational objectives and improvement targets. They develop the critical success factors: control systems, schedules, tracking mechanisms, performance indicators, and skill analysis. The outcome of each is a vision of the project that is linked to the organizational objectives, a work plan with designated milestones, a communication process for documenting key decisions and improvements, and a project completed on time and within budget.

Personal Management—Quality planning provides all employees with the means to implement continuous improvement of the above processes and systems through development of individual work functions and control. Each individual is guided through the development of a personal mission and vision.

ENDNOTES

1. Tribus, Myron (1992). "Ten Management Practices." In Voehl, Frank (1992). *Total Quality: Principles and Practices within Organizations.* Coral Springs, FL: Strategy Associates, pp. IV, 20.
2. Deming, W. Edwards (1986). *Out of Crisis.* Cambridge, MA: MIT Center for Advanced Engineering Study.
3. Tribus, Myron (1992). "Ten Management Practices." In Voehl, Frank (1992). *Total Quality: Principles and Practices within Organizations.* Coral Springs, FL: Strategy Associates, pp. IV, 19.
4. Imai, Masaaki (1986). *Kaizen: The Key to Japan's Competitive Success.* New York: Random House. He also states, "The message of the kaizen strategy is that not a day should go by without some kind of improvement being made somewhere in the company" (p. 5).

ABSTRACT

ABSTRACT 5.1
THE BALANCED SCORECARD—MEASURES THAT DRIVE PERFORMANCE

Kaplan, Robert S. and Norton, David P.
Harvard Business Review, January–February 1992, pp. 71–79

"What you measure is what you get," begin these authors. "Traditional financial accounting measures like return on investment and earnings per share can give misleading signals for continuous improvement and innovation—activities today's competitive environment demands." The remedy, they say, is a "balanced scorecard," a group of measures that summarize progress toward the objectives most important to the organization. Anything else is like trying to fly a plane by watching just the altimeter and ignoring measures like air speed, remaining fuel, and so on. The authors conducted a year-long research project with 12 companies to explore ways of finding the combination of operational and financial measures that would constitute a "balanced scorecard." They concluded that there are four important measurement perspectives:

- Financial perspective (How do we look to shareholders?)

- Customer perspective (How do customers see us?)

- Internal business perspective (What must we excel at?)

- Innovation and learning perspective (Can we continue to create value?)

Each of these perspectives implies a set of goals that in turn imply measures of performance in reaching those goals. To illustrate possible goals and measures, the authors describe how a disguised electronics firm derived its own balanced scorecard of goals and measures from these four perspectives, and the authors supplement these examples with measures adopted by other businesses. They conclude with some suggestions on how to ensure that balanced scorecard measures will result in improved financial results. (©*Quality Abstracts*)

ABSTRACT 5.2
NEW ENGLAND TELEPHONE OPENS CUSTOMER SERVICE LINES TO CHANGE

Clarke, J. Barry et al.
National Productivity Review, Winter 1992–93, pp. 73–82

When a consultant surveyed customers of the Interexchange Customer Service Center of New England Telephone, the results were not flattering. "The solution," say the authors, "was to reengineer the entire operation by establishing a customer-focused service team structure responsible for all processing and servicing support for a specific customer base." The company began by explaining the problems in very candid fashion to employees gathered in an auditorium. Reaction was extremely positive. Part of the program involved developing a vision statement which contained specifics regarding: customer loyalty, service quality, competitive edge, organizational effectiveness, job satisfaction, and training and participation. One of the key changes was involving service representatives in the billing and claims activity. Employees were offered a series of work effectiveness and change management workshops, and nonmanagement teams were formed to address job design, training, and mechanization. The redesigned workplace now includes the following elements, each of which the authors describe briefly: training, intern programs, career development programs, a mechanized report system, a managers' forum, professional development seminars, facilitator programs, support/supervisor monthly meetings, quality action teams, a quality notebook, a quality newsletter, a subject-matter expert process, a flexible work arrangements committee, and customer-centered work teams. Since 1989, the authors report, expenses have fallen, the workforce has been reduced 32 percent without any layoffs, overtime has been reduced, and the department has received quality awards for its achievements.   (©*Quality Abstracts*)

ABSTRACT 5.3
QUALITY IN AMERICA: HOW TO IMPLEMENT A COMPETITIVE QUALITY PROGRAM

Hunt, V. Daniel
Business One Irwin, Homewood, Illinois, 1992, 308 pp.

Quality in America is a readable volume that demystifies the quality movement and presents a clear plan to implement TQM in an organization. The author begins with an assessment of the global marketplace and the importance of TQM to a firm's remaining competitive. Next, he describes the fundamental concepts and vocabulary of quality. Chapter 3 is a helpful characterization of four of quality's pioneers: Deming, Juran, Robert Costello, and Philip Crosby. Then the author compares the emphases of the school of thought attributed to each of these people. "There is no one best way," says the author, but from that point on he describes and promotes his own synthesis of quality principles under the name *Quality First*™. A chart shows the relationship of Crosby's 14 steps, Deming's 14 points, and Juran's 7 points to *Quality First's* 8 tasks, which are summarized under the following major categories:

- **People-oriented tasks:**
1. Build top management
2. Build teamwork
3. Improve quality awareness
4. Expand training

- **Technically oriented tasks:**
5. Measure quality
6. Heighten cost of quality recognition
7. Take corrective action
8. Commit to a continuous improvement process

Chapter 4 describes the Malcolm Baldrige National Quality Award and recommends applying for it. This is followed by a chapter giving a thumbnail sketch of Baldrige Award winners: Federal Express, Globe Metallurgical, Motorola, Wallace Co., Westinghouse, and Xerox Business Products and Systems. Then the author provides a specific outline for implementing quality in an organization. Chapter 6 includes a complete self-assessment questionnaire and scoring evaluation system. After introducing his *Quality First* concepts and principles, the author outlines a 17-step implementation plan. The first ten steps are planning, followed by seven implementation steps. Chapter 10 consists of a brief survey of quality tools (e.g., bar chart, fishbone diagram, control chart, Pareto chart, etc.) and techniques (action plan, benchmarking, cost of quality, SPC, etc.). A final chapter reviews the steps and urges the reader to "act now." Three appendices provide basic resources: an executive reading list, a glossary of quality terms, and a list of information sources. This is a helpful "first book" to introduce the quality movement to corporate executives.   (©*Quality Abstracts*)

CHAPTER 6

STRATEGY MANAGEMENT AND QUALITY PLANNING

The essence of management is…the art of mobilizing the intellectual resources of everyone working for the company. The intelligence of a group of executives, impressive as this might be, is no longer enough to guarantee success.

Konosuke Matsushita

STRATEGY MANAGEMENT

As indicated in Chapter 5, total quality is initiated at all levels of management. Implementing the principles of quality in an organization requires rethinking the very purpose of the organization. Without senior management's full support, it is impossible to provide the leadership, change the culture in which the organization operates, and potentially alter the direction of how to serve the organization's customers, shareholders, vendors, and employees.

Defining Strategy

Before proceeding, let's understand what strategy is. *Webster's New World Dictionary* defines strategy as "the science of planning and directing large scale military operations, skill in managing or planning, especially by using stratagem."[1] Stratagem is derived from two Greek words: *straos*, meaning army, and *agein*, meaning to lead. Basically it is a term used to describe a plan or trick to deceive an enemy. Eventually the concept of strategy spread to private businesses and then to public and nonprofit organizations. The term strategy in business has come to refer to the actions taken to establish and achieve the goals and objectives of an organization. Tregoe and Zimmerman[2] define organizational strategy as "the framework which guides those choices that determine the nature and direction of an organization."

Five basic functions of strategy critical for setting and maintaining direction are driven by the principles of total quality management and continuous improvement:[3]

1. Implement *leadership* for quality.

2. Develop an organizational *mission* for quality improvement.

3. Create a *vision* that inspires everyone to seek quality in all aspects of their work.

4. Generate a *culture* that encourages quality improvement efforts at all levels.

5. Establish overarching *goals and objectives* consistent with the principles of total quality and continuous improvement.

Each of these five points is briefly explained below. They should be used as guidelines to enrich planning and decision-making efforts.

Leadership: The Will to Change

Leadership is a catalyst for change, and total quality management efforts require positive change. Deming's seventh principle stresses the importance of leadership, and a review of all 14 principles shows that successful total quality implementations require leadership. The Baldrige Award criteria[4] describe the leadership category as examining "senior executives' personal leadership and involvement in creating/sustaining a customer focus with clear and visible quality values."

Becoming a manager does not automatically make one a leader. There is a difference between being a leader and being a manager. Bennis[5] summarizes the differences between management and leadership as follows:

Manager	Leader
1. Administers	1. Innovates
2. Is a copy	2. Is an original
3. Maintains	3. Develops
4. Focuses on systems and structure	4. Focuses on people
5. Relies on control	5. Inspires trust
6. Has a short-range view	6. Has long-range perspective
7. Asks how and when	7. Asks what and why
8. Has eye on bottom line	8. Has eye on horizon
9. Imitates	9. Originates
10. Accepts status quo	10. Challenges status quo
11. Classic good soldier	11. Own person
12. Does things right	12. Does right thing

Both management and leadership skills are necessary to produce an effective, efficient plan to guide the organization. A leader is receptive to change. Leadership practices should be adopted throughout the entire company, including the information technology (IT) organization. (For additional information, see Abstracts 6.1 and 6.2 at the end of this chapter.)

Mission

The mission is the basic purpose an organization seeks to accomplish—the reason why the organization exists. A mission statement is the formal expression of a company's purpose for its internal functions, customers, and employees. The IT mission statement should focus on complementing the overall company mission. IT should aid in developing the company mission. It is important that the mission statement identify the product produced or service performed and recognize the customers who are affected and their needs. The mission statement must be shared throughout the organization, with all its members, to be effective.

Vision

> Where there is no vision, the people perish.
>
> Proverbs 29:18

Vision is the direction or common belief of what the organization should be like five to ten years in the future. A vision should define what is to be created versus what is to be accomplished. A vision statement should be creative, clear, concise, positive, credible, reasonably obtainable, and shared throughout the company. The IT organization should have a vision that is in harmony with the overall company vision.

The concept of vision is often difficult for individuals to deal with because it defies conventional management approaches or the concept is unclear to them. Nanus[6] identified six things a vision is not:

1. While a vision is about the future, it is not a prophecy (although, after the fact, it may seem so).

2. A vision is not a mission. To state that an organization has a mission is to state its purpose, not its direction.

3. A vision is not factual. It does not exist and may never be realized as originally imagined. It deals not with reality but with possible and desirable futures.

4. A vision cannot be true or false. It can be evaluated only relative to other possible directions for the organization.

5. A vision is not (or at least should not be) static, enunciated once for all time.

6. A vision is not a constraint on actions, except for those inconsistent with the vision.

The benefits associated with a clear, positive vision for an organization include:

- Greater clarity of direction, which provides a framework for organizational decision making concerning desirable outcomes and actions and identification of opportunities and threats

- Greater unity of purpose and action

- Enhanced expectational guidance, which provides guideposts for determining appropriate behavior and assessing how individuals fit into the larger organizational picture

- Increased emphasis on innovation and anticipatory management, since the future direction is provided by the vision

- Increased motivation and commitment among the members of the organization; the creation of dynamic tensions between the present and desired future provides meaning and challenges for all

- Greater potential for decentralized decision making; when individuals and teams are aware of the vision and related mission, goals, and objectives, they are able to incorporate these factors into their decision making

Experience in strategic planning has shown that vision often ignores potential opportunity and lacks creative thinking. *Creating a vision requires playing the "anything goes" game, which involves using hindsight, foresight, and insight.*

Organizational Culture

Organizational culture refers to patterned ways of thinking, feeling, and acting throughout an organization. The specific characteristics of culture include behavior, structure, actions, attitudes, and roles. For the IT organization, this means transforming its image and conceptual ways of thinking about being merely computer analysts. IT professionals must also make an effort to help change the overall company cultural thinking and become business organizational allies and business analysts versus "an expensive department with technical people."

Table 6.1 lists nine key steps identified by Carr and Littman to ease the cultural transformation process. These nine steps are guidelines to follow. Organizational culture modification does not happen overnight. Culture change takes time, and it usually takes a long-term successful track record before transformation occurs. Old habits are hard to change, but time, consistency, and patience can make it happen. (For additional information, see Abstract 6.3 at the of this chapter.)

Goals and Objectives

The goals and objectives provide the linkage between the macro-level defined mission and vision statements of the organization. They identify how

Table 6.1 Carr and Littman[7] Steps in Easing the Cultural Transformation Process

---

1. Planning for cultural change
2. Assessing for cultural "baseline"
3. Training managers and the work force
4. Management adopting and modeling new behavior
5. Making organizational and regulation changes that support quality action
6. Redesigning individual performance appraisal and reward systems to reflect the principles of total quality management
7. Changing budget practices
8. Rewarding positive change
9. Using communication tools to reinforce TQM principles

---

the vision is going to be achieved. Goals and objectives can provide a larger picture and help unite everyone in the organization. Before developing plans and making decisions, the goals and objectives of the organization should be considered.

The quality planning process can begin when the overall company strategy has been established and communicated throughout the organization.

QUALITY PLANNING

Definition and Benefits

Quality planning is the business planning process used to formulate, deploy, and achieve business objectives by concentrating resources on high-priority items. This method of management links business activities to the long-term view of the company and provides the system that propels a company toward its vision while increasing the opportunity for competitive advantage.

Quality planning provides a systematic methodology to achieve the company vision once strategies have been defined. The processes and theories used to achieve success start with five basic business and personal management principles:

1. Always put the customer first.
2. Have true respect for people; treat others as you would want to be treated.
3. Deal with facts, not rumors or gossip.
4. Strive for continuous improvement.
5. Allow and encourage teamwork between *all* business functions and customers.

Life is not always as simple as we would like; complexity is a fact of life. However, if we look at the issues facing a company, apply the five principles listed above, and follow straightforward systematic approaches, we can solve complex problems and implement strategies to make our company successful.

Quality planning does not take the place of the organizational strategic plan; instead, it provides a bridge from strategy to operational actions. *Strategic plans concentrate efforts on particular markets and specify products to offer those markets. Quality plans focus on the business processes necessary to gain and maintain competitive advantage.* The differences between strategic planning and quality planning are shown in Table 6.2. Both strategic and quality planning work together to achieve the long-term goals of a company.

Table 6.2 Strategic Planning Versus Quality Planning

Strategic planning	Quality planning
Project oriented	Process oriented
Generally not well understood by everyone in the organization	Communicated throughout the organization
Projects selected by the knowledge and experience of those preparing the plan	Improvement areas selected by those most familiar with the processes
Difficult to link one year's plan to the next in most cases	Plan is built on the preceding year's plan
Targets are selected by intuition and reflect a top-down mentality	Targets are established based upon analysis and data

Quality planning breaks down barriers and opens lines of communication. Organizations establish breakthroughs by focusing the *entire* company on the vital few. All business functions and departments are able to understand where the objectives fit into the long-term company direction. The employees are given a clear sense of where they are headed. The firefighting mode prevalent in today's business operations is eliminated.

The quality planning model presented here follows the *hoshin* methodology. Management Systems International, Inc. (MSI), a firm that specializes in continuous improvement and planning, uses this methodology and has proved that it works.

Organizations that practice total quality deal with three interacting managerial systems: management, organizational, and educational. These systems were discussed in Chapter 5. The effectiveness of an organization is measured by its managerial system. Figure 6.1 displays quality planning and its interaction with the managerial system. It is through the managerial system that work is completed.

Components and Focus

Quality planning efforts consist of formation, deployment, and diagnosis. Formation is creating quality objectives based on understanding the organization from both customer and business viewpoints. Deployment is establishing methods to improve and assign resources (e.g., deciding to automate a manual process). Diagnosis is the ongoing review of the outcome (feedback) with emphasis not only on the results but on how the results were achieved.

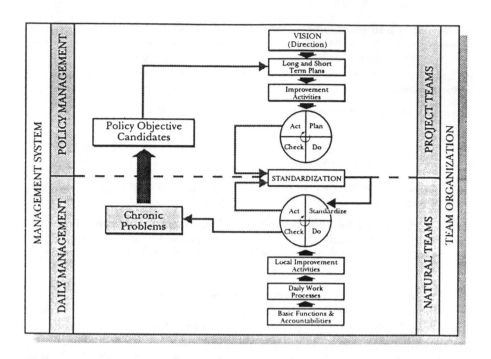

Figure 6.1 Quality Planning and the Managerial System.

Focus is the key in quality planning. There is often a difference between the apparent direction of a company and reality. It is important to understand the real focus rather than what is published in various plans. To ascertain the real focus, think back to last year's activities in your area. What items received the most attention? To assist in understanding, it is helpful to draw a pie chart divided into pieces proportional to how you spent last year. The largest slices are the real focus points.

FORMATION

Quality plan formation consists of three main sections. The sections produce customer requirements (voice of the customer), generate business requirements (voice of the business), and then develop objectives that are linked to the strategic plan. Where does IT fit into the picture during this process? Quite often, the IT professional does not have the opportunity to be involved in overall company planning or deal directly with customers, internal or external.

During the planning process, the business departments usually interact with their external customers to determine what is necessary to satisfy their business needs. IT must then rely on second-hand information and implement the technology requested without fully understanding the business need. Often the technology requested is more than what is actually needed or there may be other solutions, including preserving the status quo.

Including the IT function in the quality planning process and using cross-functional business teams will also improve the response time for delivery. It is faster, easier, and more cost efficient to make changes during the planning stage than it is to wait until product development or implementation. Every business function should be involved up front, before the customer is informed. It is embarrassing to tell customers that they will receive something at a set time and then, after discussing it with other departments, find that there is no feasible way to do it.

One suggested approach to aid in developing quality plans is to obtain the services of an outside facilitator. The facilitator is unbiased and can assure that all departments provide input and are fairly represented. Departmental representatives and the facilitator meet to determine requirements. The time required varies, but usually four to five dedicated days will suffice.

The first step in the formation of objectives is to determine the customer requirements by listening to the customer. It is important to equally weigh the customer and business interests so that one does not impinge upon the other.

VOICE OF THE CUSTOMER: CUSTOMER NEEDS

Many concepts regarding the voice of the customer fail to take advantage of information that exists within an organization. Most concepts begin with customer surveys but then do not use the information. Customers surveys are a useful tool but they should be used when customer requirements are already known.

In order to take advantage of the current body of knowledge, look for the various sources where customer requirements can be found. They include:

- Market research/surveys
- The sales force
- Warranty claims
- Customer complaints
- Customer service transactions
- Government regulations

- Technical and trade shows
- Customer site visits
- Focus/user groups

The key point is to *listen* to what customers say. It is amazing what knowledge can be gained by simply asking customers and listening to their responses.

Deriving Customer Requirements

In order to derive customer requirements, we must know how the customer views quality. The definition of quality with regard to planning and TQM is *conformance to customers' valid requirements*. This means that customer requirements are more than just quality issues; they reflect the customer's entire relationship with a company and its products and services.

Customer requirements can be broken down into four main categories: quality, safety, cost, and delivery. These categories have been derived by studying a significant amount of customer requirement data. The "Big Q" (quality) is derived from these four areas.

If we take time to reflect on the evolution of quality, from the days of the artisan craftsman, through the industrial revolution, to the present, we can see how quality consistently conformed to customer needs. When quality was controlled by the craftsman, he was responsible for building quality into the product. This was easily achieved since the same craftsman performed every step. Whether making a pair of shoes or cutting a gem, customer requirements were translated into product specifications, and the craftsman conformed to the specifications. Products were customized to customer requirements.

In some cases, customers did not know exactly what they wanted and relied upon the artisan's experience to develop specifications. Again, we see that the process involved translating customer needs into specifications and performing to specifications. The product was then either accepted or rejected by the customer. If the craftsman's interpretation of the customer need was valid, then the customer was satisfied. If not, the customer was unsatisfied.

The industrial revolution and mass production solidified the concept of conformance to specification. If the product was more complex, such as an automobile or piece of machinery, it was even more important to conform to specifications. This is also where the designer was forced to look at other aspects of quality, such as cost, reliability, and competition. If competitive pressure was light, a lower quality product could be produced and would be accepted by the customer. Once competitive pressure increased, cost became the main focus and cost reductions (many times at the expense of quality) were put in place.

The same concept applies to both services and products. Conforming to an internally derived specification will not always lead to satisfied customers. This is known as single-dimension quality, where achieving customer satisfaction is a function of conforming to specification. In actuality, there have always been two dimensions of quality. Instead of a single set of characteristics that govern quality acceptance, there are two: expected or required quality characteristics and unexpected or exciting quality characteristics.

Expected or required quality is a function of removing dissatisfaction. This means that supplying certain characteristics in a product or service does not create satisfaction but rather not supplying them can only create dissatisfaction. The best performance, or conformance to specification, only yields a neutral customer reaction. These are the items that a customer expects in the product or service.

As an example, let's consider a bank. A bank provides accurate statements to customers as an expected characteristic; by doing so, the bank does not gain customer satisfaction. When you received your last bank statement, did you call up the bank to say that it was doing a great job by providing you with an accurate statement? Of course not. But if the statement had been incorrect, how would you have reacted? You would have been dissatisfied with what you *expected* to be accurate. It is easy to see that providing an accurate statement does not create satisfaction, but *not* providing one creates *dis*satisfaction.

The question remains how to create satisfaction. Unexpected characteristics of a product or service create satisfaction. This stems from providing some feature or service that pleased and surprised the customer. By providing the *unexpected*, we can generate a sense of excitement that creates satisfaction. Looking at customer satisfaction from both points of view (*removal* of dissatisfaction and *creation* of satisfaction) is known as two-dimensional quality. This concept was developed by Dr. Noriaki Kano of the Union of Japanese Scientists and Engineers.

Let's return to our banking example. Suppose your bank manager called you and said that a review of your account showed that you could save money or time by subscribing to a new service. This unexpected service would make you feel good and give you satisfaction. (For additional information, see Abstract 6.4 at the end of this chapter.)

Obtaining Customer Requirements

The information to obtain customer requirements is usually available but, like most information, it must be translated into useful data. Gathering data

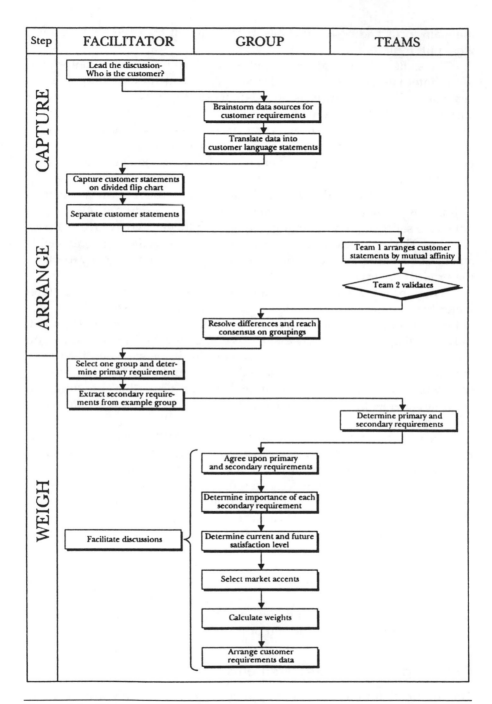

Figure 6.2 Process to Obtain Customer Requirements.

and arranging it in useful format(s) is the focus of this section. A three-step process is used to transform information into data:

- Capture the information
- Arrange the requirements
- Weigh the requirements

Figure 6.2 shows the process flow of the tasks to capture, arrange, and weigh customer requirements.

Step 1: Capture

In this step, a group brainstorms all possible data sources. All existing or potential customers are identified. The group basically asks, "Who are the customers and what do they require?" All ideas are written down and none are initially ignored. Each customer and the associated requirements are then translated into customer statements.

Step 2: Arrange

The customer statements captured in step 1 are arranged into common manageable groups. The affinity diagram is a recommended approach for documenting data. Figure 6.3 is a sample affinity diagram. The data are

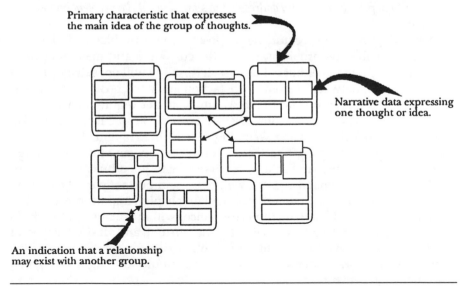

Figure 6.3 Affinity Diagram.

grouped by the primary characteristic that expresses the main idea of a group of thoughts. Each idea is documented with a narrative expressing the idea. Narrative data express one thought or idea of the group. These items are listed under the primary main idea. When primary ideas exist within another group, arrows are drawn to show the relationship.

Two teams should be created. Each team arranges the customer statements by mutual affinity. The teams then validate each other's work and resolve any differences before proceeding to step 3. The teams are a check and balance for one another and must arrive at a consensus.

Step 3: Weigh

The organization defines quality and the customer either rejects or accepts it. The customer provides two important components in determining the weight of a given requirement: importance and satisfaction. The customer indicates how important a requirement is, but this is somewhat skewed by performance, especially recent performance. The customer also indicates current level of satisfaction in terms of meeting requirements. Simply asking customers will not do, since recent performance will skew their responses.

Requirements should be weighed to achieve a balance between what the customer wants and good business practices. This means that the goal is to satisfy the customer, in fact even delight the customer, but to do so within the confines of good business practice. Anyone can throw money at a problem, but the challenge is to solve customer issues within constraints. *Throwing money at a problem rarely fixes it; it usually addresses the symptoms of the problem and not the true causes.*

Satisfying customer requirements poses certain problems, and it is a challenge to solve the problems, satisfy the customer, and maintain profitability. If a company goes out of business, it certainly will not satisfy customers. The balance between customer satisfaction and good business practice is achieved by utilizing four factors to weigh customer requirements: importance, current level of satisfaction, desired level of satisfaction, and market accent. Table 6.3 displays the weighing factors matrix and the weighing algorithm. By utilizing these factors, an organization can effectively weigh customer requirements and achieve a balance with good business practice.

Understanding what drives the weight is an important part of assessing customer requirements. In some cases, a relatively high importance, together with a rather dismal showing in performance, will make a weight high. In other cases, a significant gap between the current and desired levels of satisfaction will drive the weight. In still other cases, a combination of the above scenarios and a market accent will contribute to a highly weighted customer requirement.

The organization determines the desired level of satisfaction. For ex-

Table 6.3 Weighing Factors Matrix and Algorithm

Weighing factors matrix		

Factor	Description	Weight scale				
Importance	The degree of importance customers place on a given requirement	1 low	2	3 med	4	5 high
Current level of satisfaction	The degree of satisfaction that customers are currently experiencing	1 low	2	3 med	4	5 high
Desired level of satisfaction	The degree of satisfaction that is needed to maintain competitive advantage or parity. This becomes your quality target for a given requirement	1 low	2	3 med	4	5 high
Market accent	Selected customer requirements, usually high in importance, that yield competitive advantage when satisfied	No accent = 1.0 Medium = 1.2 High = 1.5				

Weighing Algorithm:

$$\text{Weight} = \text{Importance} \times \frac{\text{Desired}}{\text{Current}} \times \text{Market accent}$$

ample, it is not necessary to satisfy a given requirement at a level of five if customers only demand a level of three and the competition is at three. In this case, applying additional resources to achieve a higher than necessary level of satisfaction is poor business practice.

VOICE OF THE BUSINESS

Another key critical analysis, in addition to the voice of the customer, is to understand the voice of the business. This analysis is done to determine the current status of the business functions and identify which processes need improvement. The voice of the customer identifies key business functions that affect the needs of the system; the voice of the business evaluates the processes within these customer-identified business functions.

The business speaks to us differently than customers. Customers are sometimes very vocal in their demands. By watching certain indicators, such as market share, a company can get a good idea of what is needed. The voice of the business is assessed by looking at business problems in two main areas:

- *People*—Composed of employee-related issues
- *Waste*—Composed of efficiency- and cost-related problems

The voice of the business is very important because customers cannot always tell you what is wrong in the company. It is true that problem business processes generally manifest themselves through customer complaints, but many times this is too late. By thinking about the direction in which the company, business unit, or department is headed, the major problems in the organization can be assessed. What processes are broken with respect to achieving the long-term direction? What areas adversely affect the cost structure so as to make the business less competitive? (This question also applies to internal departments, since many of the functions performed by these departments are now outsourced.) Where can resources be gained by doing away with wasteful activities? These are the type of questions that assist an organization in determining the voice of the business.

All information is valuable when assessing business-related problems. Opinions are informative, but they can lead to working on the wrong things. When assessing business-related problems, one question always arises: "Compared to what?" Benchmarking can assist in identifying waste and can also help improve the situation. Finding and eliminating waste is a necessary and continuing effort.

The voice of the business analysis requires cooperation, openness, sharing, and understanding. Concerns which affect the business, such as personnel, competition, finance, technology, internal time cycles, and regulatory issues, are revealed and considered. All employee levels are included, and senior management must share future plans. The information captured is shared with work teams. This approach follows the capture-and-arrange steps identified in defining customer requirements.

IDENTIFYING THE PROBLEM

A problem well stated is half solved. This statement may sound trite but it is true. Individuals are often assigned a project and are not quite certain what is expected. A good problem statement is imperative to keep this from occurring. A good problem statement should be able to answer the following:

- *Who*—Who is affected by the problem, or the *customer* of the problem?
- *What*—What exactly is the "pain" the customer is experiencing?

- *When*—What is the time period associated with the information collected to support the problem?
- *Where*—*Precisely*, where is the problem being experienced?

Although these appear to be simple questions, they are often ignored when framing a business problem. The above checklist applies to any type of problem and should be used to assist in all improvement efforts.

DETERMINING BUSINESS PROBLEM PRIORITY

Today's business world is in a constant state of flux. Organizations must be concerned with change and change management. An inordinate amount of emphasis is sometimes placed on employee satisfaction when a company assesses the people side of the voice of the business. Satisfying employees is an admirable goal, but rapidly changing environments mandate a redefinition of people-related issues. The characteristics of the *new* organization are:

- Challenging work environment
- Encourages learning and employee development
- Values people as resources
- Encourages risk taking
- Leads rather than controls
- Leverages all parts of the organization
- Abolishes "not invented here"
- Achieves balance between processes and results
- Demonstrates consistency, integrity, and judgment
- Realizes that change is inevitable
- Seeks knowledge

An organization has many business-related problems. When prioritizing business-related problems, three factors should be considered:

1. *Urgency*—Must be solved in the next 18 months to 2 years in order to gain or maintain a competitive advantage. Weight scale is from 1 (problem does not affect competitive advantage) to 5 (problem significantly affects competitive advantage).

2. *Severity*—The level of impact the problem has on business operations. Weight scale is from 1 (problem does not take resources or time from other areas) to 5 (problem affects many areas and takes resources to support).

3. *Influence*—The level of influence the organization can exert in order to correct the problem. Weight scale is from 1 (problem is confined to one area of the organization) to 5 (problem will require involving many areas of the organization to solve).

These three factors are used to calculate the priority of the business problem using the following formula:

Business Priority Weight = Urgency × Severity × Influence

Recognizing business problems and reviewing business processes will identify areas that need improvement. The results will help management analyze the overall business and establish priorities for changing the business processes (especially those that require immediate attention). Downsizing is not always the best solution. Fewer employees may decrease customer satisfaction or eliminate resources that could be assigned to pursue new business opportunities. After all, the employees usually know the customers and the business problems.

BUILDING OBJECTIVES

Objectives are formed by taking data from the voice of the customer and the voice of the business and deciding where to focus efforts. There is no magic answer here. Only by utilizing the two voices can the confidence level be raised. There is no right or wrong choice, but some choices are better than others. Factual data, justification, and experience are the important tools.

Objectives merely provide a common focus. Each level is characterized by stating an objective and a corresponding means. An example is provided in Figure 6.4. One level's means becomes the next level's objective. In this manner, linkage is created from the formation stage through to implementation. The means to achieve objectives is through analysis based on data. Catchball is a useful technique to assist in quality planning. One of the most important aspects of quality planning is involving the individuals most familiar with the process in determining how it will be improved. This is where catchball is useful. Each level negotiates how it will support the company or departmental objectives.

The probability of achieving success is increased by having those closely associated with the work participate in the planning process. The concept is to select the most appropriate means to improve from all possible means. This is a key point of the *hoshin* planning methodology and separates it from other planning methodologies. Understanding how the results are achieved is as important as achieving the results. This allows good results to be replicated and eliminates undesirable results.

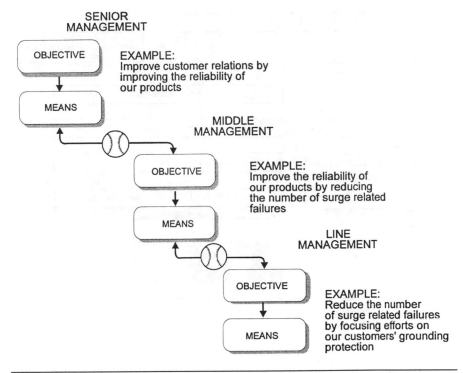

Figure 6.4 Example of Objective and Means Catchball and Leveling.

LINKING OBJECTIVES TO STRATEGY

The corporate strategy can be linked to the quality planning objectives. Figure 6.5 shows in further detail how the two interact. Monitoring and continuous feedback are important in the review process. Review steps include:

- Checking the long-term direction annually

- Building a one-year plan based upon the previous year

- Diagnosing throughout the year to provide midstream corrections and input to the next cycle

- Achieving the objectives through catchball discussions based on analysis

It is important to link the overall quality planning objectives to the business strategy plan. What use is defining objectives if the objectives are not considered in the overall planning effort? You must define what you want and be receptive to change.

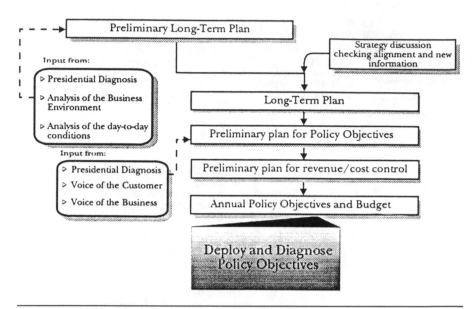

Figure 6.5 Objectives Link to Strategic Plan.

ENDNOTES

1. *Webster's New World Dictionary* (1992). Compact School and Office Edition. New York: Simon and Schuster.
2. Tregoe, Benjamin and Zimmerman, John (1980). *Top Management Strategy: What It Is and How It Works.* New York: Simon and Schuster, p. 17.
3. Lewis, Ralph and Smith, Douglas (1994). *Total Quality in Higher Education.* Delray Beach, FL: St. Lucie Press, p. 113.
4. 1993 Award Criteria, Malcolm Baldrige National Quality Award. Milwaukee: American Society for Quality Control, p. 16.
5. Bennis, Warren (1989). *On Becoming a Leader.* New York: Addison Wesley, p. 45.
6. Nanus, Bert (1992). *Visionary Leadership.* San Francisco: Jossey-Bass, pp. 31–32.
7. Carr, David and Littman, Ian (1990). *Excellence in Government: Total Quality Management in the 90's.* Arlington, VA: Coopers and Lybrand, pp. 190–203.

ABSTRACTS

ABSTRACT 6.1
WHAT IS LEADERSHIP?

Smolenyak, Megan and Majumdar, Amit
Journal for Quality and Participation, July–August 1992, pp. 28–32

What leadership type can empower employees to develop their inherent capabilities? The authors answer this question by describing three types of leaders:

- **The champion** is characterized by uncontested authority, usually resulting from a feat or event he or she has masterminded. This kind of leader is tough and determined and thrives in an autocratic, hierarchical world. The champion is normally patronizing toward followers.

- **The visionary** inspires others through a commitment to a vision of monumental proportions. This leader persuades people to follow by tapping their emotions. The visionary's relationship with followers can be described as paternalistic. The danger with this type of leadership is that the loss of the leader can mean the end of the movement.

- **The servant** attains stature through the accomplishments of followers by bringing out the "leader" in each of them. The servant is respected and admired but does not seek self-glorification. This type of leader is approachable and interactive, thriving on open communications. Most of all, the servant is an enabler who helps others develop their inherent capabilities in support of a mutually agreed upon mission. The followers then have a sense of ownership in the mission.

Many companies that practice TQM are already using servant leadership, say the authors, especially with self-managed work teams. When managers make the transition from boss to coach, they are adopting the servant style of leadership. Those who stubbornly resist this style may eventually have to leave for the good of the company. The good news, according to the authors, is that the supply of servant leaders as opposed to other types is very generous. (©*Quality Abstracts*)

ABSTRACT 6.2
INSIDE THE BALDRIGE AWARD GUIDELINES—
CATEGORY 1: LEADERSHIP

Sullivan, Rhonda L.
Quality Progress, June 1992, pp. 24–28

This first in a series of articles on the guidelines for the seven categories of the Baldrige Award focuses on leadership. "The 1992 Baldrige Award criteria are built on 10 core values and concepts," says the author. She briefly discusses each: customer-driven quality, leadership, continuous improvement, full participation, fast response, design quality and prevention, long-range outlook, management by fact, partnership development, and public responsibility. "By completing the award application's leadership section," she says, "a company will determine whether its organizational structure will support its objectives." In addition to a copy of the actual Baldrige Award criteria for Category 1, and a table of scoring guidelines, the author offers advice on areas of importance in the leadership category, such as:

• Don't rely solely on management by walking around. Develop a formal structure and strategy to ensure that leaders are accessible.

• Insist on enthusiastic personal involvement from senior executives.

• Stress two-way communication.

• Develop multiple methods for accomplishing an objective to ensure validation.   (©*Quality Abstracts*)

ABSTRACT 6.3
BUILDING A TOTAL QUALITY CULTURE

Batten, Joe
Crisp Publications, Menlo Park, Calif., 1992, 88 pp.

"People want to be led, not driven," insists the author. Providing the kind of tough-minded leadership that will produce a total quality culture is the focus of this motivational book (which includes a foreword by Zig Ziglar). Rather than presenting a formula for TQM, the book aims at developing the attitudes which support successful TQM leaders. Chapter titles are:

1. The Path to the Future
2. The New Leaders

3. Making Quality Possibilities Come True

4. Peak Performance at All Levels

5. Winners Can Be Grown

6. Tomorrow's Culture

Some of the themes include tough-minded leadership (the title of one of the author's former books), servant leadership, being a winner, motivating one's subordinates, excellence, and dreams. The author draws on the upbeat quotations from a variety of individuals to bolster his points. The book concludes with a 14-page glossary of terms which serve to spell out Batten's philosophy of leadership. For example, he defines "builder": "The CEO who stands tall is, above all, a builder. Committed to vision, stretch, empowerment, synergy, responsiveness, flexibility—toughness of mind—a builder ensures that all dimensions of each P in the pyramid are intensely focused on creation, growth, and building." (©*Quality Abstracts*)

ABSTRACT 6.4
MIS + TQM = QIS

Keith, Richard
Quality Progress, April 1994

This thought-provoking article discusses the important role of information systems in implementing total quality systems and explains how one company, Lithonia, revamped its management information system (MIS) to create "quality information systems." With annual revenues over $700 million and a workforce of 4,500, Livonia enjoyed gains in product quality and cost reduction, but remained stagnant in the "office environment." Specifically, the general business processes were being maintained in the status quo while the total quality focus was on the plant floor.

The article discusses management's realization that MIS must occupy a central focus of the company's total quality movement and must be combined in a strategic way in order to achieve a new understanding of system and service. This involves expanding the scope of the "data processors" to include the entire business process, including those that have little to do with the information systems function or department. "QIS requires the systems department to develop, implement, and champion a methodology that looks at the business goals and develops activities that might or might not include a computer system to meet those goals. Service should be the MIS department's deliverable product. This service should include setting goals, facilitating and participating in process improvements, and implementing computer systems.

The MIS function took over the business reengineering activities, and a sister group to "applications development" was formed with senior business analysts from technical and nontechnical backgrounds. Three goals were formed: (1) everyone must understand the QIS initiative, (2) MIS/QIS is uniquely suited to facilitate process improvement, and (3) the goals of the company must be the same as the goals of MIS/QIS.

The group found success using the process mapping techniques described in *Improving Performance* by Rummler and Brache (Jossey-Bass, San Francisco, 1991). Flowcharts were developed to depict the customer/server relationships and the corresponding processes being performed. These flowcharts were based upon performance metrics and standards that focused on key processes of providing price quotes to customers, developing installation drawings, and entering orders. None of the standards set by the team were met once an order was received. The marketing division was reorganized into work cells, each having total responsibility for any job assigned to its area from start to finish. Each cell was measured and held responsible for errors, quality problems, and substandard performance. Supervisors were eliminated, resulting in better information flow between the company and the customer.

Also discussed are the long-term considerations for procedural improvement focused in two areas: education of the customer and automation of the remaining streamlined processes. One of the most important aspects of the overall effort was the buy-in by division management and staff. Six months after implementation, the prime objectives were being met in all areas, leading to the author's conclusion that the combination of QIS and an improved bottom line creates a win–win situation for all. Limited references are provided.

CHAPTER 7

PROJECT TEAMS AND METHODOLOGIES

After management has reviewed the business process objectives and set priorities, these priorities are then assigned to a project. *Webster's Dictionary* defines a project as "something that is contemplated, devised or planned; plan; scheme."[1] Project management consists of the tasks involved in planning, organizing, overseeing, scheduling, and implementing a project. Teams are formed made up of individuals whose activities are linked to the company's improvement objectives. The major tasks include creating the project-centered vision, identifying critical success factors and developing control systems and estimating, scheduling, and tracking mechanisms, as well as identifying skills required and performance indicators.[2] This approach allows the company to work with facts and gives all employees the opportunity to improve the quality and level of service provided to customers.

TEAM BUILDING: ROLE TEAMS PLAY IN QUALITY IMPROVEMENT

Companies have traditionally formed organizations around work groups and specific functional tasks. Each organization is accountable for its particular area and for meeting its budget. The company's top executives manage by functional unit as opposed to business process. This tradition is slowly changing as companies are beginning to manage accountability by *process*.

A major theme of this book is that the success of every company rests on the effectiveness of work group teams. The key differences between a work group and a team are displayed in Table 7.1. That view is the basis for the use of total quality management. If a house is being built by two different contractors and there is no teamwork or coordination, one contractor might build a contemporary style house while the other builds a colonial style. When a company is changing its work flow processes, *all* business departments must work together to consider appropriate technology. The entire company must work toward and be kept informed about achieving the same vision, goals, and objectives.

The term "team" has come to describe a group of people who are goal centered, interdependent, honest, open, supportive, and empowered. Team

Table 7.1 Groups Versus Teams

Groups	Teams
Members think they are grouped together for administrative purposes only. Individuals work independently, sometimes at cross purposes with others.	Members recognize their interdependence and understand that both personal and team goals are best accomplished with mutual support. Time is not wasted struggling over "turf" issues or personal gain at the expense of others.
People tend to focus on themselves because they are not sufficiently involved in planning the unit's objectives. They approach their jobs simply as hired hands.	Members feel a sense of ownership toward their jobs and units because they are committed to goals they helped establish.
Members are told what to do rather than being asked what the best approach would be. Suggestions are not encouraged.	Members contribute to the success of the organization by applying their unique talents and knowledge to team objectives.
Members distrust the motives of colleagues because they do not understand the roles of other members. Expressions of opinion or disagreement are considered divisive or nonsupportive.	Members work in a climate of trust and are encouraged to openly express ideas, opinions, disagreement, and feelings. Questions are welcomed.
Members are so cautious about what they say that real understanding is not possible. Game playing may occur, and communication traps may be set to catch the unwary.	Members practice open and honest communication. They make an effort to understand each other's point of view.

Table 7.1 (continued) Groups Versus Teams

Groups	Teams
Members may receive good training but are limited in applying it by the supervisor or other group members.	Members are encouraged to develop skills and apply what they learn on the job. They receive the support of the team.
Members find themselves in conflict situations which they do not know how to resolve. Supervisors tend to put off intervention until serious damage has been done.	Members recognize conflict as a normal aspect of human interaction, but they view such situations as an opportunity for new ideas and creativity. They work to resolve conflict quickly and constructively.
Members may or may not participate in decisions that affect the team. Conformity often appears more important than positive results.	Members participate in decisions that affect the team but understand that their leader must make a final ruling whenever the team cannot decide or an emergency exists. Positive results, not conformity, are the goal.

Source: Adapted from Maddux, R.B. (1988). *Team Building: An Exercise in Leadership.* Oakville, Ontario: Crisp Publications.

members develop strong feelings of allegiance that go beyond the mere grouping of individuals. The productive outcome is synergistic and the accomplishments often even exceed the original goals of the task.[3]

TYPES OF TEAMS

To effectively implement total quality improvement, four types of teams are necessary: the lead project team, functional team, cross-functional team, and task team.

Lead Project Team

The lead team, also known as the quality council, leads the project. It functions as the steering committee in that it sets policy, establishes guidelines, and handles overall communication for the other three types of teams. The other teams operate under the lead project team.

A lead team is formed for a specific purpose, either in the management area for policy or for a major business process activity. Members are selected by management and membership is determined by expertise and company background. Project team members consist of cross-functional representation from each business function, including information technology (IT). The level of membership can vary based upon the project and its effect on the organization. There are three types of project team membership:

- *Executive level*—For major, critical company-wide projects, usually composed of presidents and vice presidents (e.g., CEOs, CFOs, COOs, and CIOs).

- *Activity-centered*—For a specific activity that does not affect the entire company. Usually composed of vice presidents, managers, and directors.

- *Location-centered*—For region-specific projects. Consists of directors, functional managers, and the chief manager for the location.

Every lead project team must have a project leader. The leader coordinates activity, develops project plans, communicates, and ensures that project objectives are being met. This individual is a mediator and the central contact point for the project. The life cycle of the team varies from project to project; it may be as short as one week or as long as three years. The lead project team ensures the success of the project, no matter how small or large. Unless working on an internal IT project, an IT representative should not be the team leader. The function of IT representatives is to communicate technology concerns, to be aware of what is happening, and to support the company. They should not make business decisions.

Cross-Functional Team

Cross-functional teams are often created by the project team, depending on the size of the project and its effect on the organization. When the executive-level team is formed, a cross-functional team becomes a necessity, as communication, analysis, and research among the business processes are inevitable. Membership usually consists of (but is not limited to) directors and managers from each business function.

Functional Team

Functional teams are additional teams established by the lead project or cross-functional teams to further detail specific processes. A functional team has a eclectic membership and concentrates its efforts on specific functional processes. The functional team is a subset of the lead project team and sometimes the cross-functional team. A representative from the functional team communicates requirements and status to the lead project team. The idea is to ensure that all efforts are viewed as processes with measurable results. Numerous functional teams can be generated for a single project.

Task Team

Task teams include representatives from multiple areas and are formed to complete a specific task or problem. Suppose a major computer project needed to be converted. The task team would plan and implement the conversion. Its functions are similar to a project team and are part of the success of the project. Additional functional teams might be created if additional specialized planning and research are necessary. (For additional information, see Abstract 7.1 at the end of this chapter.)

INFORMATION TECHNOLOGY TEAM REPRESENTATION

IT team representation will vary from project to project. When the executive level is involved, the senior IT manager should always be a member of the lead team. If the team activity is location centered, the IT director, project manager, or a systems analyst can be involved, based on the criticality and importance of the project. IT management has the option of sending representatives from each IT functional area or assigning a central coordinator to communicate with all areas within IT. The central coordinator is usually the systems analyst or IT team manager responsible for the project assigned to the project team. A separate cross-functional IT team should be created for any project that involves technology to ensure that each IT functional area is aware of the project. Table 7.2 shows a sample internal IT cross-functional team, its membership, and the expertise that should be involved.

Table 7.2 Information Technology Team Interaction

Function	Skill
Applications support	Project lead Systems analyst
Data center	Scheduling Systems support
Telecommunications	Telecom analyst
Information	Security/audit Business administration

When the IT function is outsourced, someone with technical expertise should represent the project and coordinate with the outsource firm. This person can be either a company employee or a consultant who specializes in project management and planning. When using an outside technical service, it is wise to choose an advisor who does not represent a particular product or vendor. This eliminates the possibility of designing business requirements to meet a particular purchase.

The role of the technical representative is to guide and assist. For example, technology vendors sometimes announce a product and years pass before it is available, even in a test mode. The technical representative investigates the various technology solutions and informs everyone. IT professionals, usually management or systems analysts, also contribute their technical expertise by offering workflow enhancements. IT should avoid telling a business department that its request is not technically unfeasible. "Can't be done" is an unacceptable answer; IT should at least provide alternatives. Communication is enhanced when business functions and IT teams define requirements together. *All* business support functions must work together to ensure the highest quality and eliminate communication difficulties.

DEFINING PRELIMINARY PROJECT CRITERIA

Before starting any project, certain criteria must be agreed upon by top management and everyone involved in the project. These criteria are the team purpose, commitment, and review processes which are to be in place and enforced.

Team Purpose

Creating empowered, effective teams requires a four-step facilitative process, as described by Schultz.[4] The lead project team is responsible for creating the vision and mission for the project. This team is the guiding light that the other teams follow. The vision and mission statements should be consistent with the direction of the company. The first step is to create the vision statement using clear, unambiguous language that is endorsed by everyone on the team. The second step is to define the reason for the team's existence. The third step is to define the principles and values that will guide the team by answering the question: "What principles and values do we find most important in meeting the vision?" The fourth step is to develop a mission for the unit, based on the principles and values. This serves as a guideline for decision making by everyone on the team. It answers the question: "How do we fulfill the vision?" (For additional information, see Abstract 7.2 at the end of this chapter.) An opportunity to create team responses is provided in Exercise 7.1 at the end of this chapter.

Individual and Management Commitment

In total quality, managing is not limited to managers; managing falls on the shoulders of every employee. Senior management's sincere involvement and participation ensure that the policies of the organization are being implemented and that the departments are continually improving. While some people feel that total quality stifles creativity, with proper use, it can encourage creativity from all levels of the organization. Employees need to know the issues, however, in order to recognize problems and offer solutions.

Care must be taken to ensure that people do not use the quality tools for unimportant issues or to meet artificial or personal goals. Total quality is total because it considers cost, delivery, safety, etc., as well as quality. Time spent on useless quality stories, four-lane highways to nowhere, and busy work (which does not add value) simply wastes time and money.

Management must commit to providing whatever the project needs. This includes people and capital. A project cannot afford to have someone involved part-time when the effort requires full-time support and this support is continually being pulled from the project.

Senior management must also endorse the project and demonstrate its full support. Direct line managers and all personnel who report to them must know that deviations from team norms or lack of teamwork will not be tolerated.

Review Process

The project review process monitors the project, making certain its goals and objectives are being met. These reviews assist management in understanding how policies are being supported, keep management informed on the status and findings, show where funds are being spent, and indicate whether the project is within budget and on time. This type of review promotes cooperation among the functions and gives meaning to the company's plan, since senior management is in the communication circle.

During review, involved individuals must speak factually. When difficulties arise, the team should give an accurate status report and attack the process instead of the individual. If there are difficulties, management should be informed and help requested. If a top manager wants information about a project, that information should be available at any time.

The review should be scheduled based on the criticality and length of the project. It is difficult to set standard review schedules because each project is different. A guideline would be no less than a weekly written report from the project team. Each subteam formed from the lead project team should report its status to the team leader, who forwards the information to the project team. (For additional information, see Abstract 7.3 at the end of this chapter.)

PROJECT DEVELOPMENT METHODOLOGY CYCLE

After the lead project team has been formed, it is time to start the project development effort. There are various project development methodologies, but they all follow the same basic rules. A company should establish and follow a methodology customized to meet its quality standards and the way it conducts business. *No one methodology is right or wrong; companies have different guidelines and business directions. Each company must develop its own methodology.* It may be advantageous to obtain outside assistance in some situations. The point is that some *standard* project methodology must be in place and endorsed by everyone. Without senior management's commitment to support the methodology, the project is doomed, no matter how good the process is.

There is no one project development methodology for developing and maintaining automated systems; there are only guidelines. Figure 7.1 shows a comparison between manufacturing a product and software development.

When starting a project, the IT professionals and businesspeople must include all of the business work processes. When a project considers only one functional area and not the entire business process flow, integration is lost and redundant information occurs. The common high-level phases for project development are:

1. Planning and defining business requirements
2. Generating functional requirements
3. Designing and building the system
4. Testing
5. Installation
6. Ongoing maintenance and feedback review

Each project development phase has teams with assigned tasks. All teams work together throughout the entire project. There are checkpoints and sign-offs between each phase. This eliminates communication breakdowns and ensures that what was requested is what is delivered. A description of each phase follows (see also Exhibit 7.1).

Phase I: Planning and Defining Business Requirements

This is the planning and business design phase. The requirements of the business and the customer are defined, feasibility determined, priorities established, and a project plan completed. Priorities are geared to company plans or, in some instances, are the result of government-mandated regulations.

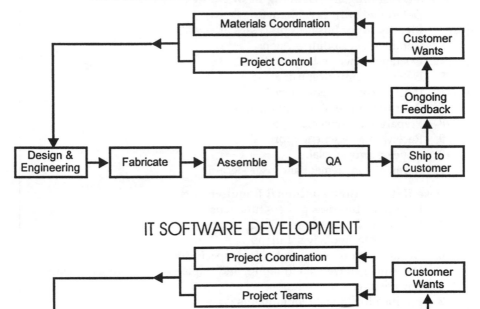

Figure 7.1 Comparison of Product Development to Information Technology Software Development.

The time needed to complete Phase I varies depending on the number of business functions involved and the complexity of the project request. There are a number of ways to conduct fact-finding sessions. The suggested method is to hold a master planning session, bringing all people involved together at the same time. Using an outside facilitator is recommended to keep the meeting on track and make sure that the objectives of the session are accomplished.

In most cases, within six to ten days, with the appropriate facilitator, complex business models can be designed, developed, and documented and "ownership" of business processes confirmed, with consensus reached as to strengths and weaknesses. Processes that deal with multiple markets

Phase I: Planning and Defining Business Requirements
1. Determine business objectives
2. Identify major business processes affected
3. Conduct fact-finding sessions
4. Document fact-finding results
5. Determine improvement areas
6. Prepare cost–benefit analysis
7. Prioritize processing requirements
8. Prepare requirements report
9. Receive management approval
10. Develop project plan
11. Receive management and user sign-off

Phase II: Generating Functional Requirements
1. Determine business process functions
2. Document business processing
3. Consider technology solutions
4. Document conceptual technology specifications
5. Determine conversion, training, and implementation requirements
6. Review alternative solutions
7. Produce functional requirements document
8. Review and update project plans
9. Receive management approval
10. Obtain user and management sign-off

Phase III: Designing and Building the System
1. Document detailed systems flow
2. Build a prototype
3. Select a package or develop in-house
4. Produce detailed systems specifications
5. Obtain user and management sign-off
6. Code and inspect programs
7. Review and update project plans

Phase IV: Testing
1. Develop testing scheme
2. Conduct technical testing
3. Conduct business process testing
4. Obtain user sign-off

Phase V: Installation

Phase VI: Ongoing Maintenance and Feedback Review
1. Conduct team review
2. Support maintenance requests

Exhibit 7.1 Project Methodology Phases.

or business departments require the same level of analysis as described for each of the initial business departments. Completing this phase takes longer, because it is usually more complex and requires outside customer information.

The information collected can be compiled in tabular format. These shared viewpoints will be the basis for identifying the system design. Evaluation of *shared* existing business strategies is critical in establishing the evolution of the system. Defining priorities for the first stage and the long-term goals of the process requires knowledge of the benefits to customers, departments, divisions, etc. This information will be integrated with appropriate technology and system architecture as the phases of the development plan are established.

This design allows management to see how the automated process aligns with its objectives and policies, as well as how it fits in with priorities within divisions and departments of the organization. It provides a shared view of the future and assures linkage to the long-term direction of the organization. When applied against four key indicators—quality, customer needs, safety, and delivery—the policy shows a balance between these factors.

Next, priorities are assigned. Management's approval follows and functional requirements can then begin.

The basic steps in planning and defining business requirements are:

1. *Determine business objective(s)*—Know what the objectives are for the business, what is important to customer service, and identify the financial bottom line.

2. *Identify major business processes affected*—Internal and external, by project request or process. Once the functions have been identified, a representative from each area is assigned to the cross-functional team for the duration of the project.

3. *Conduct fact-finding sessions*—Interview individuals involved in the business processes that are affected and learn how they conduct business.

4. *Document fact-finding results*—From all functional units using data models. Document the work flows and process; show where and how the functional units interact with each other in the process.

5. *Determine improvement areas*—Analyze facts documented for each business function. Identify the areas that are cross-functional and those that stand alone. Analyze and divide into subprojects by processing requirement.

6. *Prepare cost–benefit analysis*—Identify the costs and risks associated with each processing requirement identified in step 5. Technical con-

siderations must be included in this analysis. The risk of what would happen if nothing is done versus the risk of change must be considered.

7. *Prioritize processing requirements*—By using the company plans, cost–benefit analysis, and determining whether the requirement is mandatory or a "nice-to-have."

8. *Prepare requirements report*—Generate a report that will be presented to management for review.

9. *Receive management approval*—Review the findings with management for approval and commitment. Confirm the requirements that will be implemented and the order of priority.

10. *Develop project plan*—For the requirements that have been approved by management. This plan sets forth the tasks, what resources are needed, an estimated time frame, and the anticipated workload.

11. *Receive sign-off*—Distribute the project plan to all parties involved for sign-off and approval.

Phase II: Functional Requirements

The functional requirements phase identifies how the business requirements identified will be implemented. This phase analyzes business requirement(s) and determines particular actions within the business process affected. This may or may not include technology to enhance the process. In this phase, whether or not to automate is determined.

Always consider manual, less expensive solutions first.[5] Automating may be one solution, but it is not always necessary. If a process can be manually rearranged to meet acceptable quality standards, it may not be necessary to spend money to automate.

Team representation is revisited and any additional teams are created for the duration of the project. This phase primarily identifies the inputs and outputs on a business-user functional level. Process flows are generated by the business and technical areas. Business areas create detailed business work process flows and the technical area generates a detailed systems interface processing flow, showing the internal technical interactions. These are two separate tasks, although the efforts occur simultaneously.

The Plan-Do-Check-Act (PDCA) cycle of constant improvement (explained in Chapter 4) can be used to produce the system. Constant teamwork between the end users and the technical area is critical at this stage of the project. All planned activities are included in the continuous improvement cycle. Training requirements, conversion effort, and testing methodologies are fully explored and buy/build decisions are clearly delineated. Having defined customer needs and business issues, the natural question is: What is the best technological solution for this project? The technical area reviews available productivity tools in exploring ways to make the system more predictable and controllable.

IT evaluates currently available technology for present and future implementation. It is critical to match technology and the direction of the organization. *Business needs should dictate the technology used instead of technology driving the business.*

During this phase, quality measurements are defined and agreed to by each business process. Examples are given in Table 7.3, although the list is not comprehensive as there may be more or fewer measurements based on each individual project. The most important issue is to define standard methods for measuring the quality and overall success of the requirements and to build measurement criteria into the project. You cannot improve what you cannot measure. Measuring customer satisfaction should be included when considering technical requirements. This information will be the basis for the measurement criteria used to evaluate performance and quality at the end of the project.

Once the scope of the project is defined, it is reviewed and decisions are made about how to implement the system, in a phased, modular fashion.

Table 7.3 Functional Design Quality Measurements

Measurement considerations	Questions to ask when designing projects
System availability (up time)	When does the software/hardware need to be available to the users?
Response time	What is the turnaround time for obtaining results (online and reports)?
	Can processing be done in batch mode or must it be online in real time?
Ease of use	How user friendly is the software design?
	Is there a help function for online screens?
	Are the screens or reports easy to read and understand?
Performance criteria	How fast is the processing?
	Does the software function as the business requires?

Table 7.3 (continued)   Functional Design Quality Measurements

Measurement considerations	Questions to ask when designing projects
Reliability	How responsive is the software?
	How long has the software/hardware been in use for similar situations?
	How dependable is the software/hardware?
Transferability	How easy is it to transfer to other types of computer equipment?
Upgradability	How easy is it to upgrade the hardware or software?
Ease to install	How easy is the software/hardware to install and learn?
Documentation	What documented information is available (vendor-purchased or in-house) and how detailed is it (i.e., user procedures, computer operating procedures, programming and restart/recovery directions)?
	Is the documentation easy to read and understand?
Peak load management	How will the software/hardware function during high-volume use?
Ease of maintainability	How flexible is the software design/code for handling future changes?
	Is the design in modular, reusable segments?
	Is the information integrated and documented?
Information redundancy	Is the information reoccurring, fragmented, or stored in a central location?
Cost to operate	How much will it cost to operate?
	How many users will access the software at the same time?
	Are the users all at one site?
	Is additional hardware/software needed to support the project (i.e., modems, terminals, larger computer)?
Security	Has the "owner" been identified?
	Have access privileges (i.e., who can access specific information and functions) been established?
Business recovery	Have the business recovery requirements been identified in terms of what is needed in case of a disaster or temporary disruption to the customer?

Whenever possible, it is best to divide a system into functional processes and conduct a phased installation. Benefits of the phased approach include:

- Less risk of failure when introducing production volumes
- Responsibility for each process step is clearly defined
- Easier to measure and debug manageable-sized pieces of a system
- Users start working with the system and provide feedback
- Ease of maintenance
- As progress is reported, management has confidence that there is some quick return on investment

The basic steps followed during the functional requirements phase are:

1. *Determine business process functions and activity*—Define each business activity within the process and the information (data elements) used or needed. Define the security and business recovery criteria and identify any other system interactions, manual or automated.

2. *Determine all the inputs and outputs to the business process*—Identify by function and show their interaction within the process. Compare existing and anticipated data elements to verify that all process activity has been identified.

3. *Build processing flows*—After determining inputs and outputs, document the processing flow and system interactions, including both automated and manual systems, for the anticipated process.

4. *Define hardware/software environments*—Identify the computer hardware and software environments currently being used and what is needed to support the project or task.

5. *Document conceptual technical specifications*—Create a functional narrative by process and flow that identifies any design constraints. Determine technical requirements by showing any inputs, outputs, and cross-system interactions.

6. *Determine conversion, training, and implementation strategies*—Find out whether any existing business process or computer system requires conversion or training to use. If conversion or training is necessary, a separate task team for should be created for each to support those activities. The conversion task team starts its own subproject using the project development methodology from phase I. When preparing a conversion project plan, conversion testing should be ready for user testing and installation concurrent with the new development. The implementation strategy is how and when this requirement will be introduced in the business.

7. *Review alternative solutions*—Contemplate and weigh any other possible choices that could be considered.

8. *Produce a functional requirements document*—Write a functional document that defines all the requirements identified for the new process.

9. *Review project status and update task plans*—Compare the original project task plan to the final document and update the project task plan and status.

10. *Receive user sign-offs and management approval*—Distribute the functional requirements document for review and receive approvals from all functional user areas involved. Update management on any changes and receive approval to proceed with the project.

Phase III: Detail Designing and Building

Once the functional requirements phase is under way, the detail design of the system begins. A system is a composite of information, equipment, skills, and techniques to support a business objective. This phase is primarily an IT responsibility. While IT is working on this phase, the business teams are completing their assigned tasks, including generating test schemes, training, and writing procedures. The technical task teams are formed by project functions (systems) and consist of systems analysts, programmers, and a project leader for each team, with key business interaction continuing. The individual IT teams communicate with one another, but are divided into separate teams to expedite the system development process.

The detail design phase is where the technological advances of today and the potential benefits of tomorrow are considered. Standards, philosophies, and methods are melded to build a foundation for future evolution.

The overall architecture and design are dictated by business requirements and the status of the process. The best technical solution is designed in detail, either by purchasing a software package or writing customized programs. Today, standardization is more important than ever before. Larger companies are taking either a centralized or decentralized approach to technology but all seek central integration of information. Standards must apply across company lines when regions come into play or there will be no information integration. These standards allow each IT region throughout a corporation to present a consolidated information base. This facilitates supplying information to a corporate parent and giving top management information for the overall corporation. It is helpful for all regions and subdivisions within a corporation to calculate and report information the same way. Matching the structure of information with the design of the organization is critical. Systems must provide the correct information to the appropriate people in a timely, dependable manner and must be designed to handle rapid change.

Although it is beneficial to have a set of standard modules for analysts to use, they are expensive to develop. Therefore, to be more cost effective, reusable modules should be evolutionary in application. It takes longer and requires greater discipline, standardization, and expertise to develop such reusable code, but long-term use and the ability to expand the product must be fully explored. Standard interfaces are a must to handle the linkage between modules, technical libraries, languages, and databases.

The steps in the design and build phase are:

- Document detailed systems flow
- Build a prototype
- Select package or develop in-house
- Produce detailed systems specifications
- Obtain user and management approval
- Code and inspect programs
- Review and update project plans

1. Document Detailed Systems Flow—Business processes are documented in detail, reflecting where and how the automated and manual systems will interact. The design should be modular and divided into maintainable, manageable pieces.

2. Build a Prototype—One good approach to use when designing a system is to develop a prototype, sometimes known as a pilot system. A prototype shows how the system will flow and what it will look like in the working environment. One difficulty with prototyping is that end users working with the prototype often believe that the system is almost complete. They do not realize that the core internal processing is not included in the working model. Prototyping is helpful when users find it difficult to state their information needs. A major cause of this difficulty lies in the users' inability to see how they might use an information system. Prototyping enables users to better perceive screens and reports in the proposed system.

The distinct features of prototyping are:

- Learning and experience are integrated into the design process for both IT and the user

- Faster feedback on whether the system is functioning as requested and less time to make changes

- User involvement and the opportunity to resolve any potential communication misunderstandings before coding begins

- Lower costs, because it costs less to change a system that has not been tested or coded

3. Select Package or Develop In-House—The final decision is made as to whether a software package will be purchased or the system will be developed in-house. In many instances, even though a package is selected, it must be integrated with existing systems. Often "hooks" are needed to interface packaged software with existing systems.

4. Produce Detailed Systems Specifications—Specifications are written on a program level and assigned to the appropriate IT project task team.

5. Obtain User and Management Approval—Distribute the detail specifications document for review and receive approvals from all functional user areas involved. Update management on any changes and receive approval to proceed with the project.

6. Code and Inspect Programs—Programmers write the code per the detailed specifications given to them. When completed, the IT project teams meet and inspect the code. This quality step ensures that standards are being met, the code is efficient, and the program is functioning as requested by the customer. This step saves time by desk-checking before testing begins.

When packaged software is selected, the code should be installed and reviewed by all team members, so they all understand the system.

7. Review and Update Project Plans—Compare the original project task plan to the final document's anticipated work and update the project task plan and status.

Phase IV: Testing

Thorough testing is critical to the success of any project. The business departments and IT must work together closely to ensure that the system requested is working properly and is exactly what was requested. The IT area is not the sole judge in determining that the project request is ready to be implemented in a production environment or that the system is what the business departments requested.

Basic Test Criteria

When testing, the following four steps should be completed:

1. *Develop a test scheme—*
   a. *Devise a test plan*—Identify what needs to be tested and how it will be tested. Determine the risk of the process change and the level of

testing required. For example, will it be necessary to test quarterly and year-end processing with this system change? Will both online and batch processing require testing?

    b. *Create a test script*—Identify the specific functional activities that require testing and the sequence of testing steps.

    c. *Build test data*—Establish controlled testing conditions and build test situations that will produce specific results.

2. *Perform the test transactions*—Enter the data for testing.

3. *Run any programs required to process transactions and generate reports*—Run the programs and process as they would run under actual conditions.

4. *Analyze the results*—Review and verify the expected test results for accuracy, both batch and online.

A controlled testing environment and test cases should be used to ensure quality results.

Every project request should meet the following testing criteria to ensure minimal difficulties when the system is implemented.

Types of Testing

There are two basic types of testing: technical only and combined business and technical involvement. Each step must to be completed before the next level begins.

Technical Only

At this level, the IT functional areas verify that the project functions as a system and that all the pieces work and fit together.

IT ensures that the project request delivers what the business user has requested. Technical involvement during the business requirement and functional requirement phases eliminates the miscommunication usually associated with not delivering what the user really wanted.

This criteria level includes:

1. *Unit test*—Programmers verify that the code for each program or component works (multiple programs are usually written for each project request).

2. *Systems test*—Programs or components that were unit-tested are migrated into the existing system process to ensure that all existing system interactions remain intact.

3. *Integrated test*—*All* systems and each IT function (such as telecommunications and the data center) involved are consolidated for a thorough systems integration test to ensure reliability.

Business Functionality

At this level, the business users and the technical teams work together to verify that the project request functions as intended. Users have the opportunity to "shakeout" or work with the system before it is installed in a production environment.

1. *User acceptance*—Business departments verify that the system request meets business requirements and that the system functions properly.

2. *Stress test*—Ensures that the system request functions efficiently using real-life business conditions and volumes. This test should always be conducted before implementing a new system. Without a stress test, a contingency plan should be in place, which may be "dropping back" to the original system or proven processing method. A three-minute response time is an unacceptable quality service indicator for most companies, and a stress test will help uncover this difficulty before installing the system.

3. *Conversion test*—This step is required only when existing information needs are converted into a new format. The business departments are responsible for verifying the integrity of information. The accuracy of this function is critical to implementation of the project request. If existing data are converted inaccurately, the new process starts off with incorrect information and the project will fail.

4. *Regression test*—This test ensures that no existing system functionality is affected when the changes are introduced. The ideal situation is to retain initial test cases created for new systems and test the system using those conditions. Maintaining test cases requires discipline because any new system functionality must be added as a test condition and any enhanced system functionality requires testing against original test case conditions.

Usual practice is for the IT area to conduct and verify all the technical testing before involving business users. This verification is conducted by technical teams first because technicians need to iron out any problems before involving business users (the IT organization has multiple functions which must be coordinated). Technical checking should be completed before business users see the system, because giving users a bad first impression due to technical problems can result in loss of confidence in IT and the entire effort. This loss of confidence, in turn, can lead to user resistance to change.

Mandated project delivery dates, such as government-mandated changes, may force testing steps to be combined. In such cases, business users may become involved in technical testing and verification of test results before IT completes its testing. This commonly occurs when projects are not given time to follow proper procedures. Users are then forced to play a more active role in technical testing. Under no circumstances should any IT changes be installed before users have approved or signed-off on the installation.

Phase V: Installation

Before a project can be successfully implemented, the following tasks must take place within both IT and the business areas:

1. Educating employees about the change
2. Training conducted
3. Knowledge transferred
4. Documentation and procedures written
5. Testing completed
6. Contingency plans developed

In this phase, the project request is implemented in day-to-day production processes. All conversions take place and processing is "live."

Phase VI: Ongoing Maintenance and Feedback

The implemented project request results are reviewed. This is also considered to be the continuous improvement phase.

Measurement Review

Pertinent team members review and discuss among themselves and with the customers:

1. What could have been done differently to improve the project request development process
2. How efficiently the process is operating, both for the business and within the technical area

Operating efficiency items which should be considered and measured include:

1. Malfunctions categorized by type and how many occurrences are due to:
   * Programming
   * Equipment
   * Incorrect or misleading requirements
   * Improper work flow
   * Business process misunderstanding
   * User input error
   * Data editing
   * Conversion

2. Generate a cost–benefit analysis for the new system.

3. Review overall system response time and availability.

4. Review feedback and compare the results to the measurement indicators set during the functional design phase.

5. Evaluate whether project was completed on time and within budget. If it was not, determine why for future reference.

6. Compare original estimated cost–benefit with new cost–benefit analysis. Compare the estimated payback period to what the project delivered.

Maintenance

System maintenance is a never-ending task and in total quality is continuous improvement. Maintenance is constant after any project request is implemented. It sometimes requires following all the project methodology steps, depending on the business change request. Someone must be responsible for making sure the system continues to run smoothly. Examples of maintenance include correcting technical difficulties ("program bugs") or enhancing the system with mandated requirements or requested improvements. All installation plans should include additional time for maintenance support, especially during the period immediately following installation. Maintenance usually impacts the technical area first, but the business departments must also allow time to learn the system before installing new quality measurements.

MEASURING AND ESTIMATING METHODS

Measurements Are Needed

The quality of technology is difficult to measure, and the quality of software development is even more difficult to assess. When measuring a physical product, it is relatively easy to quantify and compare. In addition to measuring physical attributes (such as disk space, memory, and response time), software measurement should consider user friendliness, maintainability, whether results meet customer requirements, and whether the system is problem free and was delivered on time and within budget. The number of lines of code produced by a programmer is not important. In fact, measuring by lines of code can be counterproductive if programmers include extra lines to make a project appear larger. The goal is to measure software efficiency and not the programmer's technical efficiency.

The total quality concept includes having a quantitative measurement standard; otherwise, you cannot know that you are improving your process. The Gardner Group[6] reported that:

- A TQM program that is not based on a measurement program will fail within 12 months of implementation (0.8 probability).

- A TQM program that is not based on standards will fail within 12 months of implementation (0.8 probability).

- TQM programs can reduce the amount of rework required to repair defects by 80 percent (0.7 probability) and increase information systems productivity by 30 percent (0.8 probability).

- The cost of correcting a defective requirement once code has been written is at least 30 times greater than the cost to correct the defect during the requirements definition process (0.8 probability).

- Formal, facilitated review sessions of requirements will identify 90 percent of requirements defects (0.7 probability).

The benefits of implementing a measurement program include:

- Determining what resources (people and machines) are being used

- Analyzing how much time is being spent on a system or project

- Producing more accurate time and cost planning estimates by comparing previous similar projects

- Improving the overall process

- Examining effectiveness of a methodology or tool

- Evaluating where defects are occurring throughout the process so they can be eliminated in future projects

When establishing and reviewing measurements, it is important to remember that the intent is to improve the process and not to attack the people involved. Productivity gains are usually lost when people feel they are being criticized. Also, improving communication in culturally diverse teams is an important consideration when breaking down the barriers that prevent success. (For additional information, see Abstract 7.4 at the end of this chapter.)

Getting Started

The measurement program should be a consistent, never-ending circle. The IT organization must initially set goals and review whether it has any existing measurements. Sample goals might be to achieve closer conformance to requirements or to reduce software development costs and delivery time.

A measurement should be meaningful, easily obtainable, consistently reproducible, pertinent, and have system-wide business applicability. A starting point *must* be established. It is suggested that a controlled activity be identified, a unit of measure chosen, a standard value used (to compare with the controlled activity), and a method chosen to measure the performance between the standard value and the created value. Each organization must establish its own guidelines according to what best meets its budget and quality control criteria. The findings should provide feedback to the entire organization for use in determining where there is potential room for improvement.

IT performance measurements should measure productivity gains, technical quality, and whether customer requirements were met. For example, if a larger computer is purchased to improve response time, the measurement would compare the original computer response time to the larger computer results using the same volumes and conditions. The Gardner Group[6] states that the measurement process must be integrated into development and maintenance environments, so that performing measurements becomes part of the way business is done. They also say that measurements can support strategic and tactical planning and can provide information for calculating the return on investment in IT.

IT measurement programs should include tracking work effort, evaluating project change activity, reviewing post-project problems, and surveying customers.

Tracking Work Effort

This method is good for measuring the time being spent on a new or existing project by task and individual. Based on the statistics, management is able to analyze actual versus estimated project time, provide improved estimates for future projects, monitor project estimates during project development, flag existing systems that continually require maintenance support, and schedule individual work assignments. Standard time reporting must be in place in order for this to be effective. When establishing a time tracking program, everyone must follow the same recording procedure. The following standards must be in place to measure accurately:

- Establish a standard work day, which is used to determine overtime
- Designate consistent project categories and tasks for all projects
- Determine the direct and indirect hours to be reported
- Define who records their time
- Design and implement a standard time reporting sheet or automated system

Tracking work effort can give the project team a history of project time and improve estimation accuracy. The estimation accuracy (EA) can be calculated using the following formula:

$$EA = \frac{\text{Estimated Value} - \text{Actual Value}}{\text{Actual Value}}$$

The estimation accuracy would then be compared to the quality standard set by the organization. Of course, in estimating projects the goal is 100 percent, but in the real world, the variance allowed is usually 10 percent (allowing for specific deviations).

Evaluating Project Change Activity

Change activity taking place during a project can be categorized into three different types:

1. Missed functionality/customer-need requirements
2. Deviations from the *expected* original functionality requirement
3. Problems discovered during the testing phase

Tracking the number and type of changes is a good measurement indicator to evaluate where there is room for improvement during each project methodology phase. During the project, a standard log should be generated tracking each change by type, phase within the project methodology, and time spent adding to or correcting the activity. These statistics can be used to measure against other comparable projects. (For additional information, see Abstract 7.5 at the end of this chapter.)

Reviewing Post-Project Problems

Post-project problems are situations that occur after the project is implemented and delivered to the customer. A standard log should be completed for each problem reported. Suggested information includes:

- *Type problem category*—Technology area where the problem occurred and where the problem should be forwarded (e.g., data center, applications support, telecommunications)

- *Severity level*—How much time until the problem must be corrected (e.g., now, within 24 hours, by week end and by month end)

- *Project*—The application project where the problem occurred

- *Date*—Date the problem was reported

- *Description*—A brief description of the problem

- *Contact*—Individual who reported the problem

- *Person assigned*—Individual assigned to correct the problem

- *Date corrected*—Date the problem was corrected

- *Problem resolution*—Description of what activity took place to correct the problem

- *Problem code*—Code indicating the cause of the problem as determined at resolution time (e.g., hardware failure, program bug, missed functionality, or scheduling)

- *Time spent*—Time spent correcting the problem (man-hours—time actually worked)

The problem log statistics can be used to measure software reliability. This includes how much time is being spent correcting problems and types of problems by project. Newer projects should have less problem reporting. This is a good measurement indicator to evaluate overall technical quality and to determine whether additional time is needed when conducting testing. These aspects can be used to anticipate the failure rate as software ages. Failure rate is defined as the number of problems reported divided by how much time it took to correct the problems.

The problem log tracking can be used to measure the number of new problems for a specified period of time and the turnaround time to service problems. Measuring the response time for open problems (RTOP) can be calculated using the following formula:

$$RTOP = \frac{\text{Total Time of All Problems Open}}{\text{Number of Open Problems}}$$

The average time taken to correct closed problems (TCCP) can be calculated using the following formula:

$$TCCP = \frac{\text{Total Time Closed Problems Were Open}}{\text{Number of Closed Problems}}$$

Comparing measurements is based on whatever specified time period is best for your organization. The specified time could be a daily, weekly, or monthly period.

Surveying Customers

A basic survey of IT customers is prepared and conducted, asking what they think of the IT organization and its service. A standard set of questions is generated and the results reviewed. The survey can be conducted and the results compared on a quarterly basis. The same customers are surveyed each time for consistent standard measurement. What better way to improve service to customers than by asking the customer directly?

Additional Measurement Considerations

When establishing IT measurements, it is important to consider effect on the business in addition to technical efficiency. This includes comparing functionality requested to what was delivered. During the functional phase of the project, customer needs and requirements were identified. During testing and after implementation, measurement criteria consist of reviewing the requirements and then comparing the expected results with the actual results. Table 7.3 provides a sample list of functionality requirement questions; the answers can be used to measure quality standards based on what was expected.

For most projects, a cost–benefit analysis is prepared before any project approvals are given. It is important to find out whether the anticipated savings and productivity gains were achieved. A projected cost savings is generally set before a project is initiated; this figure would be used as the measurement indicator.

Estimating Software Development Projects

It is difficult to create an accurate estimate for a software project. The situation is complicated by the fact that IT is often asked to provide an estimate before the business requirements are complete. IT should be given the opportunity to revise estimates after each step in the project methodology, especially after the business requirements (phase I) and functional requirements (phase II) steps. When the business requirements have been written, the final processing functional points still have not been determined and additional processes may be identified during the final conceptual design. When the functional phase is completed, all processing points should have been identified and the estimate can be measured against the result. This is a Catch-22, situation, however, as the software estimate is usually needed before IT knows how much work will be involved. To make matters worse, management usually will not allow changes to the estimate without good reason. Often the result is that management urges IT to assign extra people to the project, but there are limits. Remember, "nine women can't produce a baby in one month."

In addition to past history, the following should be considered: the size of the effort, company environment, IT staff, and other miscellaneous factors discussed below. (For additional information, see Abstract 7.6 at the end of this chapter.)

Size of Effort

The size of the effort can be estimated by counting the number of business process activities (called function points by IBM). The basic idea is to determine how many inputs, outputs, queries, processes, and files are involved. For example, suppose it takes an average of 3 man-days (working constantly) to create an input. If there are 10 inputs, then 30 man-days would be the estimate for inputs. The same procedure is followed for outputs, etc.

The sum-of-basic-function-points estimate should then factor in extra time for multiple locations, higher volumes, performance, complexity of processes, telecommunications, reusability, external customer involvement, and changes.

Company Environment

Any project estimate should consider company culture and customer involvement in past projects. When the customer is resistant to change or has not been involved in projects, extra time should be factored into the estimate. The requirements change rate will be higher when the end user does not participate in up-front planning and design.

Information Technology Staff

The expertise and size of the IT staff are factors which should be considered. Major projects using new technologies may require obtaining outside expertise to supplement staff skills. Additional IT staff training may be required, which adds to the estimate.

Miscellaneous Considerations

New projects often entail using new technologies. The estimate should consider whether the technologies have a proven track record.

When a pre-set deadline date is mandated, the existing staff size may not suffice and temporary help may be needed, adding to the estimate.

Misunderstandings most frequently occur between IT and its customers when the customer has a mental picture of what the final result will be but fails to communicate that image fully to the implementors. As part of any specification or plan, it is always a good idea to review a "mock-up" or prototype report, screen, or process flow. Unless IT has this information, it is difficult to estimate time and difficulty. The user also appreciates the thoroughness and a chance to participate in the planning process. This same method may be used when an existing process requires change or conversion.

Some projects require a conversion from an existing system to meet the new process requirements. When this is necessary, the estimate must include the planning, designing, building, and testing time required to convert the old process to the new.

WHAT CAUSES PROJECTS TO FAIL

Inevitably, some projects will fail. Factors that contribute to failure include:

- Inexperienced management and lack of skill
- Rudimentary planning techniques
- No previous situation to compare in order to accurately estimate the project
- Relationships between business functional areas, including IT, poorly handled
- Management did not follow through on meeting its commitment
- Poor planning, follow-through, and status reporting
- Appropriate knowledgeable people were not involved
- No communication or forewarning about the project
- Project was delivered to business areas before they were involved or trained
- New tools and techniques were used without proper training or outside expertise to help teach their proper usage

SUMMARY

Every project should have a project team and subproject teams that are responsible for the project request. The teams are responsible for ensuring the success of the project and are involved from start to finish. Before any project development methodology can be successful, commitment must be received from senior management and standard methodologies set in place. There are six basic phases in the project development methodology which must be completed when quality control standards are being meet. There is no single methodology a company must follow. A successful methodology complements how the company conducts business and is consistent with company goals and objectives. (For additional information, see Abstract 7.7 at the end of this chapter.)

ENDNOTES

1. *Webster's Encyclopedic Unabridged Dictionary of the English Language* (1989). New York: Portland House, a division of Dilithium Press, Ltd.
2. Shore, Joel (1989). *Using Computers in Business.* Carmel, IN: Que Corporation.
3. Lewis, Ralph and Smith, Douglas (1994). *Total Quality in Higher Education.* Delray Beach, FL: St. Lucie Press, p. 189.
4. Schultz, Louis E. (1989). *Personal Management.* Minneapolis: Process Management International.
5. Rowan, T.G. (1982). *Managing with Computers.* London: Heineman, p. 125.
6. Gardner Group Continuous Services (1993). "AD Metrics: A Foundation for Improved Quality and Productivity." *ADM Strategic Analysis Report,* January 4, 1993.

EXERCISE

EXERCISE 7.1 FOUR STEPS FOR DEVELOPING EFFECTIVE TEAMS

1. *Vision Statement*—Create a vision statement of the ideal team three to five years into the future. Answer the questions: "What can we do?" and "Where can we be?"

   Examples—To provide top quality customer service to our clients when they request information about any of the company's products or services. To be one of the top five companies in our industry according to customer surveys conducted by outside marketing firms.

2. *Purpose*—Define why the team is needed. Answer the question: "Why does the team exist?"

   Examples—Provide multiple customer services with one central customer support center. Provide integrated sales and marketing product offerings.

3. *Principles and Values*—Define the principles and values that will guide the team members' actions. Be certain they relate to company ethical standards and values. Answer the question: "What are the principles and values we consider most important in working toward our vision?"

   Examples—
   1. Continuously seek ways to improve business processes
   2. Develop and practice listening skills
   3. Encourage open discussion and welcome everyone's opinion
   4. Encourage initiative
   5. Work as a team and support each other
   6. Continue to learn
   7. Maintain a positive approach
   8. Assist with improving other teams and business processes
   9. Serve the customer's need
   10. Provide support in seeking and conducting research
   11. Encourage creativity and innovative ideas
   12. Maintain a positive attitude

4. *Mission Statement*—Develop a unit mission that will serve as a guideline for decision making by everyone on the team. Be consistent and identify areas for which the team will be responsible. Answer the question: "How will we move toward the vision?"

   Examples—Our mission is to plan for and implement the best customer support service center in our industry. Our services will allow customers to be served in a minimum of time. Customers will be able to receive product information from one central point versus having to call multiple service areas.

Our mission is to plan and install an intercompany employee growth and incentive program. This incentive program will fairly distribute information about company work positions and expectations and will provide a way to compensate employees and teams who are exceptional performers.

ABSTRACTS

ABSTRACT 7.1
STUDY SHOWS STRONG EVIDENCE THAT
PARTICIPATIVE MANAGEMENT PAYS OFF

Lawler, Edward E. III et al.
Total Quality Newsletter, September 1992, pp. 1–4

In this excerpt from a new book, *Employee Involvement and Total Quality Management: Practices and Results in Fortune 1000 Companies,* the authors present comparisons of surveys sent to Fortune 1000 companies in 1987 and 1990, with 51 percent and 32 percent response rates, respectively. The article includes several bar graphs and charts which compare 1987 and 1990 data. There seems to be little difference between the surveys in reasons for implementing employee involvement (EI) programs: improving quality and productivity are still at the top (about 70 percent each), followed by improving employee motivation and improving employee morale (about 55 percent each). "Most employees, in a 3-year period, did not receive training in interpersonal skills or in the kinds of technical/analytical skills necessary for an employee involvement or total quality program to work effectively," say the authors, the data showing little change from 1987. Only 9 percent of the organizations recently trained more than 60 percent of their employees in TQM and statistical analysis, and only 2 percent have trained 60 percent in understanding financial reports and business results. All but 10 percent of the corporations have some employees covered by individual incentives, but they usually cover less than 40 percent of the work force. Overall, the success ratings for the pay-for-performance reward systems associated with EI programs are extremely positive. Highest ratings were for profit-sharing and employee stock ownership programs, but 43 percent of respondents were undecided with respect to the success of gainsharing. Work group or team incentives indicated 51 percent undecided, but few reported failure. While support by top management retained its lead as a condition facilitating EI (50 percent), support by middle management dropped from 39 percent to 26 percent over 3 years, reflecting the ambivalence middle managers have toward EI when they see how the programs will force behavior changes and reduce their numbers. The greatest improvement in internal processes is reported in participatory management, technology implementation, trust management, decision making, and organizational processes and procedures. Quality, service, and productivity are reported improved as a result of EI efforts in about two-thirds of companies. The relationship between TQM and EI follows no clear pattern, with slightly more than one-third of companies managing EI and TQM as one integrated program, a third managing them as separate but coordinated programs, and the other third managing them separately. Still, respondents tended to view EI as part of quality (76 percent), rather than quality as part of EI. (©*Quality Abstracts*)

ABSTRACT 7.2
THE QUALITY TEAM CONCEPT IN TOTAL QUALITY CONTROL

Ryan, John M.
ASQC Quality Press, Milwaukee, 1992, 272 pp.

"This book's intent," explains the author, "is to provide the reader with a comprehensive look at how various techniques, methods, and strategies fit together to restructure an organization's culture by building and implementing an overall team approach to total quality control/just-in-time (TQC/JIT)." The author focuses on a JIT approach to process improvement as a subset of TQC. In the first chapter, he relates JIT to TQC and discusses basic JIT terms and concepts, illustrating them with a variety of graphs. The second chapter explains how a company can organize the three types of teams required to implement and support a TQC/JIT system:

- *Top-level team (TLT)*—He explains how to select participants from the upper levels of management, and then he outlines and explains the specific responsibilities of this team to write and manage a plan for system implementation and maintenance.

- *Corrective actions teams (CATs)*—After the TLT identifies company-wide problems, it assigns CATs to solve the problems. This chapter outlines the basic guidelines by which a CAT runs.

- *Functional improvement teams (FITs)*—These teams are formed in every department to identify and correct problems which are more or less confined to their own operations. The author gives a list of guidelines for running FIT meetings, along with the responsibilities of the leader.

The next chapter gives a detailed description of how to implement a FIT. The principles, he explains, are nearly identical to those that govern the implementation of CATs. The author introduces flowcharting and the types of graphs through which to communicate information. This section also includes a number of forms and examples of implementation in various companies. The next chapter describes specialized CATs for solving specific problems, such as the pilot line, vendor relationships, value engineering, design for manufacturability, parts commonality, preventive maintenance, foolproofing, process layout and line balancing, lot size reduction, organizing and cleaning the workplace, *kanban*, line stop, SPC, visual signals (ANDON), training (certification), setup time reduction, automation review, and cycle time control. Chapter 5 deals with the principles of cost savings. A final chapter summarizes the commitment needed by top management to make the system work. This book provides practical, detailed help with team implementation. Though most of the examples are from a manufacturing setting, the author assures the reader that the principles also apply to non-manufacturing functions as well. (©*Quality Abstracts*)

ABSTRACT 7.3
TQM: A STEP-BY-STEP GUIDE TO IMPLEMENTATION

Weaver, Charles N.
Quality Press, Milwaukee, 1991, 235 pp.

While it doesn't make sense implementing TQM like making "instant pudding," this book does offer a useful step-by-step approach. The author introduces a combination of TQM and a management information system called the "methodology for generating efficiency and effectiveness measures," and he proceeds to use the acronym TQM/MGEEM throughout the book to identify this system. He suggests beginning a comprehensive education based on Deming's and Juran's philosophies to help change the corporate culture a few months prior to introducing TQM/MGEEM. The book begins with a description of the quality problem in America. Then successive chapters describe in considerable detail the steps which need to be taken to implement TQM/MGEEM, down to the content of the leaders' talks and the group processes to be used. Briefly, the TQM/MGEEM program revolves around Blue Teams and Gold Teams for each organization within a company.

- The Blue Team for a department is composed of a facilitator, the manager, immediate superiors and immediate subordinates, and representative customers and suppliers. The team uses nominal group techniques to review the department's mission statement, and then it breaks the mission into measurable parts called "key result areas" (KRAs).

- The Gold Teams, formed from the manager's subordinates and key workers, are led by facilitators to develop indicators to measure the KRAs.

These teams also build a feedback chart for each indicator to be used for periodic feedback on the KRAs' progress.

* Members of each department participate in monthly feedback meetings, where they (1) review progress on their charts, (2) share ideas on how to improve the process by which work is accomplished, and (3) discuss how to eliminate unnecessary bureaucracy. Suppliers and customers can attend these meetings to provide input on their expectations and ideas for improvement.   (©*Quality Abstracts*)

ABSTRACT 7.4
AFTER PRODUCT QUALITY IN JAPAN: MANAGEMENT QUALITY

Yahagi, Seiichiro
National Productivity Review, Autumn 1992, pp. 501–515

This is one of the most important new articles to come out of Japan in 1992, and the implications are enormous. The author proposes the use of expert systems featuring a 12-factor model organized into 41 "elements" of measuring subfactors. Japanese management has moved beyond product quality, says the author, to an emphasis on total integrated management (TIM)— management concerned about each facet of the company and interrelating them into a concerted, comprehensive corporate management policy of innovation. The author has developed an expert system which measures the 12 factors that determine management quality, divided into 41 subfactors:

* Corporate history: past, present, and future

* Corporate climate: core climate and culture

* Strategic alliances: objectives and coherence

* Channels: suppliers and buyers

* Management cycle: vision, strategy, planning, organizing and implementing, and controlling

* Environment: economic, societal, and global

* Management targets: inputs, markets, technologies, and products

* Business structure: business fields, business mix, and market standing

* Management resources: money, materials, information, and people

* Management design: system, organization, authority, and responsibility

- Management functions: decision making, interrelationships, and quality
- Management performance: growth, scale, stability, profit, and market share

He sees six factors as critical to the success of a company: management cycle, business structure, management resources, management design, corporate culture, and management performance. These six factors are interrelated in a circulatory system of Management Quality factors which have a cause-and-effect relationship as follows. The management cycle acts as the driver and influencer of the four factors of structure, resources, design, and culture, which in turn affect management performance. If the quality level of the management cycle is low, then the six factors generate a negative or bad feedback loop which finds management passively waiting until poor results of management performance force reactionary feedback into the management flow.* If the quality level of the management cycle is high, then these six factors generate an excellent feedforward loop in which management perceives the strategies and plans needed for success of each management factor and then proactively formulates and implements them.

The author's consulting organization conducts an annual survey of the management practices of Japanese firms, and in this article he presents the results of the most recent survey, which represents input from about 200 firms. Graphs and charts show comparisons between the worst-scoring and best-scoring companies, and he uses creative graphics to illustrate his analytical technique and to summarize questionnaire responses. From this comparison, he deduces a number of principles: (a) management quality factors must be well-balanced, (b) management cycle is the key to the management quality loop, and (c) the dynamics of TIM must be considered. He then goes on to describe the management cycle, which consists of the following key components: vision, strategy, planning, organizing, implementing, and controlling. The author recommends using an annual questionnaire to first analyze management factors within a company and then develop a multiphase action plan to restructure an organization for TIM. This article by Yahagi is must-reading for anyone who wants to remain on the leading edge of new application-oriented technology.

---

*According to Yahagi, the circulatory aspects of the management quality system are a key to understanding the relationships of this system to others, such as the Malcolm Baldrige National Quality Award.

ABSTRACT 7.5
THE PHASES OF DATA ANALYSIS

Cleary, Michael J. and Tickel, Craig M.
Quality Progress, February 1992, pp. 57–59

With Deming's claim that Japan's economic success has stemmed from the proper use of statistical analysis in its production process, U.S. organizations have developed a strong interest in statistical process control. But rather than making frantic efforts to master these particular skills, say the authors, an organization should expect to go through four distinct phases in implementing data analysis techniques:

1. *Hand calculation*—Manual data collection and preparation of control charts is a fundamental way to learn how a process works. However, it is prone to errors and does not make it easy to apply more advanced analysis techniques.

2. *Computer applications*—Readily available PC software packages will help the user chart more accurately, and they contain enhanced statistical tools for analysis.

3. *Data collection devices*—Data collection devices which allow data to be collected directly from the production process provide timely and accurate data.

4. *Online systems*—When automatic collection systems are connected directly to the computer, immediate analysis is available. The authors warn, however, against overcontrol from automatic adjustment systems.

The authors also caution against letting data collection become an end in itself. Successful programs emphasize problem solving and analysis, not charting. These should be seen as tools to address the issue of continuous improvement.   (©*Quality Abstracts*)

ABSTRACT 7.6
QUALITY CONCERNS IN SOFTWARE DEVELOPMENT:
THE CHALLENGE IS CONSISTENCY

Perry, William E.
Information Systems Management, Spring 1992, pp. 48–52

Current software quality levels in the United States are 4.5 defects per 1,000 lines of code, compared to Japanese levels of 1.5 per 1,000. The difficulty in improving software quality, says the author, is in defining what quality is. "If quality means meeting specifications and standards, the definition of those specifications and standards is the definition of quality. In essence, every organization establishes its own quality definition." The remainder of the article concentrates on the information systems (IS) department's own internal standards. While critics argue that standards inhibit creativity, the author contends that standards produce a vital consistency. Internal characteristics of software which must be controlled by standards, according to the author, include: correctness, reliability, efficiency, integrity, usability, maintainability, and testability. However, in organizations with finite resources, these quality attributes must be prioritized so that programmers will emphasize those that reflect the users' needs rather than their own. Moreover, the author faults unrealistic scheduling with degradation of software quality. He concludes the article with three major suggestions:

- The IS standards committee should develop the standards it believes are necessary to meet each of the quality attributes listed above, making quality rather than uniformity its main objective.

- The user should be asked to prioritize each of the quality attributes so the developers can create the structure that best meets the user's needs.

- The estimating system should be designed to produce a schedule to build the software, but once the estimate has been established, meeting the estimate should not be the major concern of IS management. Instead, they should focus on those quality attributes.

ABSTRACT 7.7
TEAM DEVELOPMENT: THIS IS HOW IT'S DONE

Gold, Jeffrey (editor)
Executive Development, Vol. 5 No. 3, 1992, pp. 1–32

This entire issue of *Executive Development* is devoted to the process of developing teams—both training members of a management team and training members of work teams. The individual articles include:

- "Building Our Team—From the End of a Rope"—Explores training a management team through outdoor training.

- "Measures Which Help You Work Together as a Team"—Discusses three different feedback instruments: the Types of Work Index, the Team Management Index, and the Linking Skills Index.

- "Improved Teamworking Using a Computer System"—Reviews the computer-based Belbin *Interplace III Expert System* that is used to help determine and understand an individual's team role.

- "From Public to Private: The Team Approach at Scottish Hydro Electric plc"—Outlines a development program for 130 senior managers.

- "Management Team Building: An Experience at BT"—Explains a management team development workshop at British Telecom.

- "Organizational Change Through Team Development at BICC"—Describes a senior management team development exercise at a company implementing work teams throughout its organization.

- "Team-Built Teams"—Reviews three-day team-building workshops at Colworth House Laboratories as part of a total quality initiative.

- "Developing the Team at Northamptonshire Police"—Describes a management team development effort.

- "Know Thy Team—and Play Your Trump Card!"—Outlines the *TeamBuilder* analysis of five team roles used at a London-based design company.

- "Improvement Teams at Champion Spark Plug"—Describes workshops to train total quality management improvement teams at a manufacturing plant.   (©*Quality Abstracts*)

CHAPTER 8

"HOW-TO"
TECHNIQUES
AND TOOLS

The purpose of this chapter is to present a "how-to" methodology to define and design processes using various techniques and tools available to implement quality. These tools and techniques are used internally and jointly by the business and information technology functions. It is important to mention at the outset that *methodology* is a *way for people to approach solving problems* in an organized, team-oriented fashion, whereas *techniques and tools* are *used to deliver improvements* that are envisioned and planned when using the methodology.

DEFINITION OF TECHNIQUES AND TOOLS

Techniques are a method used in performing functions or tasks. Tools are implements used to perform the functions or tasks. Techniques and tools work hand in hand to improve quality and productivity. A tool is usually given a name denoting the type of work performed. Tools can be equipment, computer software, or a standardized, codified series of steps to accomplish a specific end. Many other definitions are possible for both techniques and tools, but the above will suffice here. Even pencil and paper can be defined as tools.

CONSIDERATIONS WHEN USING TECHNIQUES AND TOOLS

It is important to remember that there is no one right or wrong way when deciding which techniques and tools should be used to improve business and technical functions. Each company must implement the techniques that will work best for that particular organization. Companies have different goals and objectives. Any technique being used should be periodically reviewed and modified to meet changes in philosophy, business, or technical areas. If the proper tools and techniques are carefully selected, a company can achieve success.

Companies of all sizes should use some type of technique or tool to document and standardize processing and communications methods. A technique can be as simple as a business plan. Every company, even the one-person owner, should have a business plan to define the goals and objectives of the business.

When a small company experiences sudden growth, the CEO can no longer keep tabs on all day-to-day events and processing. Without standard techniques, the employees and company no longer function efficiently. Once a firm reaches approximately 60 employees, the "way it's always been done" is no longer acceptable if the company wants to grow and develop. The company must reassess business plans and workflows to implement techniques and tools that complement business goals and objectives. Standard written communication methods and policies *must* be developed as the company outgrows the "word of mouth" communication that is no longer effective in a larger organization.

Smaller companies can use techniques and tools to a lesser extent, but since both communication and control are tighter, a small firm must beware of overkill when determining which methods to utilize.

There are many different products available representing various techniques and tools. Each vendor says, "We will meet your business needs!" or "You must have this; it's the newest thing out and everyone has it!" The reality, however, is that someone is trying to make a sale instead of addressing the company's best interests. Firms often purchase products that are inappropriate for their size and business processing needs or products that allow for future growth. Once a company identifies its business needs, a thorough vendor product evaluation and selection analysis should take place before investing money in any product. There are many products defined as techniques and tools from which to choose. These choices are *business decisions* that must take information technology into consideration (not the other way around). A firm can save money by knowing what it really needs and taking the time to do comparison shopping.

Whatever techniques and tools a company selects, they must be installed and used in a standardized storyboard fashion throughout all departments.

It is critical that every employee be thoroughly trained in the use of the tools, the techniques, and the storyboard before going into production mode. Any benefit is negated when one department uses one method and another department uses another method or an employee is told to use a tool or technique without being trained. This creates an organizational "Tower of Babel." *Consistency*—in communication, measurement, and method—can be lost in this manner and any attempt to achieve true progress is also lost. (For additional information, see Abstract 8.1 at the end of this chapter.)

TECHNIQUES AND NONSTATISTICAL TOOLS

The following represents a sampling of available techniques and tools. The list is intentionally not product name specific. Our purpose is to provide a guideline and create awareness that a product or method exists. The intent is not to endorse any product or vendor, since numerous companies offer these techniques and/or tools. A company should conduct a thorough analysis and feasibility study before implementing anything new in its quality control process. Not doing so only courts disaster.

Business Plan

A plan is a scheme for action to accomplish a specific purpose. A company may have many plans, each a part of the master corporate business plan. Each department should have its own plan. Departmental business plans must tie into the overall corporate plan and show appropriate linkage to corporate quality systems.

The goal of the business plan should be to:

- Provide a method to translate customer needs into specific action
- Focus business activities to achieve customer satisfaction
- Align control/improvement activities at all levels of the organization with corporate policy
- Communicate chronic high-priority problems and target them for improvement

Planning and communication of the plan gives everyone in the company a common direction.

Change Management

This methodology is used to track and communicate changes. A commonly understood plan for modification preserves a "business as usual" attitude as project development takes place within the company.

Information technology should have a separate change management process to handle software code, documentation, equipment, and data.

When everyone in the company knows what is going on and is aware of any changes taking place, fear and uncertainty are minimized.

Education and Training

TQM begins with education and training that never ends. The Japanese philosophy is to first train your employees and *then* you can make changes. The integration of training into system building and conversion is very important. There is a cost to good training, but any other alternative is more expensive.

Employees must be involved and educated before using any newly introduced processes or systems. Employees should be introduced to and trained in a new process before starting to serve customers. Quality service can be greatly affected when training occurs during process introduction.

Any company success is based on employee acceptance. You cannot please everyone, but most people can be less fearful and less resistant to change. Investment in education and training can pay rich dividends.

Management-by-Walking-Around (MBWA)

MBWA is a very positive management tool. Using the Plan-Do-Check-Act cycle, MBWA, and formal reviews educates everyone involved and creates understanding of issues/concerns faced by the entire organization. Senior managers, for instance, should not sit in their offices and only speak with their immediate links in the chain of command. If you really want to know what is going on within the company, talk to all employees, at all levels. It is surprising what information can be gained and the amount of feedback that is shared once trust is established. Managers should recall what it was like before they reached their present positions and stay in touch with employees. This is an excellent means to continually improve.

Benchmarking

Benchmarking is used to measure and to compare work processes, equipment, systems, or individual performance (of people or a department) with others either inside or outside the organization. This helps establish standards of excellence. Benchmarking helps groups/individuals to learn the innovations and best practices of other groups or companies, set targets based on data, and convince people that "we can do better, measure performance, and be a more outside-world-focused instead of inner-focused company." It leads to significant improvements in cost, quality, cycle time, and competitive ability.[1]

Brainstorming

In this technique, ideas are generated by a group. The ideas are not open to discussion and every idea is considered. A team of representatives from all areas, including information technology, is assembled for a brief period of time. The participants offer suggestions and consider "what if" situations. The reasoning behind the technique is "two heads are better than one."

Nominal Group Technique (NGT)

This tool is a structured group decision-making process used to assign priorities or rank order groups of ideas. NGT is used where agreement about a decision is lacking or where group members have incomplete knowledge of the details of a problem. It was developed by Delbecq and his colleagues in the 1970s[1] and has been used for a wide variety of organizational development and improvement activities. For example, it was used to obtain responses from a focus group of business faculty on the type and relative importance of changes that were needed in a comprehensive revision of an MBA program at a state university.

The process for performing the NGT is as follows:

- Silent (written) generation of ideas in response to a focused question

- Round-robin recording (usually on a flip chart) of one idea at a time from each group member by a designated recorder

- Clarify ideas through questions from group members as to the meaning of various listed items

- Vote on ideas to prioritize importance; uses a one- or two-stage process

- Closure on a decision of what to do about the prioritized items

For additional information, see Abstract 8.2 at the end of this chapter.

Joint Application Development (JAD)

In this method, all business and technology areas participate in planning and designing the system. It is usually divided into two separate phases which can consist of multiple sessions. A skilled outside facilitator should be used to facilitate the sessions. This technique is used during phase I (project development) and phase II (functional requirements) of the project development methodology.

The benefit is that everyone in the company is working in the same direction and toward the same purpose. All areas involved are working together, at the same time, planning and designing. This technique enhances the communication process and speeds development time because all participants are brought together as a company team.

Computer-Aided Software Engineering (CASE)

CASE is a collection of techniques and tools directed toward developing and maintaining software systems of all types. It provides project management as well as project development life cycle analysis, design, implementation, and maintenance support.

CASE is not recommended unless a company has already installed a proven project development methodology. A company can have the best CASE tools in the world to document and support product development, but if requirements are not defined in detail up front, the tools will not be effective. When CASE tools are used, they must blend in with some process and employees must be properly trained in their use. Numerous vendors sell CASE tools, but the tool purchased must meet a company's needs. Senior management must make an initial heavy investment and allow time for processes to be changed when using this new way of developing and maintaining systems.

Object-Oriented Design/Programming (OOD/OOP)

Object-oriented is "breaking into parts" functions that are performed in the same way and have common behavior. Each module is related to and communicates with another. Each module is considered "reusable," which benefits information technology by allowing the same modules (programs) to be used for other similar processes. Once the modules have been identified and the initial development efforts have taken place, reusing modules can expedite making changes and decrease maintenance time. This is similar to the top-down method, but there is more emphasis on how modules communicate and are related to one another versus emphasizing program development and testing modularity.

Structured Design/Programming

This was the trend in the 1970s, but it is being replaced by the object-oriented methodology. The method is directed more toward helping information technology program development and testing efforts. The overall process is designed, programmed, and tested in a modular fashion by function. The concept is to design programs that are reusable when performing common functionality. The premise is why reinvent the wheel when an existing process meets the need. Object-oriented methods expanded on this concept by including more information about how the modules communicate with and are related to each other. Top-down is mentioned only as a "nice-to-know."

Graphical User Interface (GUI)

This is a display format which enables the user of an online system to choose functions from pictures (icons). Instead of pressing a key to request an option, the user points to his or her request and clicks using a mouse. This method forces a modular design by business processing functions. This format is excellent, particularly when developing systems that support customer service inquiry.

Prototyping

Prototyping is the creation of a preliminary model that the business and technical areas try out to determine whether the system meets request objectives. This would be comparable to a sample in manufacturing. Everyone is given the opportunity to identify any difficulties before full technology development efforts are completed. An example would be designing the online screens and letting the customer navigate from one process to another. Prototyping saves time and money because the customer receives a preliminary preview and design problems can be addressed before coding begins. It should be used far more than it is.

Data Dictionary

This is a central repository for all the data elements. It can retain information about files, data definitions, fields, edits, and variables as well as whatever information the user wants to know about a data element. A company must generate standards for usage before a dictionary can be used efficiently and effectively. This is an excellent tool for decreasing information technology change-response time because it defines data element usage throughout the company. When developing a system, it can be an invaluable reference. It is difficult to see how earlier data processing existed without a data dictionary; in fact, COBOL was very popular in particular because it demanded a "data division" (at least on a program-by-program basis) that defined inputs and outputs in a dictionary-like manner.

Plan-Do-Check-Act (PDCA)

The PDCA cycle is a critical part of the management system and provides a means to gain knowledge from all employees, to communicate plans and activities, and to negotiate contributions to corporate policies.

Quality Function Deployment (QFD)

QFD is tied to customer needs and is an excellent method to systematically focus on the most important issues from the customer's viewpoint. What the customer wants and how this project will solve the problem are clearly stated, keeping technology in mind. This is an excellent method for helping to identify detailed project requests and for measuring improvement.

STATISTICAL TOOLS

Organization and resolution statistical tools are used when a project includes a large amount of varied data and the issue requires analysis. (For additional information, see Abstract 8.3 at the end of this chapter.) The basic statistical tools are as follows.

Control Charts and Graphs

Control charts and graphs are means to present information in the form of a picture. One example would be to show the variance between actual and estimated. This method monitors the ongoing performance of an activity. It can be immediate or over time. The type of analysis conducted and each presenter's personal preference determines which type of graph will be used. Each graph has its own application value. Some of the types of graphs are:

- Bar
- Line
- Circle or pie
- Radar

Flowchart

Flowcharts are commonly used and are a natural for the information technologist. They are not, however, an accepted way to stratify and recognize variation. Stratification is the arrangement of components within a whole.

A process flowchart is a visual representation of the steps in a given process (business or technical). The steps are sequential and the chart reflects how the process functions.

Upon reviewing a documented flowchart, it is easier to recognize redundant activities or missing steps. A flowchart shows:

- How the process works, like a factual "road map"
- Where there are interfaces with other key activities
- Where control points and measurements should be developed

Check Sheet

A check sheet is used to identify tasks and measure their status using a standard format. This tool is used when it is extremely important to capture the correct information in a timely manner and over a period of time. Check sheets provide a means to record events in a concise manner. The degree of accuracy achieved is dependent upon the number of people collecting the data and the level of detail they provide. It is a good tool for analyzing information.

The check sheet provides a means to simplify a process by preprinting the items to be checked. It serves three major purposes:

1. Makes the task easy
2. Standardizes and reduces variation
3. Arranges the information for future ease of use

Scatter Diagram

The scatter diagram is an analytical graph in which data items are plotted as points on an X–Y coordinate axis. Real-world conditions require us to study many variables. A scatter diagram is a graph showing the relationship between two variables. It helps to show:

- Cause and effect
- Relationship between characteristics
- Patterns and pictures of the variables

Histogram

The histogram is used to measure frequency of occurrence, which is displayed as a frequency distribution. It is represented as a vertical bar chart. The column widths are the interval ranges and the lengths are the frequencies.

If all data were constant and predictable, the world would be very orderly and probably very boring. However, data, like nature and people, do not always remain in a constant state. One of the basic principles of TQM and continuous improvement is management by facts. The histogram is a means to collect data and determine facts.

Pareto Diagram

The Pareto diagram is a technique to graphically display the ranking of causes from the most to least significant. It provides a means to break down the "countless many" in order to identify the "vital few."

Cause-and-Effect or Fishbone Diagram

The cause-and-effect diagram is a visual display illustrating the relationship of various causes and symptoms to a specific effect. It helps identify the root causes of a problem. The cause-and-effect and Pareto diagrams can be powerful allies when used properly.

Gantt Chart

This is a horizontal bar chart that shows the project plan over a period of time. It can show the tasks, areas of responsibility, milestones, critical paths, start and end dates—the list can go on and on. The content will be the factors that are necessary to manage and keep track of the progress of the project over time and ensure that it is on schedule and within budget. It a way to measure project status. A documented project plan keeps all involved parties aware of their deliverables and when their portions must be completed. It is a superior communication tool.

Program Evaluation and Review Technique (PERT)

PERT is commonly used to monitor large, long-term projects and their critical paths. It involves analysis of the time frame required for each step in a process and the relationship of the completion of each step to activity in previous steps. The chart is shown as circles (work elements against time) and connecting lines.

Graphical Evaluation and Review Technique (GERT)

This procedure is used for the formation and evaluation of systems using a network approach. The relationships between project activities, tasks, and events are documented. This method is used to organize data in artificial intelligence systems.

Data Flow Diagram

This is a graphical analysis and design tool that represents the flow of data through a system.

Hierarchy Plus Input–Process–Output (HIPO)

The standard format is divided into three basic categories using document work flows or system processes. All process inputs are shown, the process function(s) are delineated, and all outputs are defined in detail.

Affinity Diagram/KJ Method

This method organizes pieces of information into groupings based on the natural relationships that exist among them. It is used when large volumes of information are being gathered.

PERIODICALS AND NEWSPAPERS

The following is a list of nonindustry-specific periodicals and newspapers. They provide articles to assist management in remaining up-to-date with business and technology issues, services, and products.

- *Business Week*
- *BYTE (sometimes more technical)*
- *CIO (Chief Information Officer)*
- *Computerworld*
- *Datamation*
- *The Economist*
- *EDI World*
- *Entrepreneur*
- *Forbes ASAP*
- *Fortune*
- *Harvard Business Review*
- *IBM Systems Journal*
- *Information & Management Journal*

- *Information Week*
- *PC World* (sometimes more technical)
- *Profit*
- *Sloan Management Review*

ENDNOTE

1. Delbecq, A.L., Van de Ven, A.H., and Gustafson, D.H. (1975). *Group Techniques for Program Planning: A Guide to Nominal and Delphi Processes.* Glenview, IL: Scott Foresman.

ABSTRACTS

ABSTRACT 8.1
STORYBOARD: A CREATIVE, TEAM-BASED APPROACH TO PLANNING AND PROBLEM-SOLVING

Shepard, Dick
Continuous Journey, December 1992–January 1993, pp. 24–25, 31

The storyboard is a creative problem-solving tool which allows teams to assemble and process information and ideas in an efficient and effective way, says the author. An illustration pictures a typical storyboard layout on a wall or portable bulletin board, with colored cards affixed with pushpins. A *topic card* (5" × 7") defines the subject of the session. *Header cards* (4" × 6") provide column headings for major subjects under which *subber cards* (3" × 5") expand the ideas, with occasional *sider cards* (2 1/2" × 3") which modify other cards. Colored yarn is used to frame, divide, or connect ideas. The author recommends assigning one of the group to serve as facilitator, rotating this assignment every 30 to 45 minutes. The facilitator switches the group from creative (right-brained brainstorming) to critical (left-brained analysis) modes as the storyboard develops. During the creative times, participants write their ideas with marker pen on the cards and pin them to the board. The critical periods organize and provide opportunity for objection and countering. The article concludes with a discussion of four specialized types of storyboard approaches: idea, planning, communication, and organization.   (©*Quality Abstracts*)

ABSTRACT 8.2
TAKING QUALITY BEYOND THE AWARENESS STAGE

Wetzel, Charles F. Jr. and Yencho, Nancy M.
Journal for Quality and Participation, January–February 1992, pp. 36–41

"How can we get real performance with results from TQM?" The experiences of the RENEW team at Boeing Materiel exemplify how one can put the theory of quality into practical terms and actually improve work processes. Continuous quality improvement (CQI) is the term Boeing uses to represent its commitment to a total quality environment. When it set up the new entity of

Boeing Materiel, it saw an opportunity to pilot test innovations and extensions of the CQI concept. A team was assembled from eight Boeing Materiel employees and three consultants from the firm of IRD/Macro International. The primary objective of their pilot study was: "Improving the cycle time of major information processes, ensuring the effective utilization of people and improving information quality flow." To accomplish this, a PC-based software program called *RENEW* (from IRD/Macro International) was used to:

1. Gather and analyze data on organizational processes

2. Make recommendations for improvement

3. Create action plans to implement the improvements

Considerable detail is given here on the several surveys conducted, the functions the program performs, and the subsequent data analysis. Nonvalue activities were eliminated, processes were improved, and more emphasis was placed on "taking time to do the job right the first time." The pilot program allowed all the employees to see CQI in action with open channels of communication and a set of measurable goals.   (©*Quality Abstracts*)

ABSTRACT 8.3
MEETINGS ANONYMOUS: IBM DOES IT WITH COMPUTERS

Grimaldi, Lisa
Meetings & Conventions, January 1992, pp. 100–102

This author suggests that trainers may find themselves as facilitators of "silent meetings," if IBM's *TeamFocus* software gains wide acceptance in corporate America. IBM developed the silent meeting to brainstorm and process ideas several years ago, but the company found it so successful—cutting the time of the average business meeting by 60 percent—that it has begun to market the computer program on which the silent meeting is based. The program, installed on a file server, links up to 24 desktop PCs. The typical meeting follows the sequence below:

1. During a brainstorming session, participants are given the topic to be "discussed" and are asked to type all their ideas into the computer.

2. The server collects and sorts the comments and sends them back to the participants so each can see what colleagues have written.

3. The facilitator and participants arrange these ideas into 10 to 15 categories.

4. Categories are then sent to participants who rank the categories in order of importance.

5. Finally the information and votes are printed out, eliminating the need for notetaking.

The power of the method seems to reside in: (1) allowing ideas to be shared without fear of reprisal and (2) saving time that would be taken up with socializing. However, computerphobia limits the enthusiasm of some top executives for this concept. (©*Quality Abstracts*)

CHAPTER 9

ELECTRONIC
DATA INTERCHANGE

Technology continually offers new and innovative techniques that affect companies and individuals. The cordless telephone, video games, facsimile (fax) machines, answering machines, notebook computers, electronic mail (E-mail), and calculators are a few examples that were not affordable or available ten years ago. With an ATM card, you can visit another state and obtain or transfer funds from your bank account. We are in the midst of the electronic communications era, which will determine how we communicate in the future. One innovation is electronic data interchange, which is causing major changes in how companies conduct business.

WHAT IS ELECTRONIC DATA INTERCHANGE?

The term electronic data interchange has many definitions. The description used by the Data Interchange Standards Association (DISA), a division of the American National Standards Institute (ANSI), is:[1]

> Electronic Data Interchange (EDI) is the transmission, in a standard syntax, of unambiguous information of business or strategic significance between computers of independent organizations. The users of EDI do not have to change their internal data bases.

EDI is the common "language" used to get information from one computer system to another. Users must translate this information to or from their own computer system formats, but this translation software has to be prepared only once.

In simple terms, EDI is computer-to-computer communication using a standard data format to exchange business information between companies. As an example, consider the postal system. A sender places a document in an envelope; the envelope is stamped and placed in a mailbox; it is picked up by a mail carrier, sent to the appropriate post office, and delivered by a mail carrier to your mailbox; you retrieve the mail from your mailbox, open the envelope, and read the document mailed by the sender.

EDI allows a company to rethink how it can improve its business processes and competitiveness. It is a means by which companies can become innovative in changing traditional methods used to conduct business. EDI allows companies to pursue new strategic business directions and visions. These efforts include reengineering business processes and implementing or revising the direction of total quality. Types of business processing improvements would be eliminating paper, faster turnaround, allowing data to be automatically entered into computer systems, and eliminating human data entry. The full benefits of EDI are realized when a company is creative in streamlining its business processes to make them more efficient and cost effective.

There are many definitions of EDI, and they vary based upon what article you are reading or who you are speaking with. Some people consider fax transmissions to be EDI, while others see it as using magnetic tape or diskettes. The key point when utilizing EDI is for a company to rethink how it conducts business and where it can continually improve.

EDI USERS AND TYPES OF ACTIVITIES

Who Uses EDI?

Companies of all types and sizes are able to utilize EDI. Some large corporations specify EDI as the communication method of choice. Businesses such as the federal government, K-Mart, and the Big Three automakers are nudging their suppliers to send all purchase orders and invoices electronically. EDI is being applied in many industries and is not limited to high-tech companies. Industry examples include banking, healthcare, retailing, travel, manufacturing, insurance, government, and utilities. Sample EDI application areas include purchasing, inventory, billing, distribution, price notification, financial, freight rate notifications, and sales and cash management, among others. A sampling of industries that are using EDI is provided in Appendix 9.1.

Based on a detailed study[2] conducted among firms using EDI, the majority suggested that EDI will be used as a competitive weapon. Dominant firms will choose to make alliances with a few suppliers rather than adopt an open market philosophy.

Types of EDI Activity

Currently EDI is primarily used for purchase orders, bills of lading, invoices, healthcare claims, and financial exchanges. The applications are limited only by imagination. As long as a standard data format is designed or in place and another company is willing to receive the information, any document can potentially be transmitted electronically. There is often confusion about the difference between EDI and electronic funds transfer (EFT), since EFT is also used to exchange information electronically. Financial EDI is the exchange of payment and bank balance information between a company and its bank or another company. EFT is the exchange of information between two banks that results in value being transferred.[3] It is possible for financial EDI to be bank to bank, but EFT does no bank-to-company exchanges. Examples of financial EDI would be bank account statements and payment orders; examples of EFT would be Automatic Clearing House (ACH) debit and credits or wire fund transfers. Realistically, EFT uses EDI as a means to transmit information.

One concern about using EDI arises when a company transmits information electronically and the receiving company does not simply print the information received. Someone in the process verifies and rekeys the information into another automated system, which means that the transaction continues to flow internally. Benefits of EDI should include elimination of paper and automatic information entry without manual intervention. Before this benefit can be achieved, companies must readdress their business processes and existing automated systems.

Business Processing Considerations

EDI is changing the way companies do business, shifting the ordering process from a snail-like, paper-intensive system to a computerized one.[3] One objective of using EDI is to align business transactions with business processes, not business functions. The nature of business relationships, both internal and external, is changing. EDI is evolving from transmitting orders and invoices to becoming a management tool used to reengineer business processes. Roles and tasks are changing as firms are changing their work process flows. A salesperson who used to receive and write orders has become a product advisor. Customers conducting business with firms that have multiple divisions now request centralized electronic transmission. These new concepts are forcing companies to build information technology (IT) organizational infrastructures that allow their divisions to exchange information and cooperate with one another.

Firms using EDI are in a position to consider reengineering various business activities, since EDI is faster and paperless. A company's information flow needs to be rethought. This change in thinking may necessitate revising operating procedures or eliminating procedures that do not support company strategies such as total quality management and just-in-time (JIT). With JIT, inventory is available as needed. EDI has assisted in this process by providing expedient inventory reporting to suppliers that continuously replenish stock. Many firms have eliminated warehouse space and allow manufacturers to resupply directly to the using location. Instead of storing products at a warehouse and having the location obtain inventory from the warehouse, the location is automatically stocked by the product manufacturer. (For additional information, see Abstract 9.1 at the end of this chapter.)

WHERE DOES INFORMATION TECHNOLOGY FIT IN?

EDI is not merely a technical tool or technique; it offers change and new ways of conducting business. The information provided and stressed throughout this text can also be applied to EDI projects. The involvement and role of the IT organization would be the same as for other business projects but entails crossing company boundaries. IT cannot be the sole implementor of EDI; it must be a business and technical team effort. An EDI effort involves thorough planning by the business and technical sides and requires technical functional support from all the IT areas identified in Chapter 2 (telecommunications, applications support, data center, and administrative planning).

EDI should have its own architecture tied to the company's strategic direction. This EDI architecture at a minimum should be designed to handle any system integration elements, systematically know the data format, address security levels, and know which communications connectivity to use. The real EDI world has many different criteria and needs; this preplanning allows for handling multiple data formats and multiple system interfaces and provides better support to the various business processing areas using EDI. It may be necessary to designate an EDI coordinator, who will be responsible for planning and coordinating all EDI activity within the company. The size of the firm and the extent of EDI activity are the basis for deciding whether an additional full-time position is necessary. It is recommended that someone coordinate the EDI effort, regardless of the size of the effort, so that results are not fragmented throughout the company.

An information architecture and systems integration should be in place to support the business before implementing EDI. In larger companies with multiple divisions, this interrelationship becomes even more critical, as the trend in customer service is "one-stop shopping" and dealing with a single entity for all products and services. Separate islands of information could easily be created as the result of EDI activity if there is no plan or technical platform to handle multiple data format standards and communication connections. Without planning within the IT organization, EDI will become fragmented and difficult to maintain, much like the antiquated computer systems many companies maintain today. When implementing EDI, or any new technology, planning is critical, to allow for business growth and to keep the systems modular and maintainable.

Using EDI for process reengineering and implementing a total quality program forces a company to examine itself by workflow process instead of functional unit. The business functional areas and technical functions must work together to develop an EDI strategy. EDI alone could be a company's mission that would generate numerous projects and subprojects for years.

WHAT IS NEEDED TO IMPLEMENT EDI?

Some companies and vendors make implementing EDI sound simple, but in reality there is more to it than electronically sending information to another company. In addition to top management's commitment (which is a *must* for all projects), other considerations include using a methodology, addressing standard data formats, and establishing electronic connections.

EDI Methodology

The EDI project methodology guidelines are the same as for any project. The stages are:

1. Planning and business requirements definition
2. Functional requirements
3. Design and build
4. Testing
5. Installation
6. Feedback and review

The above phases and their steps are the same as those discussed in the project development methodology presented in Chapter 7. The steps and considerations are the same, but the following are some additional factors to consider when implementing EDI.

EDI Implementation Considerations

Business Strategic Planning

Before starting any EDI adventure, it is important to establish a vision and mission for the company and its EDI commitment. The EDI project team should include a representative from each business functional area. No potential future user should be excluded. Questions that must be answered are:

- Why are we pursuing EDI?
- What do we expect from its usage?
- Who will be our EDI partners?
- What information do we want to exchange?

Based upon the answers to these questions, the scope of the project and the effort required to successfully implement EDI will vary. If the objective is solely to electronically communicate information but continue entering information into the existing business systems, then the project would not entail redesigning the work process to better utilize the technology. The effort would be minimal and the benefits of EDI would not be fully realized. On the other hand, a business may want to continually improve its work processes to take advantage of technological innovations, including EDI. In that situation, the firm's vision would be to phase in implementation of EDI by initially installing the data communications piece, which would eventually be incorporated into a new work process. It is always best to keep it simple by installing a project in small manageable pieces, using a pilot program.

Build External Company Relationships

One major factor that distinguishes an EDI project from other company projects is that EDI entails teaming with another company, known as a trading partner. When selecting a trading partner, it is important to survey potential firms to determine their level of interest in EDI and to find out if they are leaders or followers in implementing EDI. A trading partner must be an active participant in each phase and both partners must cover the same activities. A partner company must be included in the process as part of the project team and part of the project plan. EDI data formats and transmission method, checks and balances to confirm the receipt of information, volumes, and frequencies are critical requirements for both companies and must be defined and agreed upon up front. The user acceptance test must include both companies and must be signed off on by both before installation. Any EDI installation will be unsuccessful unless both parties involved are in sync with what is expected from the other. Timing, cooperation, and coordination between the trading partners are critical components of a successful implementation. (For additional information, see Abstract 9.2 at the end of this chapter.)

Ensure Commitment and Acceptance

It is important that all levels of management, employees, and team participants be educated on EDI and its capabilities. This helps define business requirements in solving business concerns. Education also helps in overcoming the fear of change and promotes eventual acceptance. The overall goals and objectives of the project must be explicitly defined and top management must commit to the project before moving on to functional requirements.

Legal and Tax Implications

Before implementing any EDI project that eliminates paper, a company should seek advice from legal and tax experts. The IRS is trying to help auditors eliminate paper files, but records must still be kept. IRS rules vary based on the company and its involvement with EDI. It is important to make certain the paper files can be eliminated when defining business requirements. Some basic questions (not an all-inclusive list) that must be answered are:

- Is the original document required?

- Are original signatures necessary?

- What information must be retained for tax or legal purposes?

- How long must the information be kept?

- How long does the company have to present the information?

- Will a copy of the document need to be recreated or will a report displaying the required information suffice?

One suggestion that should help in a tax audit or financial audit is to have well-documented processing explanations that include document flows and systems interaction flows.

It is better to be safe than sorry; consult appropriate authorities for clear, concise answers before eliminating paper. Microfiche and imaging are other alternatives when storing archival information.

Standard Data Formats

One benefit of EDI is that it forces industries to standardize terminology and usage and how information is recorded and presented by creating a dictionary of industry terms and usage. The data transmitted must be clear, concise, and unambiguous between companies. For example, on a bill of lading it would be important to clarify whether the port of discharge is the site where the product was unloaded or the location where the product was actually received.

EDI Data Standards History

The EDI data standards process began in the United States with the transportation industry during the mid-1970s. The transportation (ocean, air, motor, and rail) and other associated industries (banking, shipping, customs, freight forwarders, and brokers) created the Transportation Data Coordinating Committee (TDCC), which defined a standard electronic representation based on paper forms used within the industry. The initial effort created 45 transaction sets for the transportation industry. In the early 1980s, the American National Standards Institute (ANSI) initiated efforts to define a single set of standards for EDI that could be applied across industries.[4] These standards are known as the ASC X12 standards. Refer to Appendix 9.3 for an example.

Standardization is also growing internationally. The International Organization for Standardization (ISO) creates standards that are equivalent to the ANSI X12. This equivalent, called EDIFACT (Electronic Data Interchange For Administration, Commerce, and Transportation), was designated by the United Nations to support a global standard. Although the X12 and EDIFACT groups work together closely, the standards are different, which forces many companies to support multiple EDI formats.

Standard Group Types

Various standard groups have been formed to establish standards unique to their industries. These groups usually consist of major companies that communicate electronically with each other or compete with one another. The purpose is to establish a common language throughout the industry. This text will not attempt to explain all the different standards and meanings of the data. Appendix 9.2 provides a list of various industry standard groups and their addresses. Because each industry is unique and standards are rapidly changing, it is best to become involved with an industry standards committee to stay up to date.

Implementing Standards

An attempt to implement standard data formats is underway, but many firms still use proprietary formats. This forces companies to support multiple formats for the same business document. When implementing EDI, a company must be able to identify the sending company, determine the type of business transaction, and recognize the standard being used to translate the data into a format acceptable to the business system. When sending, the opposite occurs; the sender must "speak" in the format that the company addressed uses. Why have standards if multiple formats exist? One master format per business document would be the best of all possible worlds, and standards committees are striving to achieve that goal; however, some companies will insist on using proprietary formats, primarily because they have EDI formats in place and changes are costly. Another reason is that some firms are not team players and do not want a standardized format that would share competitive information. Regardless of any changes that may occur in the future, a firm should plan on handling multiple formats unless it has the clout to insist that it will only conduct business in its own format.

Data Standards Software

The cost of software that supports translating information into the standard data formats has dropped. As more and more firms pursue EDI software, vendors are offering products that perform this function. This eliminates the cost of developing in-house customized programs and maintaining reformat programs. As of this writing, it would take up to a year, at a cost of up to $60,000, to duplicate the function of a software package that retails for $4,000. The reason is standardization. The software vendor has already produced the product and has recouped initial development costs. (For additional information, see Abstract 9.1 at the end of this chapter.)

Some of the questions to ask when considering a software vendor are:

• Does the vendor provide current and future support of EDI standards?

- Does the software support handling multiple versions of the same standard, while going through the approval process?

- How long from approval of standards until the software is upgraded?

- How flexible is the communications support?

- How does the software handle auditing of the document life cycle?

- What mapping capabilities are supported (i.e., flat files, online, user-defined interface or menu driven)?

- Is the software upgradable for larger hardware (i.e., personal computer to mainframe)?

- What hardware platform is needed?

- What are the mailbox capabilities?

- What security features are offered and are they used at the recovery site?

- Are any formal software implementation plans available?

- How does the software handle network and/or mailbox transmission difficulties?

- What are the detailed guarantees and controls (checks and balances) that the entire transmission was delivered?

- What reports are available?

- What are the archive facilities? Where is the information stored? How available is it? How long must the information be retained? Can the information archived be selected by the user?

- What are the hours for support?

- What is the response time if difficulties arise?

- Will the vendor provide a complete client list that can be contacted?

- What is the maintenance cost after purchasing the package?

- Does the price include the entire package or is it modular?

- What is the cost to obtain multiple copies for other locations?

- Is the source code included?

- Can the package handle generating proprietary nonstandard formats?

Establishing Electronic Connections

In addition to a standard data format, it is mandatory that the companies' computers are able to "talk" to one another. This sounds simple but it can be complex. EDI entails the use of special translation and communications software. When connecting computers, companies must consider the communications method and protocol that will be used to transmit information, as well as security and business recovery. Much of this will be determined by the company with which a firm exchanges information. The following definitions are from the *Computer User's Dictionary*:[5]

- *Protocol*—A set of standards for exchanging information between two computer systems or two computer devices.

- *Communications protocol*—A list of communications parameters (settings) and standards that govern the transfer of information between computers using telecommunications. Both computers must have the same settings and follow the same standards to avoid errors.

- *Communications program*—An application program that turns your computer into a terminal for transmitting data to and receiving data from distant computers through the telephone system.

Protocol standards are different than data format standards. Protocol is used to communicate data formats. Industry groups are trying to implement protocol and communications standards.

Choosing the type of electronic connectivity is usually an economic decision. There are basically two choices: direct communication with a company or a value-added network (VAN). Recently, VANs have become compatible and more reliable, but it is important to make certain that the trading partners will be able to communicate. A firm may have to support multiple networks and communication connectivities. The most widely used VANs today are operated by such firms as AT&T, MCI, Sprint, General Electric, and IBM. Using a VAN usually eliminates concerns about protocol, security, data receipt acknowledgment, and recovery.

When deciding which type of communication connectivity to use, the following is a sampling of factors to consider:

- What are the data volumes?

- How often will data be transmitted?

- Will data be accumulated and transmitted at preset times or will transmission occur when processing activity takes place?

- Is data transmission dependent on system loads?

- Do security levels prevent data interception?
- Does data require encryption for security?
- What is the data recovery plan?
- How reliable is the connectivity?
- What are the costs?
- What equipment and software are necessary?
- What are the line speeds (BPI)?

Based on the answers to these questions, a company will be able to make a good decision. Often the trading company will dictate the choice.

Each situation is unique, and there is no way to choose the type of connectivity without knowing all of the details. The purpose of this discussion is to heighten awareness of the factors that must be considered. The telecommunications field is rapidly changing, and it is wise to include someone with a strong telecommunications background as part of the EDI project team.

INTERNATIONAL CONSIDERATIONS

Standards

EDI is not used only in the United States or North America. Data format standardization efforts are taking place in the United States (ANSI) and internationally (ISO). As mentioned earlier, ASC X12 is the American standard and EDIFACT is the international standard format. The committees work together but it will be years before one common standard is used throughout the world. This may seem like a simple task, but cultural differences, different ways of conducting business, different industry priorities, and egos must be taken into consideration. Until there is one common standard base, EDI implementation must be flexible enough to handle multiple standards for the same type of document.

Communication Connectivity

When dealing with international communications, there are numerous concerns other than the obvious language and cultural barriers. At the tenth annual EDI Strategies Conference, Dan Petrosky of EDI Partners stated: "As soon we leave North America, the involvement of governments in EDI becomes significantly important."[6] In some countries, telephone lines are

Table 9.1 Advantages and Disadvantages of EDI

Advantages	Disadvantages
Reduces the flow of paper between organizations	Standardizes programs and procedures
Improves productivity	Lack of a common understanding and limited education
Allows for more efficient disbursement of information (speeds up the transmission of information between organizations)	Complex to use
	Difficult to quantify return on investment
	Significant impact on organizational culture
Improves accuracy of information and reduces errors	Standards still in a state of flux
Allows for reduction in personnel	Requires a high initial capital investment
Enhances relationships with customers and suppliers by creating opportunities to take advantage of new technology	Lacks the security that some companies need
	Legal ramifications have not been tested
	Most trading partners do not use EDI
Reduces inventory and inventory costs	Impacts organizational structures, procedures, and controls
Complements and enhances marketing efforts	Requires high-level management commitment to be successful
Reduces data entry	Requires high-volume use before benefits are realized

Source: *Information & Systems Journal.*[7]

government regulated and are not as efficient as in the United States. When the government runs the show, acquiring permission from telecommunications authorities for equipment connection often causes delays. Another concern is the level of data security available and the right of ownership during transmission. Before conducting EDI business in other countries, regulatory requirements, hardware availability, types of telephone lines, etc. should be addressed on a country-by-country basis.

IS EDI FOR YOU?

EDI offers many advantages in addition to standardization and elimination of paper, but first a company must determine if it is ready for EDI. Table 9.1

shows the result of an industry study[7] to identify advantages and disadvantages of using EDI. The findings are self-explanatory.

Use of EDI is expected to continue to grow. More and more companies are being forced into the world of EDI as customers redesign processes to eliminate paper and to take advantage of the speed and ease of use of EDI. The initial capital cost to implement EDI can vary from $2,000 to over $500,000 depending on complexity and level of involvement. A firm must have data available in machine-accessible format, software to translate into data formats, communications connectivity, and computer hardware. Companies should be wary of vendors that try to convince them how easy and inexpensive it is to implement EDI. This is partially true, but before spending money, *all* implications and expenditures should be considered. Communication costs, ongoing maintenance, hardware costs, data volumes, and data availability should be investigated before investing. A word of warning: it is difficult to quantify costs and determine a return on investment for using EDI because it is a complex system which affects multiple business functional areas.

For firms interested in EDI, a list of organizations that support EDI or other electronic interfaces is provided in Appendix 9.2. Appendix 9.1 lists various organizations by industry that can assist with EDI standards and implementation.

ENDNOTES

1. Data Interchange Standards Association (DISA) (1994). *1994 DISA Information Manual.* Alexandria, VA: DISA, p. 6.
2. Blackman, Ian, Holland, Chris, and Lockett, Geoff (1992). "Planning for Electronic Interchange." *Strategic Management Journal.* Vol. 13, pp. 540–550.
3. Parkinson, Kenneth (1992). "It's Time to Get Involved in Financial EDI." *Corporate Cashflow.* July 1992, p. 46.
4. McGee, James and Prusak, Laurence, The Ernst & Young Center for Information Technology and Strategy (1993). *Managing Information Strategically.* New York: John Wiley & Sons, p. 83.
5. Pfaffenberger, Brian (1992). *Computer User's Dictionary*, 3rd edition. Carmel, IN: Que Corporation.
6. Sutton, Judy (1994). "In the Little Dragons: Varied EDI Use Calls for Different Approaches." *Global Trade & Transportation.* January, p. 42.
7. McGrath, Roger Jr. and Scala, Steve (1993). "Advantages and Disadvantages of Electronic Data Interchange." *Information & Systems Journal.* August, pp. 85–91.

APPENDICES

APPENDIX 9.1   EDI SOURCES BY INDUSTRY*

This list is by no means all-inclusive. If you require information about an industry not listed, contact DISA for assistance.

Automotive

Automobile Industry Action Group (AIAG), 26200 Lahser Road, Suite 200, Southfield, MI 48034; phone: (313) 358-3570

Motor and Equipment Manufacturers Association (MEMA), P.O. Box 13966, Research Triangle Park, NC 27709-3966; phone: (919) 549-4800

Educational Institutions

American Association of Collegiate Registrars and Admissions Officers (AACRAO), AACRAO SPEEDE/EXPRESS Project, One Dupont Circle NW, Suite 370, Washington, DC 20036-1110; phone: (202) 293-7383

Arizona State University (AACRAO) (post-secondary schools), Box 870312, Tempe, AZ 85287-0312; phone: (602) 965-7302

Council of Chief State School Officers (CCSSO), One Massachusetts Avenue NW, Suite 700, Washington, DC 20001-1431; phone: (202) 336-7054

Washington School Information Processing Center (WSIPC) (pre-kindergarten through grade 12), 2000 200th Place SW, Lynwood, WA 98036; phone: (206) 775-8471

Financial

Federal Home Loan Mortgage Corporation (Freddie Mac), 8609 Westwood Center Drive, P.O. Box 5000, Vienna, VA 22070; phone: (703) 760-2465

National Automated Clearinghouse Association (NACHA), 607 Herndon Parkway, Suite 200, Herndon, VA 22070; phone: (703) 742-9190

Treasury Management Association (TMA), 7315 Wisconsin Avenue, Suite 1250 West, Bethesda, MD 20814; phone: (301) 907-2862

Government

Department of Defense (DOD), Defense Information Systems Agency (DISA), DISPO-HVE, 5111 Leesburg Pike, 9th Floor, Falls Church, VA 22041; phone: (703) 681-0219

*Source: *1994 DISA Information Manual*, Data Interchange Standards Association (DISA).

Grocery

Uniform Communication Standard (UCS), c/o Uniform Communication Council, 8163 Old Yankee Road, Suite J, Dayton, OH 45458; phone: (513) 435-3870

Health and Healthcare

Health Industry Business Communications Council (HIBCC), 5110 North 40th Street, Suite 250, Phoenix, AZ 85018; phone: (708) 872-8070

Insurance

ACORD (Property and Casualty), One Blue Hill Plaza, 15th Floor, P.O. Box 1529, Pearl River, NY 10965-8529; phone: (914) 682-1700 ext. 421

Petroleum

Petroleum Accounting Society of Canada (PASC), P.O. Box 1403, Calgary, Alberta, Canada T2P 2L6

Petroleum Industry Exchange (PIDX), c/o American Petroleum Institute (API), 1220 L Street NW, Washington, DC 20005; phone: (202) 682-8491

Pharmaceutical

National Wholesale Druggists Association (NWDA), P.O. Box 238, Alexandria, VA 22313; phone: (703) 684-6400

Publishing

American Newspaper Publishers Association (ANPA), NAA, 11600 Sunrise Valley Drive, Reston, VA 22091-1412; phone: (703) 648-1224

Book Industry Systems Advisory Committee (BISAC), 160 Fifth Avenue, New York, NY 10010; phone: (212) 929-1393

Serial Industry Systems Advisory Committee (SISAC), 160 Fifth Avenue, New York, NY 10010; phone: (212) 929-1393

Purchasing

National Association of Purchasing Management (NAPM), P.O. Box 22160, Tempe, AZ 85285; phone: (602) 752-6256 ext. 401

Retail

National Association of Retail Dealers of America, P.O. Box 9680, Denver, CO 80209; phone: (303) 758-7796

National Retail Federation (NRF) (NRMA/ARF), 100 West 31st Street, New York, NY 10001-3401; phone: (212) 244-8451

Voluntary Interindustry Communications Standard (VICS) EDI, c/o Uniform Communication Council, 8163 Old Yankee Road, Suite J, Dayton, OH 45458; phone: (513) 435-3870

Transportation

Air Transport Association of America (ATA), 1301 Pennsylvania Avenue NW, Washington, DC 20004; phone: (202) 626-4000

American Truckers Associations/Management Systems Council (ATA/MSC), 2200 Mill Road, Alexandria, VA 22314-4677; phone: (703) 838-1721

Association of American Railroads (AAR), 50 F Street NW, Washington, DC 20001; phone: (202) 639-5544

Container EDI Council (CEDIC), 251 Lafayette Circle #150, Lafayette, CA 94549-4342; phone: (510) 763-9864

International Air Transport Association (IATA), IATA Centre, P.O. Box 672, Route de l'Aeroport 33, CH-1215 Geneva 15 Airport, Switzerland; phone: (41) (22) 799-2683

National Industrial Transportation League (NIT League), 1700 North Moore Street, Suite 1900, Arlington, VA 22209-1903; phone: (703) 524-5011

Rail Industry Group of National Association of Purchasing Management (NAPM), Subcommittee on Information Standards, c/o Union Pacific Railroad, 1416 Dodge Street, Room 200, Omaha, NE 68179; phone: (402) 271-5607

Utilities

Utility Industry Group, c/o Southern California Edison, P.O. Box 800-Procurement, Rosemont, CA 91170; phone: (818) 302-5347

APPENDIX 9.2 EDI ORGANIZATIONS

United States

ANSI Accredited Standards Committee (ASC X12), c/o DISA, 1800 Diagonal Road, Suite 355, Alexandria, VA 22314-2853; phone: (703) 548-7005
Formed in 1979 to develop interindustry standards for the electronic exchange of business transactions. The data areas are shipping and receiving information, order placement and processing, invoicing, payment and cash application, and so on.

Data Interchange Standards Association, Inc. (DISA), 1800 Diagonal Road, Suite 355, Alexandria, VA 22314-2853; phone: (703) 548-7005
Formed in 1987 as the secretariat and administrative arm of ASC X12. A nonprofit organization that handles the administrative functions and communicates with ANSI for ASC X12.

Electronic Data Interchange Association (EDIA), 225 Reinekers Lane, Suite 355, Alexandria, VA 22314-2853; phone: (703) 838-8042
Promotes and educates individuals about benefits and impacts of EDI. Does not specialize in standards such as ASC X12 but provides an overall EDI information base.

International

Pan American EDIFACT Board (PAEB), c/o DISA, 1800 Diagonal Road, Suite 355, Alexandria, VA 22314-2853; phone: (703) 548-7005
DISA undertook support in 1988. Provides a forum for representation and consensus for Pan American representation relating to EDIFACT standards development, promotion, and maintenance.

International Organization for Standardization (ISO) Technical Committee 154, U.S. Technical Advisory Group, c/o DISA, 1800 Diagonal Road, Suite 355, Alexandria, VA 22314-2853; phone: (703) 548-7005
Administrates the U.S. technical advisory board for matters pertaining to the EDIFACT syntax before ISO.

UN/EDIFACT UN/ECE, Trade Division Palais de Nations, CH-1211 Geneva 10 Switzerland; phone: (41) (22) 917-2457
Develops and maintains international EDI standards. Operates under United Nations sponsorship.

APPENDIX 9.3 ASC X12S/94-172 FORMAT*

ASC X12 FORMAT	SAMPLE INVOICE CONTENT/NOTES				
ISA*00*0000000000*01*01*PASSWORDME *01*123456789*bbbbbb*987654321*bbbbbb* 890714*2210*U*00204*000000008*0*P*N/L	**Outside Envelope** (Interchange Control Header, ISA)				
GS*IN*012345678*087654321*900509 *2210*000001*X*002040N/L	**Inside Envelope**				
ST*810*0001N/L	**Invoice**				
BIG*900713*1001*900625*P989320N/L	DATE 7/13/90 ORDER DATE 6/25/90 INVOICE # 1001 CUSTOMER ORDER # P989320				
N1*BT*ACME DISTRIBUTING COMPANYN/L N3*P.O. BOX 33327N/L N4*ANYTOWN*NJ*44509N/L	CHARGE TO Acme Dist. Company P.O. Box 33327 Anytown, NJ 44509				
N1*ST*THE CORNER STOREN/L N3*601 FIRST STREETN/L N4*CROSSROADS*MI*48106N/L	SHIP TO The Corner Store 601 First Street Crossroads MI 48106				
N1*SE*SMITH CORPORATIONN/L N3*900 EASY STREETN/L N4*BIG CITY*NJ*15455N/L	REMIT TO Smith Corporation (Selling Party) 900 Easy Street Big City, NJ 15455				
PER*AD*C.D. JONES*TE*6185558230N/L	CORRESPONDENCE Accounting Dept. TO C.D. Jones (618) 555-8230				
ITD*01*3*2**10N/L	TERMS OF SALE 2% 10 days				
	QUAN	UNIT	NO.	DESCRIPTION	UNIT PRICE
IT1**3*CA*12.75**VC*6900N/L	3	Cse	6900	Cellulose Sponges	12.75
IT1**12*EA*475**VC*P450N/L	12	EA	P450	Plastic Pails	.475
TDS*4395N/L	Invoice Total				
CAD*M****CONSOLIDATED TRUCKN/L	Via Truck				
CTT*4*20N/L	(4 Line Items, Hash Total 20)				
SE*21*000001N/L	Transaction Set—Trailer				
GE*1*000001N/L	Function Group—Trailer				
IEA*1*000000008N/L	Interchange Control—Trailer				

b = Space Character   ] = Data Element Separator   N/L = Segment Terminator

*Source: *DISA 1994 Publications Catalog*, Data Interchange Standards Association, Inc., Alexandria, VA.

Smith Corporation
900 Easy Street
Big City, NJ 15155
(618) 555-6765

INVOICE
No. 1001

CHARGE TO	INVOICE DATE 7/13/90	SALES PERSON NTO

	SHIP TO	
Acme Distributing Co. P.O. Box 33327 Anytown, NJ 44509		The Corner Store 601 First Street Crossroads, MI 48106

YOUR ORDER NO.	CUST. REF. NO.	ORDER DATE	TERMS
P989320	66043	6/25/90	2% 10 Days

QUAN.	UNIT	NO.	DESCRIPTION	UNIT PRICE	TOTAL PRICE
3	Cse	6900	Cellulose Sponges	12.75	38.25
12	Ea	P450	Plastic Pails	.475	5.70

Please direct correspondence to:

C.P. Jones

(618) 555-8230

PLEASE PAY THIS AMOUNT   43.95

DATE SHIPPED 7/13/89	SHIPPED VIA Truck

ORIGINAL (from paper format)

ABSTRACTS

ABSTRACT 9.1
HOW ARCHITECTURE WINS THE TECHNOLOGY WARS

Morris, Charles R. and Ferguson, Charles H.
Harvard Business Review, March–April 1993, pp. 86–96

The global computer industry is undergoing radical transformation, the authors wrote in 1993, and three years later the beat goes on. Success today flows to the company that establishes proprietary architectural control over a broad, fast-moving, competitive environment. The authors contend since no single vendor can keep pace with the outpouring of cheap, powerful, mass-produced components, customers have been sewing their own patchwork quilt of local systems solutions.

The architectures in open systems impose an order on the system and make interconnections possible. It is the architectural controller who has power over the standard by which the entire information package is assembled. The popularity of Microsoft Windows is used as an example to show how companies like Lotus must conform their software to its parameters in order to have market share. Thus, the concept of proprietary architectural control has broader implications in that architectural competition is giving rise to a new form of business organization. The authors contend that a small handful of innovative companies will define and control a network's critical design.

It is necessary to cannibalize old niches in order to evolve to occupy an ever-broader competitive space. The Silicon Valley model is used to show four important operational features that underlie the overall basic theme of the article: inventing—and reinventing—the proprietary architectures for open systems is critical to competitive success and can serve as the platform for a radiating and long-lived product family. Overall, the five basic imperatives that drive most architectural contests are: (1) good products are not enough, (2) implementation matters, (3) successful architectures are proprietary but open, (4) general-purpose architectures absorb special-purpose solutions, and (5) low-end systems swallow high-end systems.

Of added value are three sidebars featuring scenarios for architectural competition: (1) graphical user interfaces, (2) video games, and (3) page and image description standards.

The article ends with a look at Xerox's failure to capitalize on its pioneer xerography niche and create spin-off industries and business lines. The authors conclude with the challenge: "We think that similar strategies are available to companies in other complex industries—aerospace and machine tools, among others. If so, the information (technology) sector's strategic and organizational innovations might prove as interesting as its technology." This is one of the better *HBR* articles to come along in the information technology field in the 1990s. No references are provided.

ABSTRACT 9.2
THE ROAD TO 2015: PROFILES OF THE FUTURE

Peterson, John L.
Waite Group Press, 1994, 372 pp.

In this best-selling view to the future, Peterson takes us on a scientific and technological roller-coaster ride that often defies the imagination. The author is the founder of the Arlington Institute, a well-known futurist organization, and the issues are well developed and provocative. The basic theme is that scientific discoveries, information systems, and technological advances will push a renaissance toward a knowledge society that will dwarf every previous revolution in the history of mankind. Information access, on a parallel with lifespan extension, will reach unprecedented levels. Ironically, says the author, the very global system that sustains our basic life requirements will be in danger. The work revolves around three views as to how the world systems will shift: optimistic, pessimistic, and realistic. The book is illustrated and well researched and is must reading for every information systems professional.

CHAPTER 10

HORROR STORIES
AND HOW TO
AVOID THEM

This chapter presents real-life situations and the lessons learned: the do's and don'ts of implementing new projects using technology. The cases are real; only the names have been changed to protect the guilty.

SOFTWARE SELECTION COST OVERKILL

Rebe Enterprises is a small, growing manufacturing business with sales under two million dollars. The firm handled its inventory manually and decided it was time to automate the function. The owner, Kay Rebe, attended a trade show where she encountered a firm selling prepackaged computer software. The salesperson assured Ms. Rebe that his package would meet her company's inventory business needs, other manufacturing firms were using this package, and the software could be customized to meet any special requirements. She purchased the software for $10,000.

When the package was being installed, it was found to be incompatible with existing computer hardware (PCs), and additional money was spent to purchase new PCs. The package offered multiple inventory processing components, which allowed for expansion and company growth, but only one of these functions was used. The package was difficult to use and required continual vendor support in the form of training at an additional cost. More money was spent on vendor programming assistance and customization. Ms. Rebe, the managers, and the employees were unhappy with the software, especially considering the investment (over $20,000).

One day, while sharing her frustration with another company owner, Ms. Rebe found out that her peer was using a software package purchased for $75 which would have met her company's needs and anticipated growth through the next two years.

Lessons Learned

The owner purchased software processing capabilities that were unnecessary for her company's size, projected growth, and financial position. The owner did not realize that other software packages were available for substantially less money that could meet her company's existing volume and growth plans for the next two years. Due to the owner's lack of planning and computer knowledge, hardware compatibility was not taken into consideration, which cost extra unbudgeted dollars.

1. Comparison Shopping for Software Packages

The owner should have shopped around for other software packages instead of buying on impulse. The salesperson convinced her that other companies in the same type of business were using this software and that it was the best. The owner was also convinced that the salesperson had her company's best interests in mind, when in reality the salesperson was simply making a sale. The package purchased was overkill for the small business and money was wasted.

When selecting software, the purchaser has to consider functionality, type of hardware needed, and training offered, as well as maintenance/support costs. A complete product reference list should be obtained, and it is a good idea to speak with peers in the industry about their experience with technology in general. Companies share human resource information. Why not technology?

2. Hardware Compatibility

The ideal situation would be to purchase software and then buy the appropriate hardware, but often a company must utilize existing hardware. It is easier to find hardware that meets software needs than it is to find software that meets a specific business need. Evaluating software means considering the hardware needed to run it as part of the cost.

HIGH TECH TO BE HIGH TECH

Joe Sams, CFO of a retailing company, returned from a high-tech conference excited about the new voice-response systems he saw. His impression was that his company could realize immediate savings and easily eliminate two clerical support people and a receptionist. The company would also project an image as a state-of-the art organization. He decided to purchase a voice-response system immediately. After the system was installed, customers started to complain, and after six months the system was removed. Customers hated the automated system—they wanted to talk to a human being. Many customers decided to take their business elsewhere. Sales dropped 17 percent in one quarter.

Lessons Learned

A customer survey would have revealed that a voice-response system would not be readily accepted. Many customers still had rotary phones and could not use a system that required a touch-tone phone. The customer base was an older group that did not like high-tech machines; they wanted to talk to and place an order with a real live person. These customers decided to do business elsewhere.

BUSINESS END USERS NOT INVOLVED

The top management of JCB, Inc. decided that a new and improved accounting system was needed. The CFO approached the information technology (IT) manager and said, "Give us what we need and you have my support." The managers and the business users were informally asked what they wanted in an accounting application but were otherwise uninvolved until installation. The programmers evaluated accounting software packages and purchased one that met all the technical requirements. The package was installed and the users were suddenly told to start using the new system. There was no formal training or documentation before the system was implemented. Converted information was found to be incorrect, and customer service suffered until the difficulty was corrected three weeks later.

The business users hated the system and complained, "The technology people did it to us again! We asked for one thing and received something totally different."

Lessons Learned

The technical people thought they knew what was best for the business or may have felt that the business users did not want to be involved. It does not matter who was at fault; this type of miscommunication should never happen. IT professionals and businesspeople must work together as a team to consider both business and technical concerns. There must be coordination of information and a solid connection to the purpose of the organization. IT professionals must be both business and computer analysts. Businesspeople must get involved with the technology. If IT does not customarily include business users in planning, business users should express their concerns to senior management. Any project that succeeds will be the result of a team effort. (For additional information, see Abstract 10.1 at the end of this chapter.)

A QUESTION OF SIZE AND UPGRADING

Four manufacturing firms and one distribution firm were owned by a central corporate entity called Group, Inc., which in turn was owned by Havasu, Inc. Each of the five small companies had its own computer. Those computers were all of the same type with the same operating system software, although each company had different application software.

The officers of Group, Inc. did not know what to do about their data-processing needs. The computers at the five firms were aging and money would have to be spent to update the hardware. The officers also felt that new application software was needed. A committee was formed to investigate. The committee was made up of the financial officers from the five firms and the IT manager from Group. Group's IT manager supplied programming services and personnel from Group to the five companies; none of the five companies had IT personnel of its own.

The committee hired one of the big financial consulting firms to help in its search for hardware and software. For a year the committee traveled periodically to various other firms to see software and hardware in action. At the end of the year, both the committee and the consulting firm recommended that Group, Inc. buy one large computer and a well-known application software package and consolidate all computing at one site. The software vendor indicated that each of the five companies could "tweak" the software to customize it for their particular needs.

Before any decision was made, the IT manager from Group was fired. A new manager, Harris, came on board and learned of the plan. The initial cost of the projected system was $1.2 million. Since Group, Inc. did not have $1.2 million to spend, the money would be borrowed from Havasu, the parent company.

Harris was intimately familiar with the type of hardware at the five companies. Although he had only been on board a couple of weeks, he went to the CEO of Group, Inc. and told him that it made no sense to get rid of all the existing hardware and spend $1.2 million that Group did not have. Harris explained that they could spend $200,000 and be better off. With $100,000 they could buy a new computer for the largest of the five companies and send its old computer to the next largest firm. Each firm would, in turn, receive the hardware from the next largest firm. Every firm would end up with a larger computer, with the smallest old computer being discarded. With the other $100,000, they could buy new software that would be individually customized for each of the five firms. Harris added that if Group spent $1.2 million, it would probably have to spend another million for custom software and staff expansion. Also, once the expenditure of $1.2 million was agreed to, there would be no turning back. On the other hand, if spending $200,000 did not work, Group could still elect to spend $1.2 million. Harris was opposed by the financial officers of Havasu, who wanted a single large computer and new software. In effect, Harris was betting his job that the less expensive alternative would work.

Harris's idea was accepted by the Group CEO and, after some wrangling at Havasu, Group was allowed to spend $200,000. Installation of the new hardware and customization of new software began at all five sites. Havasu kept close watch on the software customization, which was incrementally installed and proved to work well.

Two years later, only one of the five companies was profitable, and Havasu decided to sell all five. Because each firm had its own self-contained computer and software, the sale of each company was easy to accomplish. Group, Inc. was dissolved, the CEO was forcibly retired, and Harris lost his job.

Lessons Learned

One knowledgeable man knew more about the company's IT needs than a big name consulting firm, a committee, and a group of financial executives. Studies, evaluations, and estimates by people who do not have pertinent experience are useless and expensive. The idea that one big computer can solve all problems is often an unreal but tempting fantasy. In most cases, small and distributed is better. Each of the five firms had its own IT needs and handling them separately would have been a better approach. Harris being hired was a fortunate coincidence. Havasu and Group should have originally outsourced their problem to an expert who knew their old hardware and software intimately, as well as what technology developments were taking place in regard to that hardware and software. There is no substitute for pertinent experience.

An additional lesson is that although an IT function may be solid, its continued existence and that of the company depends upon financial factors beyond IT's purview. It is also significant that Harris, who saved Havasu at least $2 million (and made the sale of the five companies much easier), made himself persona non grata with the financial executives from Havasu by doing a good job. It is worth noting that an individual who persists in doing what he or she knows to be correct sometimes loses out personally and financially.

REENGINEERING INFORMATION SYSTEMS

The corporate computer systems at XRAY, Inc. were antiquated; they were no longer in sync with the direction of the business, and they were difficult and costly to maintain. After conducting a thorough study and cost analysis, it was determined that the best approach would be to reengineer the information systems and business process workflows. XRAY, Inc.'s top management committed to becoming a state-of-the art organization and the effort began. Together IT and business management teams evaluated and chose a project development methodology which was standardized throughout the company. In addition, they purchased CASE tools, upgraded the computer hardware, obtained a data dictionary, and changed the database software.

A project team was formed to coordinate and monitor overall corporate departmental functions and to be responsible for the success of the project. Additional task teams were formed with representatives from each functional business department. The team members represented every facet of the business, including technology, business processing, and marketing. The initial plan was to convert all existing processes and implement them all at the same time. As the project moved along, most of the time and effort were spent in up-front planning and defining requirements.

Everything appeared to be working well except that the project was continually over budget and behind schedule. Three years passed and nothing was installed. Top management was naturally concerned about the lack of results, and the decision was made to phase in the new system. Implementation plans were changed. After a fourth year, user training was conducted, but only one piece of the new system was put into production.

Business users were unhappy with the lack of friendliness and business functionality of the new system. They were spending more time trying to get their work done. The audit controls of the new system were not as rigid as the old system, which led to extra work. When the new system could not handle mandatory processing requirements, "quick and dirty" techniques were introduced. The business support staff increased by ten people, although the new system was supposed to reduce head count. Special "SWAT" teams were created to analyze the new system and implement new audit controls and procedures. None of the remaining systems was ever implemented.

Lessons Learned

The project started off on the right track. All the proper studies were conducted, the right people were involved, and management was committed, but the project failed in three critical areas.

1. Failure to Review and Document the Processing and Information Capabilities of the Existing Systems

During the business planning and requirements identification phase, the capabilities of the existing system were not reviewed. True, the existing systems were antiquated and the way the company conducted business had changed since they had been implemented, but their information and processing capabilities should have been considered in the new design. No comparison between the old and new systems was ever made to determine whether any of the capabilities of the old system were still necessary.

2. Lack of a Project Change Management Methodology

Although IT had a change review process, there was no *change control* for enhancements made to transform activity from the old systems to the new systems. Sample enhancements included electronic data interchange for customers and improved quality control. These changes could have saved a lot of time and reduced costs, but they were never implemented.

3. Planning the New Project without a Modular, Phased Approach, or Pilot Project

The initial plan was to convert and install all systems at the same time. This puts a company at greater risk and does not show top management any ongoing return on investment. Modular implementation would have facilitated existing business users working with the new system sooner. Phasing in would have shown that required functionality was missing.

Roughly $20 million was expended in an effort that was largely ineffective. The main lesson learned in this debacle was there should have been teamwork between existing system personnel and the new project development teams. (For additional information, see Abstract 10.2 at the end of this chapter.)

THE MAGIC SOFTWARE SOLUTION

Complex, Inc. was a large utility company with many PCs in its main office and in the offices of its subsidiary companies. The IT director and the CFO were impressed by a demonstration of new PC financial software. As a result, they advocated buying the software for all of the company PCs. Upper management at Complex concurred with the CFO and the IT director.

All PCs had to be upgraded with more disk space and larger memory in order to use the new software. All employees who used the PCs had to attend training classes. All this was accomplished, but a year later very few people were using the new software. The conclusion was that the money spent for hardware, software, and training had been largely wasted.

Lessons Learned

This was a top-down decision, made without the benefit of consulting with the people who actually used the PCs and the software. The actual users had no personal stake in making the project a success. Also, management did not monitor the use of the software and did not mandate that any particular standard reports be generated. As the saying goes, "You can lead a horse to water, but you can't make him drink." Success does not "just happen"—it has to be ensured by involving the people who actually do the work and by management's insistence on, and measurement of, particular requirements. (For additional information, see Abstract 10.3 at the end of this chapter.)

THE SOFTWARE PURCHASE

Sudley, Inc. was a manufacturing firm that had outgrown its hardware and had a considerable investment in its customized software. Sudley called in a consultant to assist in its search for a new hardware/software configuration that would be able to use its existing application software. The consultant and the IT staff at Sudley concurred on the hardware decision. A new operating system also had to be purchased and there were two main vendors: Firm A and Firm B. Either operating system could do the job, but the consultant firmly backed Firm A.

Firm A offered a money-back guarantee. Firm B was $12,000 less expensive. A survey revealed that some other companies had changed from Firm B's product to Firm A's product; there was no evidence that any company had ever changed from Firm A to Firm B. Firm A's software had a much more open architecture with more options for future computing, but Sudley elected to purchase Firm B's less expensive software. The hardware and software were successfully installed and seemed to work well.

Lessons Learned

Most firms will choose hard-dollar savings over a technically superior product (even a superior product with a money-back guarantee) because everyone understands saving money now, but few understand the money to be saved by working with a better product that allows for technical expansion in the future. If one assumes that the consultant was correct in preferring Firm A's product, Sudley, Inc. will probably remain forever ignorant of the advantages it might have offered. If at some point in the future Sudley finds that Firm B's software cannot do something it needs, which Firm A's software would have been able to handle, it would probably be identified as a brand new problem with no reference to the past purchase. Firms often pay large sums of money for technical advice, only to ignore it. Also, no one can expect to succeed in business without compromise. Ideals are seldom realized.

ABSTRACTS

ABSTRACT 10.1
THE HIGH PERFORMANCE ENTERPRISE: REINVENTING
THE PEOPLE SIDE OF YOUR BUSINESS

Neusch, Donna R. and Siebenaler, Alan F.
Oliver Wight Publications, Essex Junction, Vt., 1993, 380 pp.

The promise of the 1980s was that if your company listened to the voice of the customer, implemented JIT and TQM, and empowered its people, it would achieve world-class success. But by the mid-1990s, ask the authors, what happened to the High Performance Enterprise? "We wrote this book," they explain, "because we deeply believe that opportunities for improved performance have been placed off limits for many companies. Not because they are powerless, but because they don't really know how to go about improving performance." The authors seek to integrate the "bits and pieces" of the High Performance Enterprise into a workable whole, and in doing so they present a book consisting of two parts. The first section describes the strategic process, gives an overview, and discusses how to establish an organizational context, a strategic direction, a habit of continuous improvement, and a new work covenant. The second section is built from chapters discussing each of the ten steps in the authors' High P·e·r·f·o·r·m·a·n·c·e·s People Systems™ Process:

1. Create the target and baseline organizational profiles.
2. Define flexibility.
3. Redesign work: redesign jobs and define teams.
4. Define the roles and scope of supervision.
5. Design a skills development process.
6. Design the p·e·r·f·o·r·m·a·n·c·e·s feedback system.
7. Design NewComp™.
8. Prepare a blueprint, and develop major design components.
9. Plan for implementation and implement.
10. Monitor, evaluate, and continuously improve.

What emerges is a step-by-step process purported to create a High Performance Enterprise. Several themes are key to the authors' approach:

- *Performance* needs to be addressed in terms of p·e·r·f·o·r·m·a·n·c·e·s, the thousands of daily performances, individual activities, decisions, and transactions taking place every day and at every level among the company's employees.

- *Leadership* is an acquired craft which comes from establishing a work environment that embodies strategic direction and empowers employees.

- *NewComp*™ is a compensation approach consisting of strategy-based pay, which reshapes base pay to ensure a return on human assets, and performance-based rewards, which reinforces shared business goals among all members of the organization. (©*Quality Abstracts*)

ABSTRACT 10.2
THE JOBLESS FUTURE: SCI-TECH AND THE DOGMA OF WORK

Aronowitz, Stanley and Difazio, William
University of Minnesota Press, 1994, 392 pp.

The authors lay down the challenge to the popular belief of a utopian, knowledge-based, high-tech economy with plenty to go around. Instead, their message is that there will be massive displacement of workers at all levels in the future economy. The premise that the good life is possible based upon full employment must change radically, the authors assert. They offer alternatives for what they call our dying job culture in order to sustain ourselves and our well-being in a future economy based upon science and technology. Interesting reading.

ABSTRACT 10.3
QUALITY IN AMERICA: HOW TO IMPLEMENT
A COMPETITIVE QUALITY PROGRAM

Hunt, V. Daniel
Business One Irwin, Homewood, Ill., 1992, 308 pp.

Quality in America is a readable volume that demystifies the quality movement and presents a clear plan to implement TQM in an organization. The author begins with an assessment of the global marketplace and the importance of TQM to a firm's remaining competitive. Next, he describes the fundamental concepts and vocabulary of quality. Chapter 3 is a helpful characterization of four of quality's pioneers: Deming, Juran, Robert Costello, and Philip Crosby. Then the author compares the emphases of the school of thought attributed to each of these people. "There is no one best way," says the author, but from that point on he describes and promotes his own synthesis of quality principles under the name *Quality First*™. A chart shows the relationship of Crosby's 14 steps, Deming's 14 points, and Juran's 7 points to *Quality First*'s 8 tasks, which are summarized under these major categories:

People-oriented tasks:
1. Build top management
2. Build teamwork
3. Improve quality awareness
4. Expand training

Technically-oriented tasks:
5. Measure quality
6. Heighten cost of quality recognition
7. Take corrective action
8. Commit to a continuous improvement process

Chapter 4 describes the Malcolm Baldrige National Quality Award and recommends applying for it. This is followed by a chapter giving a thumbnail sketch of Baldrige Award winners: Federal Express, Globe Metallurgical, Motorola, Wallace Co., Westinghouse, and Xerox Business Products and Systems. Then the author provides a specific outline for implementing quality in an organization. Chapter 6 includes a complete self-assessment questionnaire and scoring evaluation system. After introducing his *Quality First* concepts and principles, the author outlines a 17-step implementation plan. The first 10 steps are planning, followed by 7 implementation steps. Chapter 10 consists of a brief survey of quality tools (e.g., bar chart, fishbone diagram, control chart, Pareto chart, etc.) and techniques (action plan, benchmarking, cost of quality, SPC, etc.). A final chapter reviews the steps and urges the reader to "act now." Three appendices provide basic resources: an executive reading list, a glossary of quality terms, and a list of information sources. This is a helpful "first book" to introduce the quality movement to corporate executives. (©*Quality Abstracts*)

INDEX